Meaghan Marie Hackinen

Shifting Gears

Coast to Coast on the Trans Am Bike Race

— — —

Library and Archives Canada Cataloguing in Publication
Title: Shifting gears : coast to coast on the Trans Am Bike Race / Meaghan Marie Hackinen.
Names: Hackinen, Meaghan Marie, 1985- author.
Identifiers: Canadiana (print) 20230158862 | Canadiana (ebook) 20230158900 | ISBN 9781774390801
(softcover) | ISBN 9781774390818 (EPUB)
Subjects: LCSH: Hackinen, Meaghan Marie, 1985-—Travel—United States. |
LCSH: Bicycle touring—United States—Anecdotes. | LCSH: Cyclists—Canada—Biography. |
LCSH: Women cyclists—Canada—Biography. |
LCSH: United States—Description and travel. | LCGFT: Autobiographies.
Classification: LCC E169.Z83 H33 2023 | DDC 917.304/934—dc23

Editor for the Press: Anne Nothof
Cover and interior design: David Gee
Author Photo: Matthias Rau

   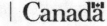

NeWest Press wishes to acknowledge that the land on which we operate is Treaty 6 territory and a traditional meeting ground and home for many Indigenous Peoples, including Cree, Saulteaux, Niitsitapi (Blackfoot), Métis, and Nakota Sioux. || NeWest Press acknowledges the support of the Canada Council for the Arts, the Alberta Foundation for the Arts, and the Edmonton Arts Council for support of our publishing program. This project is funded in part by the Government of Canada.

NeWest
Press

201, 8540–109 Street
Edmonton, Alberta T6G 1E6
780.432.9427
www.newestpress.com

No bison were harmed in the making of this book

Printed and bound in Canada.

For the Prairie Randonneurs
who infused me with their love of distance.

Table of Contents

Prologue

Condor Flight 2455 touches the tarmac at 12:45 p.m., Central European Summer Time. The abrupt deceleration causes the aircraft to shutter violently, mimicking the turbulence of my own anticipatory state. Though vibrations smooth as we taxi across the landing strip, my heart thrums faster. After ten hours in the air—and several months of planning—I've finally arrived in Frankfurt, Germany.

A canned message issued in both German and English reminds passengers to remain seated; cellular devices may now be used. I flex my legs, eager to move. To get started in this new chapter of my life. A much-anticipated ding indicates we can unfasten our seatbelts and collect overhead bags. On the tarmac, a shuttle waits to transport us to the main terminal. I twist my head back toward the plane as we file onto the bus, keen to spot my baggage—in particular, my bicycle box. For a second, my thoughts whirl in panic as I imagine scenarios preventing my precious cargo from following me across the Atlantic. Luckily, I spy it—a rectangular cardboard box scrawled with the word *Fragile* in Sharpie marker—my anxiety instantly replaced by glee.

. . .

I came here to ride my bicycle, and to embark on a relationship with someone I met on the side of the highway last summer. I've secured a year-long work visa, so I have plenty of time to do both. That someone is a quietly determined—yet fiercely funny—German cyclist and eco-friendly entrepreneur named Matthias. To get to know each other better, we will ride from North Cape, Norway, to Tarifa, Spain, along Europe's highest paved roads and most iconic alpine passes.

I perch over my daypack as we wind through the terminal, awestruck by the scale of Frankfurt Airport and my first glimpse into the bustling continent I hope to call my home for the next twelve months. After four years on the Canadian Prairies, I've become accustomed to Saskatoon's modest airport, a terminal boasting only ten gates—compact enough to punt a soccer ball from one end to the other. Already, my hometown is falling away, those final days of farewells, packing my belongings into storage, and boxing my bicycle a world apart.

The shuttle comes to a stop outside the main building, and we snake toward customs. A vibration on my cellphone reveals a notification about roaming rates, followed by a text message from Matthias: he has arrived at the baggage carousel and promises coffee to ward off impending fatigue. I imagine his bearded grin, the reassuring weight of his arms thrown over my shoulders—it's been months since we've last seen each other. From Frankfurt, we'll drive 160 kilometres to his flat in Freiburg, a picturesque university city in the Black Forest. In a few days, the two of us will board a plane bound for Norway to begin our journey from the Arctic Circle to the most southern tip of the European continent.

At last, I reach the front of the queue. A customs officer waves me through with a cheerless *Willkommen* and I take off, stride gaining pace as I forfeit the battle to constrain my excitement for the unwritten future that awaits behind a pair of frosted glass doors exiting to the arrivals lounge.

. . .

If you told me one year ago that I'd be embarking on this transcontinental journey-romance, I wouldn't have believed it. Until recently, I'd been living contentedly in Saskatoon—the Paris of the Prairies—with my partner, a revolving cast of roommates, and three cats: meal prep on Sundays, work during the week, and road trips to my partner's out-of-town family on long weekends.

A lot can happen in a year, though. I didn't arrive here by chance, but through a culmination of events. The one that set everything in motion, and changed my life irrevocably, was entry into the 2017 edition of the Trans Am Bike Race.

Pre-Race

Two days before the fourth edition of the Trans Am Bike Race rolled out of Astoria, Oregon, I found myself among a handful of prospective riders converging at Fort George Brewery under the pretense of a meet-and-greet. In reality, it was the promise of settling our collective pre-race nerves with the aid of free-flowing craft beer which drew us out—or at least, that's how I felt about it. The brew pub would hold another gathering the following night—on the eve of the race—though I wasn't planning on attending that second meetup. Consumption of liquor directly prior to a cross-continental sojourn didn't appear to be a wise strategic move. Yet two days beforehand, anything remained fair game.

Race organizer Nathan Jones was clearly onto something when he devised the Trans Am Bike Race in 2014, setting riders out with a goal as simple as it was daunting: get on your bicycle and ride across the country, as fast as you possibly can. Hailed as America's premier self-supported road race, the Trans Am takes participants from Astoria, Oregon, to Yorktown, Virginia, following the American Cycling Association's oldest bicycle route: the TransAmerica Trail. Covering 4,267 miles, ten states, several mountain ranges—from the Western Cascades to the Appalachians—and over 150,000 feet of vertical gain, it is, as Trans Am finisher and *Inspired to Ride*-star Juliana Buhring succinctly put it, a race "only for the crazies."

Aside from a modest entry fee and a GPS tracker, there are no prerequisites other than a willingness to venture into the unknown, and an inclination toward boldness or stupidity. Unlike stage races, like the Tour de France, the Trans Am operates as a continuous event: after rollout from Astoria, the clock doesn't stop ticking until you reach the Atlantic Coast. No drafting, stages, or non-commercially available support permitted. Media attention is minimal, and the only prize up for grabs is bragging rights. Unless you're lucky enough to have friends or family fly out, no one will even be there to hand you a beer when you cross the finish line at Yorktown Victory Monument, Virginia.

The Trans Am isn't for everyone, but to those craving an experience outside the norm, the race harbours an allure—a mystique. The promise of something so epic, it resonates more as aspiration than description: the opportunity to venture into the beating heartland of America and discover what you are *really* made of. Mere mention of the Trans Am has become a siren's call ensnaring the mind of the intrepid, adventure-seeking cyclist. You can probably guess, dear reader, that I was one of those starry-eyed cyclists.

Now, however, I was second-guessing. At Fort George Brewery, I sat somewhere in the middle of a long table of prospective racers. Across from the Crossleys, a perpetually upbeat father-daughter team who also hailed from Canada (Halifax), and next to a bristly-bearded Californian named Eric Fishbein staying with the same local host as me in Astoria. Wafts of hops mingled with the aroma of grilled meat from the kitchen; the room held the optimistic golden light of late afternoon. I glanced down the table— past amber pints and plates of thin-crusted pizza topped with prosciutto and arugula—examining the racers, mostly men over forty. Farther afield, tables displayed a similar age/gender breakdown: of the 131 entrants, only thirteen were women. While others discussed gear setups and expected finishing times, I remained tight-lipped. Intimidated by the sea of beards and expensive Rapha cycling jerseys, petrified a single word might reveal my complete and utter ineptitude.

"What's the riding like in Saskatchewan?" asked Eric.

My mouth opened and closed like a gasping fish. A sip of beer finally released the floundering words from the net of my tongue.

"Winters are rough," I admitted. "But summers are outstanding."

In fifteen minutes, I could be breezing along the highway away from the city. No stop signs or traffic lights. Saskatchewan doesn't have hills, but we do have uninterrupted road that stretches for miles, and wind—the flat-land cyclist's ultimate training partner. The downside: my preparation had been on pancake-flat prairie. While I wasn't sure how those miles would translate to more varied terrain—the Trans Am route accumulates enough elevation to equal six ascents of Mount Everest—I hoped my hours in the saddle might provide a requisite endurance base to weather the climbs.

. . .

I registered for the Trans Am before having ridden a road bike. Though aware of the race since its inception, I had no interest in participating myself until Alaskan ultra-endurance cyclist Lael Wilcox won the 2016 edition. Funny how inspiration plays out: seeing my gender reflected in a race winner instantly transformed how I thought about my own limitations. As I scanned online post-race interviews with Lael, I wondered if someone like me—with years of touring and commuting experience—could compete as well.

But I harboured no delusions of grandeur.

I knew from the start I had zero chance of winning. Instead, I became possessed by the newfound conviction that I was capable of more than I'd previously imagined. I decided to throw my hat in the ring, and use the race as an opportunity to test my limits.

By October 2016, I had paid my registration fee and purchased a member-ship at a local spin studio, where I planned to put on the bulk of my winter training. The bicycle came a month later: I opted for a Cannondale Synapse, a carbon road bike built with a relaxed endurance fit meant for long days in the saddle, and a price tag that exceeded my credit card limit. Luckily, I convinced my boyfriend to pay for it, promising to transfer the money later. My new bicycle was black and white like an elegant tuxedo and I named her Epona after the patron goddess of horses— also the name of Link's horse in my favourite childhood video game, *The Legend of Zelda: Ocarina of Time.* Unfortunate timing, however, saw Saskatoon's streets buried under snow just days after Epona's maiden ride, and I thrust my precious steed into storage until spring thaw.

· · ·

Eric and I continued to discuss riding conditions in our respective homelands. Both transplants from elsewhere, him from Boston, me from Vancouver. He was sixty-one and vibrant, flashing an easy smile that exuded a Californian warmth I imagined came from living down the coast in San Luis Obispo— though he hadn't lost the outspoken nasal of his Boston hometown. While Eric had come to the West Coast, I had left it to complete a Master of Fine Arts in Writing in Saskatoon, staying after I'd landed a position at a non-profit and a prairie boy to settle down with.

When Eric disappeared to the washroom, I ordered another beer from the bar and found myself in easy conversation with a racer from Portland named David Barstow Robinson—DBR, for short. DBR was infectiously likable, an in-person manifestation of grungy-bike-courier-cool: aloof, gifted with an insider's cheeky smile and calm demeanour, and chest hair that purled from his collar like the love-sick curlicued doodles of a teenager.

DBR had organized a group ride from Portland to Astoria that morning. Around thirty riders took part, including myself. Trans Am participants hail from all corners of the globe, and because Astoria lacks an international airport, most opt to fly into neighbouring Portland. Aside from being the thriftiest option, cycling the 120 miles to the coast felt like less of a logistical headache compared to renting a vehicle, or interpreting complicated bus schedules.

I suffered a series of frustrating setbacks upon my arrival in Portland, however.

After landing, I unboxed my bike in PDX Airport to discover that in late-night packing haste, I'd forgotten both my helmet and my cycling gloves. Then I managed a flat en route to the hotel. After patching it, I spent the remainder of the afternoon hunting down replacement gear. Tangled up in Portland's rose-studded roundabouts as I navigated between shops, all I could think of was how much I missed my boyfriend, Tyler, and the cycling friends in Saskatoon who I too often relied on to guide the way.

For me, the pre-ride wasn't simply about getting to the start, but a chance let go of the previous day and arrive in Astoria with a clean slate.

We rolled out of Portland among early morning commuters, careening en masse through backroads as twisted as the roots of the trees we'd later pass in moss-laden woods leading toward the coast. After a stint on the paved Banks-Vernonia rails-to-trails path, it was an easy haul through farmland— past charming red silos and emerald bursts of crops—before a series of hills deposited us in Astoria at the mouth of the Columbia River.

"Nervous?" DBR asked me now.

"Yeahhh," I drawled.

Those Portland mishaps were glaring back at me: my forgotten gear, navigational errors, and flat tire.

"I still have to grab some stuff," I explained. "I don't have lithium batteries for my GPS tracking device yet, or snacks for day one."

"You mean day zero," he corrected me. I'd forgotten that the race clock begins with zero, and only after twenty-four hours—an entire day—did day one commence. It was a confusing concept I struggled to wrap my head around, as if the first day somehow didn't count at all.

"Right, day zero," I said.

"Don't worry," said DBR, raising his glass to meet mine. "There'll be plenty of time for all that tomorrow."

. . .

Suddenly, everything became easier.

With DBR's reassurances echoing in my ears, I threaded through a dozen conversations. Names and faces changed, yet I was reassured to discover—in most of my fellow racers at least—some degree of uncertainty that paralleled my own. It might be masked by false bravado or laughed aside, but I sensed the shadow of apprehension lurking like a sea snake beneath the surface.

Among others, I chatted with a young woman with a grand nonchalance from Massachusetts named Simone Bailey; and Thomas Camero—at seventy-six years old the Trans Am's slowest, and perhaps oldest, finisher to date, which earned him the title of *lanterne rouge,* a French term that celebrates the last finisher in a race. Thomas had received this designation twice when I met him, and would add another year to his reign in 2019. Slight and exuberant, Thomas gushed about the kindness of folks who offered him sweet tea or a spot to pitch camp on their front lawns. Regardless of whether he was competing or not, Thomas travelled from Hood River to Astoria for the Trans Am's send-off every year, collecting signatures on his oversize coffee-table book, *America's Bicycle Route: The Story of the TransAmerica Bicycle Trail,* and providing race veterans with name tags so that newbies like myself knew who to aim their questions at.

As the night wore on, it became easier to forget what we were up against. We raised our glasses to adventure—"To the Trans Am!"

The time for training and preparation was over. We were ready to celebrate, scream a last goodbye to our quotidian lives and nine-to-five jobs. On the cusp of the American continent, we spoke of the next month in heroic terms, something bigger than ourselves we couldn't yet comprehend.

. . .

My final day in Astoria passed in a whirl of last-minute preparations, punctuated by shots of espresso and giant café cookies, and interspersed with conversations with cyclists I might never see again. The glorious fresh air backdrop accompanied by one-hundred-plus visiting cyclists felt something akin to summer camp for adults, all of us bubbling excitement, our new-found friendships cemented in the blink of an eye. I marvelled at winding hilltop roads, peaked with green, as ocean air infused my lungs. I hadn't realized how landlocked I'd been in Saskatoon—how much I missed the coast. Astoria's streets were overrun by Lycra-clad men and women, their shiny bicycles outfitted with Apidura gear bags and clip-on aerobars. In addition to providing an aerodynamic advantage, aerobars, also known as tribars—a type of handlebar extension with padded forearm rests that allow the rider to reduce wind resistance by drawing her body forward—are popular among endurance cyclists because they offer an alternate hand position with reduced strain on the hands and wrists. I say this as if I know what I'm talking about, but in reality, I had just clipped my first pair of aerobars on a month or two before starting the race.

Eric joined me as I frantically checked items off my to-do list: lithium batteries, race snacks, sunglasses to replace a pair I managed to lose on the pre-ride after I absentmindedly set them down on a rock when I peed in the woods. His presence provided reassurance. The constant company was a reminder that I was neither alone, nor unrealistic. In matching highlight-er-yellow helmets, the two of us sped over the high bridge toward Fred Meyer hypermarket, faces to the wind and hearts leaping in imitation of the white-caps below. At a downtown barbershop we drank tallboys of beer while waiting for two chairs to open up, soaking in the ambiance of local gossip, the buzz of electric razors and quick-shearing scissors. Eric and I joked that our new haircuts were sure to increase aerodynamic efficiency—give us both an edge on the competition by shaving off unnecessary grams. Once word spread among the staff and other clientele that we were racing, we revelled in the minor celebrity status bestowed upon us, and walked out feeling unstoppable. I forgot to bring cash, but Eric covered me, teasing that my side-shave should have been half-price since it only required half the work compared to the full buzz he had opted for.

After we'd knocked off our errands, Eric and I parted ways. Soon, we would join the others at a hilltop column to pick up our race packages, which included numbered cycling caps and GPS tracking devices. But I had one more thing to tend to first—a pilgrimage, of sorts.

. . .

I headed along the waterfront and veered uphill just before the Safeway where I'd stocked up on protein bars at a few hours earlier. A left on Franklin Avenue, then a few easy pedal strokes until I eased to a stop in front of John Jacob Astor Elementary. For most, the elementary school wouldn't register as a tourist attraction, but the location held personal significance. John Jacob Astor Elementary featured as a set location for *Kindergarten Cop*, the 1990 cheesy blockbuster crime-comedy starring my all-time favourite action hero, Arnold Schwarzenegger, as Detective John Kimble.

Ever since my days as a video store clerk in high school, I have harboured an obsession with Schwarzenegger. Despite a general preference toward musicals and comedies, I found myself drawn to the machismo, the fantasy of a larger-than-life hero who could end any conflict with a few punches and well-placed kick—or, failing that, a loaded bazooka. Schwarzenegger's muscular silhouette has decorated more than a few of my birthday cakes over the years. I went so far as to rename myself after his likeness when I took up flat-track roller derby (a full-contact sport played on old school quad roller skates) in my twenties, choosing the pseudonym Schwarzemegger as my skate name—Schwartzy for short. Sure, I was 5'6" and barely capable of a chin-up while Schwarzenegger was 6'2" and built like a tank, but I hoped that by taking on the Austrian bodybuilder's namesake, I could channel his strength.

I parked my bicycle on the grass in front of John Jacob Astor Elementary and snapped a few photos before settling on the steps. All day my mood had fluctuated between pulse-quickening excitement and stomach-churning doubt, a vicious entourage of tiny voices hissing nasty self-criticisms besieging my confidence whenever my mind had a moment to drift. Now, it was time to shut them up—and what better inspiration for a pep talk than tough-city-cop-turned-school teacher, Detective Kimble. I imagined him stomping around the entrance way, hyping me up like the kindergarten classroom for a weekly fire drill, veins bulging like massive rubber worms on his neck and forehead.

"You can do this, Meaghan! You've been training for months and now look: you have calves of steel; quads so huge, they're liable to shred your shorts to pieces. America is nothing but a puny, insignificant hiccup on the globe—forget about it. You've got this, girl."

With my inner doubts silenced by the imagined encouragement of an entirely fictional character, I set a determined chin and whizzed off toward the hilltop column.

. . .

Once I picked up my race kit, I pedalled back to Mike's place. Mike was a lovably scruffy local bike enthusiast who hosted visiting cyclists on the hospitality website WarmShowers.org. To accommodate the influx in out-of-town racers, he had opened his second-floor apartment to five Trans Am participants, including myself. While the men crowded the living room alongside our bikes and sprawling gear, I had the guest room entirely to myself, by virtue of being the only woman. All six of us—Mike, Eric, myself, a couple of Kiwis, and a red-headed musician from Florida—climbed up the rickety fire escape ladder to the rooftop for sunset. I paired my recently acquired race cap (number ninety-nine, just like Canadian hockey legend Wayne Gretzky, a coincidence I took as a good omen) with an oversized T-shirt and pair of jogging shorts belonging to Mike while my own clothes spun clean in the washing machine for the last time in who knows how many days. We each carried a stemless wineglass that Mike poured dark, heady porter into. Behind the tremendous bridge which spanned the Columbia River, the sun slipped away.

"I'm not worried about you," Eric told me, impromptu of nothing. "When we first met, I thought 'Oh boy, does this girl know what she's getting into?' But now, I can see that you're going to be just fine."

"Thanks," I said, buoyed by his affirmation. I didn't mention my bouts of self-doubt, or unorthodox pilgrimage to the set of *Kindergarten Cop*. "Good luck on your race."

The conversation ebbed. Others drifted downstairs to wrap up last-minute preparations, while Eric and I remained: legs hinged over the rooftop's edge as we silently sipped the dregs of our porter; eyes fixed to the point where the sun collided with the bridge. Everything had already been said.

Who did we think we were? I wondered, my heartbeat quickening in anticipation of tomorrow's early start. What kind of person races a bicycle across a continent? The sheer audacity of it, I thought, grinning inwardly. I looked to the horizon for some hint of the future, a prophecy spelled out in Alpha-Getti clouds.

Instead, between water and cloud cover, a band of sky. A length of shimmering, blazing gold.

Later, I would look back on this moment and wonder if I'd missed something. If there actually had been some clue that escaped my keen eye. But I've gone back to Mike's rooftop again and again in my mind—nothing. There was absolutely no way to predict the tragedy to come, during that enchanted rooftop sunset on the eve of the race.

Day Zero

JUNE 3, 2017

ASTORIA TO PEORIA, OREGON

DISTANCE: 202 MILES

RACE MILEAGE: 202 OF 4,264 MILES

The 2017 edition of the Trans Am Bike Race rolled out after dawn in Astoria, Oregon. No banners, no signs. Just a legion of Day-Glo, Lycra-clad cyclists in the parking lot of the harbour-front Maritime Museum listening to race organizer Nathan Jones bellow final reminders from a bullhorn against the backdrop of a massive bronze propeller blade.

"This is a bike ride, all right? It's a race, but really nobody cares," he said, pausing as nervous laughter leapfrogged through the crowd. "Nobody cares. Your family barely understands what you're doing, your friends have no idea, and the people you don't know, they're gonna think you are idiots—and you kinda are idiots."

Nathan continued, but I found myself distracted—head weary from fitful, night-before-the-big-day-sleep—scanning the crowd for the reassurance of familiar faces and sizing myself up against the competition: based on previous race results, only fifty per cent of us were likely to finish. Eric, who had accompanied me from our host's apartment, had wound up on the opposite side of the propeller blade, sharing a laugh with a couple of guys I didn't know. Closer, I caught the eye of DBR. With a brisk nod, he rolled by to wish me luck.

"Remember, rubber side down," he said. Then, as an afterthought: "D'ya think that's the best place for your Spot?"

I had attached my Spot Tracker, an orange and black GPS tracking device the size of a coaster and the thickness of a paperback, under my seat post. I'd struggled to find a fitting location for it among frame bags and aerobars, having only picked up the device during the pre-race meeting at the column the night before. Used correctly, the Spot would broadcast my live location to a website called Trackleaders, where family, friends, and race fans—collectively known as dotwatchers, a name derived from the popular pastime of watching racers' "dots" inch across a course when viewed on a computer, tablet, or cellphone screen—could follow. In an event where participants span several states, GPS tracking services provided a handy replacement for the army of officials that would otherwise be necessary to maintain the integrity of the race, and deter anyone hoping to skim off a few hilly miles by taking a faster alternate route.

"You might not get reception with it aimed at your butt," DBR helpfully pointed out.

I stood back to examine my bike, bracing the frame with both hands.

"Maybe I could strap it to the handlebars?"

"Be quick," said DBR, wheeling toward another face in the crowd.

Just then Thomas Camero marched by with a bottle of champagne, a tower of plastic cups protruding from his jacket pocket.

"Hold my bike?" I pleaded.

He agreed, tucking the bottle precariously under an arm as he reached for Epona. I felt light-headed: only five minutes left now. My trembling fingers struggled to pinch the zipper of the top tube bag where I'd stored my Swiss Army knife. Stupid nerves. I popped open the blade and nicked my thumb attempting to cut the zip ties attaching my Spot to the seat post.

"Here," said Thomas, seeing the smidge of blood, my electric anxiety. We traded places. He took the knife from my hand, passing the champagne off to a nearby racer. As Thomas sliced my Spot free, I instinctively stuck my thumb in my mouth and sucked hard. The taste of metal. A few seconds later he had secured the device to my handlebars with another set of zip ties I directed him to pull from my larger frame bag.

"Thanks," I said, grateful but blushing embarrassment for failing to complete even this small task alone. I didn't need anyone to remind me that once we rolled out, I'd be solely responsible for taking care of my own problems. This was DIY racing: low budget, no support. Either you figure it out or go home.

Thomas grinned, retrieving the champagne and ceremoniously tipping an inch of bubbly into a plastic cup for me. The fizz sloshed in the cup between my jittery palms like the tumultuous Columbia River. Other racers clinked rims in delight; I wondered how I even got there, struck yet again—for the umpteenth time in the past week—by the incalculable magnitude of the challenge I'd so cavalierly signed up for.

Suddenly, we were counting down to the grand depart. I slugged back the champagne, crushing the plastic cup into a jersey pocket. A cheer erupted; bystanders snapped photos. We were off.

. . .

For the initial five miles we rode together in a neutralized start, jostling shoulders in our high-vis vests like a school of yellow snapper fleeing Astoria's misty shores. Mingling words of encouragement, apprehension. But when we hit the first bridge, a handful of cyclists shot forward, a cue that the race had officially begun; I would see none of those riders again.

The pack continued to splinter as we pedalled inland toward Seaside, carving through a barren cemetery of stumps under shifting grey clouds. A spiky tang of fresh-cut wood infused the dewy morning air. Between passing conversations with nearby riders, I focused on finding my rhythm, repeating Nathan's words like a mantra: "This is a bike ride...nobody cares." To remain calm, it became necessary to maintain the illusion I was merely out for a spin, just as I had done thousands of times before. Then it hit me that sustaining race pace over nearly 4,300 miles was nothing like anything I'd previously attempted. My neck stiffened in anticipation of an impending siege from the barbs of doubt creeping up my backbone.

I took a deep breath, relaxing my grip on the handlebar hoods. Asphalt scrolled beneath me. I appreciated how my legs were fresh on the hills, the dynamic interplay of power and cadence effortlessly adapting to every subtle change in gradient.

Enjoy this, I said to myself. It's the last time you'll feel this good until you're back in Saskatoon.

But I couldn't outpace my inner critic. As I struggled to swat away the tiny cannonballs of insecurity that breached my purposefully upbeat exterior, one thought took hold—a persistent question. Would I return home ebullient in success, or shrouded in the grim cloak of failure?

· · ·

Not far past the coastal town of Cannon Beach, my rear tire flatted—barely twenty-five miles into the race. Three riders passed as I hauled a spare tube and tire levers from my frame bag, their gazes lingering long after lollipop-bright helmets bobbed over the hillcrest. My quivering hands mimicked alder leaves overhead as I reached for the rear quick release. Nerves, again.

Then I remembered: this was not my first Oregon flat. Eight years prior, toting panniers of pilfered apples, my younger sister Alisha and I pedalled from British Columbia to Mexico. For two waterlogged weeks, we twisted along the Oregon Coast, tackling fierce headwinds and never-ending flat tires with a cheerful, unwavering gusto. It was in Oregon, after over a month of bear-filled dreams on Haida Gwaii and Vancouver Island, and another week dodging storms in Washington, that my confidence surged. The winding highway transforming from a source of unseen terrors into a trove of adventure, begging to be explored.

On recollecting these adventures, my composure returned. A racer buzzed by, but I ignored him, hands moving mechanically as I recalled the countless flats that had come before. Within minutes, I slotted my rear wheel back into the frame, pumped the tire, and set off, cranking up the steep pitch with a grin—and whatever the two-wheeled equivalent to a skip in my stride might be. Wind pummeled my chest as I summited the hill and emerged at Neahkahnie Viewpoint, where the ocean spilled out in front of me.

I love the Pacific Coast: its salty air and sheer immensity of blue. The contrast between foaming seas, fern-hemmed woods, rocky shores, and sweeping bays repeated in limitless configuration. I gazed south toward Neahkahnie Bay, the shoreline extending into the horizon like the edge of a mirage, or the unplaceable border of a dream. My excitement swelled like the waves rolling in, building momentum as memories of that journey with my sister intermingled with curiosity about the unknown ahead. I remained uncertain if I could pull this off, but that was where the challenge lay. With one last glance into the pelagic depths I cast my doubts aside, channelling Austrian-accented encouragement from none other than my beloved Arnold Schwarzenegger—*You can do this!*—before I geared down for a fast descent into Manzanita.

. . .

Rockaway Beach and Bay City; Cape Meares and Sand Lake. Places familiar, yet breezing through in rapid succession remained a novelty. I didn't stop for photos—I had an entire album from my previous tour. At the McDonald's in Tillamook, I plunked down next to a racer named Aaron Ehlers from Saint Paul, Minnesota, who brought to mind a lumberjack in his plaid jersey and bushy beard. Between slugs of coffee we chattered excitedly. Despite the flat tire, that morning I'd covered a distance it took my sister and me nearly four days to pedal. Now, I wondered what else I could accomplish.

The route continued south from Tillamook, clinging to the coast toward the Three Capes Scenic Drive under blue skies and billowing clouds. Since the grand depart, I'd followed the tracks of others, another racer always in sight. When the cyclist ahead of me had missed the turnoff to Cannon Beach, I ripped by as well, hauling a U-turn only when a backtracking cyclist (who also passed the turnoff) pointed out our mistake. Now, I rolled out of the McDonald's onto southbound Highway 101 without directional concern, snaking a right after the rider ahead of me through cow-studded pastures, then west to Cape Meares. I chased seagulls over coastal capes to the soundtrack of the frothing Pacific and quicksilver winds before plunged inland at Neskowin, an idyllically situated shoreline town that features the storied Proposal Rock.

By Neskowin the pack had dispersed enough I could no longer discern any other cyclists. For the first time, I checked my digital navigation device to determine the whereabout of the turnoff, only to realize my unit wasn't even turned on.

As I waited for the map to load, I wished, in my impatience, for a rider to come by so I could follow his wheels. Finally, the route appeared onscreen, and I traced the directional line inland, grinding uphill, away from the salty coast.

. . .

I should confess: my expertise with electronic navigation was limited. Until the Trans Am Bike Race, I'd used paper maps or guidebooks, my experiences characterized by frustration, hours wasted in search of the correct route, and an unhealthy reliance on others.

I was determined that would change with the Trans Am, however. While possible to navigate from coast to coast using the American Cycling Association's (ACA) paper route guides, I didn't want the weight of a dozen maps bogging me down. Nor did deciphering paper maps on the go—unfolding them in the rain, sleet, wind, and darkness—appeal to me. Instead, I purchased a GPS navigation unit and downloaded the route, using a digital version of the ACA maps on my iPhone as a backup. I chose an eTrex 20x GPS, primarily because it was relatively inexpensive, but also because it wasn't cycling specific: I could use it for a host of other activities, including hiking, kayaking, and cross-country skiing. If I'm being completely honest, that Lael Wilcox had opted for an eTrex in her 2016 race win may have also been an influencing factor.

. . .

It was twenty minutes before I noticed the thin blue line on my digital map—showing my real-time location—no longer aligned with the pink route line I should have been following. Even then, I wishfully assumed some technological glitch was at fault: obviously I was on route—there was only one eastbound road, wasn't there?—and continued, concern growing as my track further diverged. At a hilltop, I stopped to investigate my position. As I toggled the joystick of my eTrex back and forth, an exuberant Brazilian rider I recognized as Nuno Lopez—who coincidentally rode the exact same model of Cannondale bicycle as me—crested the hill from the opposite direction, breathing hard.

"Wrong way," he announced, waving one hand to signal a turnaround. His green and gray jersey—emblazoned with the word RIDE! in capital letters—still had that glossy just-off-the-rack sheen.

I spun to pedal alongside him.

"How long did you continue off course?" I asked.

"Too long," he said, panting out the words as he flashed a high-spirited grin. Sweat beaded on his forehead like fresh raindrops on a fern frond.

I laughed as I kicked into gear to chase him down the hill we had both pointlessly ridden up.

. . .

That wouldn't be the last I saw of Nuno Lopez. We continued to bump into each other every hour or so, always off course. I was clearly lacking navigational skills, but what was his excuse?

The first few times, the two of us chuckled, chatting breezily as we returned to the predetermined route.

By evening, however, these encounters had ceased to be amusing. I wondered if there could be a curse, some voodoo set in motion by our matching Cannondale bicycles that caused us to veer off course whenever we approached—like how magnets of the same charge propel each other away. Nuno had apparently come to a similar conclusion: when we met for the sixth or seventh time, a few hundred feet off route somewhere in farmland between Monmouth and Corvallis, he didn't acknowledge me, nor I him. In fact, I promptly pulled over for a pee break. The more space between us, the better.

. . .

Once I realized I'd missed the turnoff after Neskowin, it was easy to reroute to the correct course. Under towering evergreens plush with moss, the route—which followed an old, now defunct highway—more closely resembled a meandering forest trail than a road. Sunlight sifted through lofty branches to paint the crumbling pavement in a soft, hazy light. After my brief foray on the fast-paced highway, I felt as though I had trading the modern, industrial world for an enchanted one. A quieter place imbued with a soothing, sedative magic.

It turned out, unfortunately, to be a run-of-the-mill bout of post-lunch sleepiness I was experiencing, my eyelids growing heavier with every revolution of the wheels. *Focus on the work*, I told myself, heaving my weight behind the pedals in an effort to raise my heart rate and shake the lethargy.

. . .

Prior to the Trans Am, I had hallucinated just once. Day two of the Swan River 1200: a 1,200-kilometre (746 mile) loop ride that starts and finishes in Winnipeg, Manitoba, traversing prairie lake country and remote parkland north of Manitoba's capital. Somewhere around 1:00 a.m. on the second night, while tackling a lonesome stretch of backroad en route to a checkpoint in Dauphin, I lost touch with reality.

First, it was the blazing lights of a towering farm building that I envisioned as a landing UFO, search lighting for humans in crop fields. While part of me recognized there had to be a legitimate explanation, I advanced with mounting hesitation, my paranoia manifest in accelerating heart rate and convoluted thoughts. The relief in passing—and the realization that space aliens were not casting for the role of abductee—was replaced by further confusion as the yellow dotted centre line transformed into a conveyor-belt of super-sized fries, peeling from the roadway on approach.

I reached Dauphin after 5:00 a.m. Legs cooked; brain fried; eyes bloodshot from floating particles released by nighttime combining in the fields. The next morning—or, more accurately, when I awoke two hours later with a cramped neck from sleeping on the floor—I realized just how recklessly out-of-it I'd been the night before. Lucky that no vehicles had passed. Aside from the aliens and vivid fast food apparitions, the episode read like a liquor blackout: I recalled nothing. I vowed never to skirt that close to the edge again.

I recognized when I registered for the Trans Am that I'd be pushing myself to new limits—both physically and psychologically—inviting situations similar to that hallucinatory night in Manitoba as I grappled with the effects of sleep deprivation, hypoglycemia, and the toll of hundreds of thousands of pedal strokes. So, I devised a safer course of action: if I saw the Hamburglar chasing french fries down the highway, I vowed to pull over and rest until my head was straight again. A fast finishing time was not worth risking my life over.

. . .

Thankfully, my strategy of upping the intensity to stay alert on a peaceful Oregon backroad proved successful. Soon, I was fully lucid, enjoying the subtle change of scenery as woods transitioned to farmland. As the miles ripped by, I reviewed my target for the night, and my overarching game plan for surviving nearly 4,300 miles in the saddle.

Since I wasn't racing the Trans Am to win—I didn't even expect to make top ten—my goal was simply to ride across America as fast as I could. Winners typically finish in sixteen to eighteen days; anything over a month is considered touring. A looming return-to-work deadline constrained my efforts to a one-month timeline as well. If I could finish in twenty-five days, I'd have time to recover on a sandy beach in Yorktown for a day or so before boarding a plane home. I used the Swan River 1200 as a pacing guide: I completed that event in four days, averaging 186 miles (300 kilometres) each day. While I had the advantage of support at the overnight control points, I remained hindered by the distinct disadvantage of a heavier touring bicycle, built for comfort over speed and ill-equipped for riding from dawn until dusk (and then some).

Now, armed with a real road bike—made of carbon, no less—clipless pedals and proper frame bags, I hoped to sustain my Swan River pace for the duration of the Trans Am. From the comfort of my kitchen table in Saskatoon, months before the race, I glanced over the route and told myself that goal was entirely attainable. Bring on the hills and heartache; the out-of-your-seat climbs and lonely switchback roads. I would be ready.

. . .

My pre-season training went well: I managed regular attendance at a local spin studio throughout the winter, and despite a slow spring start hindered by sub-zero temperatures and frosty roadways, I'd completed several 100-mile-plus days without difficulty, although none of them back-to-back. By June, I'd refined my kit choices and hacked out a nutrition strategy. The only thing left to do was try, and adjust my plan accordingly. If I could maintain my intended pace of 186 miles a day, I would be on track to finish within twenty-three days. However, my more relaxed objective of a sub-twenty-five-day finish accounted for likely delays caused by mechanicals, weather, and accumulated fatigue.

To stay on course for my ambitious goal, I packed light, and for the first few days set daily destination targets based on my mileage goals. Since aerodynamics also play a role in enabling a faster pace, I situated my bags close to the bike frame, where they would incur the least resistance—a common practice in bikepacking and ultra-endurance racing. In addition to items of basic hygiene, bike maintenance, and electronics charging, I brought one full set of kit. On top of the clothing I was wearing—new padded shorts and an equally new geometrically patterned black and blue jersey featuring a silhouette of a stag—I included arm warmers, leg warmers, long-fingered and short-fingered gloves, shoe covers, a neck warmer, a merino wool base layer, a raincoat, and a pair of rain chaps that I would later discover to be next to useless. My clothing, along with my sleep set-up, were stored in my rear seat pack; small, heavy items went in my frame bag; frequently used or easy-to-misplace items (like my wallet, headphones, and multitool) lived in my top tube bag.

On day one—I mean, day zero—I'd hoped to make it past Corvallis, Oregon; day one, near Mitchell; day two, Richland; and day three, White Bird, Idaho. I didn't necessarily envision myself staying in these communities. Whatever side-of-the-road hide-away I found to pitch my bivy (a compact, weatherproof sack that wraps your sleeping bag, eerily similar to a body bag) would suffice.

My race plan ended at White Bird, where I hoped to re-evaluate my progress and sketch out the following days, breaking the journey into manageable chunks. With countless unknowns—topography, weather, not to mention my own bodily limitations—advanced route planning seemed futile.

Had I known then what I know now, however, I would have spent more time researching the route—in particular the elevation profile. With a little digging, it would have quickly become apparent that much of the terrain lies above 4,000 feet, bringing nighttime temperatures near freezing. I would have also discovered that, while the bulk of the elevation appears in the first half as the route heads over the Cascade Range and the Rocky Mountains,

the states of Missouri and Kentucky—with their jagged, spikey rollers—
have more accumulative vertical gain. It is not all downhill from the high
point in Hoosier Pass, Colorado, as I'd wishfully imagined.

On day zero, I set my tires toward a tiny blip on the map called Peoria.
A cursory survey of Google Maps showed little more than a collection of
houses, a church, and a rest area by the river—perfect for my intended
purposes of bivying down unnoticed. Only ten miles past Corvallis and
thirteen miles from the next town of Harrisburg, Peoria was ideally situated
to stock up on supplies before bed, and access services again in the morning.
It seemed like the perfect setup, aside from one small hitch: it had been years
since I'd stealth camped. It was also the first time I'd opted for a bivy sack
instead of a more spacious tent. The prospect of plunking myself down for
the night in a strange place, alone, instilled anxiety—a tight pinch in my
chest—a sensation amplified by visualizing myself hostage to the suffocating
close quarters of a bivy sack. Given a moment to dwell on these scenarios,
the darker corners of my mind unspooled a frightening narrative of limb-
chomping bears, predatory men, and gun-brandishing farmers whose
property I might accidentally trespass on.

To ease these fears, I should have taken the bivy for a dry run in Saskatchewan to gain some familiarity with both the bag, and the act of stealth
camping. Instead, I found myself consumed by work, the closest simulation
being a night in the backyard in which I barely made it until 4:00 a.m. before caving to the cold, and darting indoors to the comfort of my boyfriend's
arms. Still, I tried to reassure myself: despite failing to endure even a night
outdoors in Saskatoon (which, in my defense, experiences surprisingly cool
nighttime temperatures, even on the verge of summer) I'd stealth camped—
often solo—on cycling trips plenty of times before without dire consequenes.
Hopefully, my fears would abate after a few nights on the road, and the
practice of stealing sleep in out-of-the-way places became once again part of
my daily routine.

. . .

I reached the outskirts of Corvallis as the light waned toward dusk. A couple cheered me on from the curb as I approached a gas station just north of the city, their lit-up faces vanquishing any trace of fatigue or stiffness that had worked its way into my muscles. This was my first encounter with a dot-watcher, or more accurately, a pair of them. Surprised, I smiled and waved. When the dotwatchers called my name, I pulled over to chat.

"Good job, Meaghan!" said the man, a rangy fellow in shorts that re-vealed well-defined quadriceps. He clasped my sweaty hand between his, grinning as if I'd just won a spelling bee.

"We've been watching your dot—if you hurry, you can still get some-thing to eat."

Relieved to know my Spot had been broadcasting properly after that last-minute relocation from seat post to handlebars, I left my bike in the care of the two dotwatchers and rushed inside, where the gas station manager was handing out free provisions to Trans Am racers. I'm unashamed to admit that I took full advantage of his generosity. Minutes later, I emerged with an armful of what would become race staples: Gatorade, chocolate milk, and bananas. This, in addition to the protein bars I'd carried from Astoria, would see me through until I reached the next resupply the following morning.

I chatted with the couple before pedalling on to Corvallis, intrigued by their enthusiasm and curious to understand what attracted them to the arm-chair sport of dotwatching.

"Ya'll are simply amazing," said the woman, whose sporty physique led me to imagine her as a high-performing recreational tennis player or colle-giate swimmer. "We just can't believe what you're doing."

They lived in Corvallis and came out every June to cheer on the racers, planting themselves alongside the highway to offer words of encouragement.

"At this pace, you should be over McKenzie Pass by noon tomorrow," said the man. "I'm heading up the climb myself—first time this season."

I sailed toward the city in high spirits, a grin plastered ear to ear and my heart skipping rope like a gleeful sixth-grader in my chest, excited about the prospect of tomorrow's ascent over McKenzie Pass, with treats bulging from jersey pockets as the skyline burned dusky orange. I was also, perhaps, flattered by the thought of someone other than my mother and boyfriend keeping tabs on my progress. I wondered how many other dotwatchers were out there, glued to their screens as racers' dots marched from one side of the continent to the other like a parade of determined ants.

. . .

Luxuriously wide bike lanes under leafy green boulevards guided me through Corvallis, nearly 200 miles from Astoria. I intended to keep rolling until I found a spot to bunk down, yet couldn't help but stop when I was showered with rose petals crossing a bike-pedestrian bridge over the Willamette River. I traced the scarlet polka dots across wooden slats, stamped in place by footprints or bike tires, until I encountered the source: a woman with wind-tousled hair, an arm lifted overhead after another proud flourish of petals.

"Welcome to Oregon!" she said. "Enjoy the Rose State."

Who are you? I wondered. With only ten miles to go, I could afford to find out.

The lip of her patchwork skirt floated an inch above the bridge deck. Dark lengths of silken hair cascaded around the basket's handle, rippling behind her shoulders as she reached for another handful of petals and gleefully tossed them in the air—a crimson flurry raining down upon us.

That's when I noticed the man in the red raincoat leaning against a wooden railing, like a cowboy from an old Western.

"You've made it," he said. He stood about my height, the brim of a cap shading his eyes. "What, you don't recognize me without my bicycle?" he added, his voice softly accented. Barely detectable over the river's crash and tumble below.

Something clicked: Swiss racer, Rolf Moser. I'd seen him around Astoria. I eyed him up again—clean-shaven, about fifty—this time noticing his cycling cleats and standard issue Trans Am cap that matched my own. Rolf mentioned he was staying in a hotel overlooking the river.

"I decided to go for a stroll before bed," he said, satisfying my curiosity about how he got to the bridge, though the question of why he wasn't on the road hung in the air—it wasn't even dark.

The three of us chatted for twenty minutes, Rolf and I enthusing about the glorious coast before turning attentive as Flower Lady expounded her love for Corvallis, her animosity toward recently elected President Trump. No other racers came by, leading me to believe that I must be at the tail end of the pack—I would check the Trackleaders website later. I had a particular interest in the whereabouts of Nuno, who I thankfully hadn't crossed paths with for over an hour.

A pair of commuting cyclists whisked through.

"You should get going," said Rolf.

A gust of wind swept over the bridge, plucking petals from the slats and dropping them into the sparkling river beneath. The air became perceptibly cooler, my legs stiffening with the momentary drop in temperature.

He was right. Daylight stretched thin. It was still a race, even if I was bringing up the back of the pack. At least Rolf was behind me. I said goodbye to both Rolf and Flower Lady—cheeks flushed to match the petals in her basket—before slipping into the surrounding farmland. Already envisioning a riverside nook in Peoria, the stream's reassuring surge rocking me to sleep.

. . .

I rolled out my bivy for the first time in a churchyard in Peoria. A deficiency of flat sleeping space had thwarted my plan for a riverside camp spot, and an unscheduled hunt for a dropped glove between that first place, and when I noticed its absence at the church, had set me back another fifteen minutes. Luckily, I located the glove, and took such care that I did not lose another until the final days in Virginia, when everything fell to pieces. The rural placidity of the churchyard—located a couple blocks off the main road—

calmed any lingering anxieties I had about solo camping. I imagined the simple, white steeple guarding over me as I slept. It was just after 10:00 p.m. when I climbed into my bivy and opened Trackleaders to discover how I stacked up against the competition.

I wasn't actually doing too poorly. Plenty of racers had opted to overnight in Corvallis, some further back still. I silently cheered for Eric, en route to Harrisburg, my proposed morning resupply point. DBR's dot showed up in Corvallis. A handful hadn't slowed after nightfall and appeared to be smashing their way through an ocean of darkness toward McKenzie Pass.

With knowledge of where I stood, I congratulated myself on making it this far—212 miles in one day, if you counted detours—though I remained annoyed about wasting precious minutes off course, in addition to the hassle of combing the roadside with my bike light in search of a carelessly dropped glove. But this was only day zero—it would take time to settle into a groove, I reminded myself. At least I'd caught my errors early. Plus, I hadn't gone off route since Corvallis, evidence my navigational abilities were indeed rising to the challenge.

The trouble now was that knowing my overall standing had left me wired. Too excited for sleep. My decision to stop at this arbitrary mile marker seemed foolish—why not keep going? My legs felt great. I could roll up my bivy bag in one quick minute and catch Eric in Harrisburg.

I plugged my cellphone into a battery pack and set it next to me inside the bivy, the foil crinkling like Christmas wrapping in response to the slightest positional adjustment. From a neighbouring backyard, a dog barked.

Should I continue?

But within seconds of my head touching the makeshift pillow of bundled clothing, I slipped into an unshakable slumber.

Day One

JUNE 4, 2017

PEORIA TO MITCHELL, OREGON

DISTANCE: 214 MILES

RACE MILEAGE: 416 OF 4,264 MILES

It was not my alarm, but the painful urge to urinate to which I awoke. I tromped behind some rhododendron bushes on the fringes of the churchyard to empty my bladder, teeth chattering by the time I returned to my bivy sack. Not yet 4:30 a.m., but already time to hit the road.

Unfortunately, the fiasco of dressing in the dark, in addition to the discovery of a smashed yogurt cup in my seat-post bag—what to do with six messy ounces of dairy?—delayed my departure. I considered licking the bag clean, but the possibility of self-inflicted food poisoning so early in the race seemed like a terrible tactical decision. I used the last of my precious napkins to wipe up the spill.

Morning light burned on the horizon, a fiery tangerine against the dark outline of cornstalks anchored in hushed fields. I sloughed off the night. Legs limbering with every revolution of the pedals. As I reached for a banana, a pair of tires sidled up alongside me.

"Nice morning for a little ride, isn't it?"

I recognized the voice as Rolf Moser's. Though dismayed about being caught so early, I was delighted to see Rolf and his red raincoat again. He possessed an understated kindness that put me at ease; a reassuring calmness. His voice carried the soothing, unhurried rhythms of a fairy-tale narrator. We chatted in the pre-dawn light until the shadowed outskirts of Harrisburg, when I had to let him go.

"See you down the road," I said, unconvincingly.

Rolf maintained a pace much quicker than I could sustain. He had only stopped the night before, I discovered, because of a hotel reservation in Corvallis. If not for his booking, he might have put another twenty miles on before packing it in.

As Rolf glided from sight, I vowed this would not be the last we met.

. . .

I continued alongside serpentine creeks and pretty vanilla horses, the sun still tucked behind a thickening treeline. McKenzie Pass—the race's first major hurdle—loomed large. Unseen, yet legendary. A 3,668-foot climb over the Cascade Range topping out at an elevation of 5,325 feet, McKenzie Pass promised to be an early predictor of podium favourites, most of whom ascended the night before with little or no sleep. This morning would take me through lush wilderness on the western slope, the road curling up an ancient lava field before flying down the other side, the Three Sisters range standing sentinel over ponderosa pines below. Already, the throng of racers had thinned. Every once in a while, I'd shoot past a guy relieving himself in the trees, but mostly, I rode alone.

After breakfast in McKenzie Bridge, about sixty miles from the church in Peoria where I started that morning, I turned off for the climb. Temperatures surged as the sun bobbed above the treeline. It was a stretch of the imagination to believe the pass had opened less than a week ago, when the plows came through to remove several feet of snow. Seven days earlier, I was still accumulating training miles in Saskatchewan.

. . .

May had been a pleasant month. Regular shifts at work topped up my bank account, while long days with little wind presented opportunities to roll out before dawn and ride until supper on weekends. But early spring—March and April—posed serious training challenges. Eager to ride outdoors, I hit the pavement as soon as the highway shoulder cleared, disregarding the fact that spring temperatures routinely fell below freezing. Once, I headed out at 5:00 a.m., covering quick ground in anticipation of a greasy diner breakfast at a gas station forty-five miles east of the city. I arrived to find the gas station closed, and reversed course to confront a bone-chilling prairie headwind. I pulled over at the first sign of shelter—an outhouse in the Elstow rest area— to call my boyfriend, Tyler.

"Help!" I cried. It was 9:00 a.m. on a Sunday morning. He'd been at the bar watching a UFC match the night before. "I'm stuck in a shitter and can't feel my feet."

Tyler picked me up an hour later, bringing a Tim Hortons double-double and two cream-cheese bagels. The ground hadn't thawed, so my time in a roadside outhouse wasn't as malodorous as it might have been. I apologized for conning Tyler into a hungover rescue mission. It took hours for my extremities to regain sensation, even longer for my ego to heal.

. . .

A series of tight, switchback turns traced an old wagon trail up McKenzie Pass deep into woods, the mountainside a study in green. Thin-needled conifers mingled with leafy maples, the roadside skirted by salal and huckleberry. Bird calls were joined by a chorus of rustling leaves.

The top half of the pass remained closed to vehicle traffic. I found myself overtaken instead by road cyclists—Sunday warriors with fresh legs and no superfluous gear. They zipped by, leaving me gasping in their wake. One of these riders happened to be the enthusiastic dotwatcher from Corvallis's

Chevron gas station. This time, it was me offering encouragement when he passed, as I stood munching a granola bar on the road's edge.

Gradually, the trees diminished. First in height, then altogether. Frenetic green was replaced by volcanic debris, a moonscape of lava-rock. I donned my jacket as snow accumulated, its crusty skiff blanketing the rubble. As I neared the summit, the snowbank was piled high enough to form a sheer vertical wall to my right. A chill bit my ankles. Tiny hairs on my arms and legs buzzed electric in the frigid air as yesterday's coastal capes and sea lion bellows evaporated from memory like dissolving clouds. My presence on this mountaintop of extremes—summer snowdrifts coupled with the remnants of a volcanic eruption—elicited a thrill. A sensation of almost criminal delight. I tuned into the mountain's frequency: the crackle of snow melt under radiant sunshine, the surge of wind mingling with the wheeze of my own strained lungs.

. . .

I reunited with Eric at a Mexican restaurant in Sisters, the first town after the pass. Alongside several other famished racers, we tore into burritos, rice, and beans, amassing origami mountains of soiled napkins during the friendly bonhomie. The two of us swapped stories as we tipped back glasses of ice water: after a brief respite of high mountain air, temperatures had crept even higher on the descent into Central Oregon.

"Where are you heading tonight?" asked Eric. "Know about the hostel in Mitchell?"

I'd planned on wilderness camping: bivying down and rising early, same as the night before.

"Are you really prepared for that?" asked a young American rider as he pushed an empty plate away. "It'll be a hell of a lot colder at elevation."

The others nodded in agreement.

Admittedly, I'd given little thought to the effects of mountain ranges on temperature. Accounting for massive gains in elevation was simply not something I'd had to consider while living on the Prairies, but as I reflected on the piles of snow flanking the road only an hour ago, it suddenly seemed like the consequences of elevation would be unwise to ignore. In the Mexican restaurant, I googled the distance from Sisters to Mitchell: ninety miles. It was past two o'clock, and McKenzie Pass had already taken a toll on my legs—was it possible to reach the hostel tonight? Maybe. Suddenly, our bill couldn't come soon enough.

We set out together, a loosely tethered pack of five. The others fell away as the wind picked up, and soon, it was just Eric and me, pedalling hard toward Prineville. The hot, dry air clobbered my lungs; giant pinecones scattered the road's edge. Then the trees gave way, and the landscape opened up like the glossy pages of a coffee-table book: high country. This was the wild west, and we were cowboys on metal horses—blasting off in search of untold adventure.

I was determined to make it to Mitchell now, and my speedometer ticked higher as a tailwind took hold. I tucked low and kicked into the pedals. Eric leapfrogged ahead as we reached a hillcrest, unleashing a spirited shriek into surrounding red rock. "Yorktown, we're coming for you!"

Eric pumped a fist in the air, breathing hard. Grin wider than his face. Riding purely for the thrill, immune to every obstacle in his path. I fed off his kineticism, ignoring the stifling heat and sweat marinating my sports bra. On seeing Eric's undisguised glee, I couldn't help but feel the tug of the road on my own heart—*carpe diem*. Instead of taking a breather, I gripped the bars and prepared for a fast descent.

I chased Eric down, then back up again. Hill after soaring hill. My legs grew heavy—hammering might not have been the best strategy, I'd later admit—but I was too full of adrenaline to ease off.

In that moment, there were no fences.

. . .

Darkness blanketed the highway. As Eric and I disappeared into the Ochoco Wilderness, our tones became hushed, conspiratorial. The steady ascent meant our pedalling grew torpid, inhalations laboured. During steeper sections, I barely mustered the energy to keep moving. Nighttime temperatures steadily fell. We layered up to ward off the increasing cold as we gained elevation, alternately clenching our hands into fists to drive blood back into fingertips. We never mentioned that stopping no longer remained an option: we needed to make it to the hostel in Mitchell now. As we pressed on, Eric and I exchanged stories about tenacious headwinds and torrential deluges, double centuries and 400-kilometre brevets. The inference was that this—assailed by cold and fatigue, unmoored in the darkness—was nothing we couldn't handle.

"I've never understood night riding," pondered Eric. "You can't see anything."

Indeed, that evening, we witnessed nothing. What I do recall was Eric's company, the quiet back and forth between us. So mundane, I nearly forgot we were racing. Therein lies the beauty of riding at night, I realized. A shift of focus from sights distant to close at hand.

· · ·

We crashed into Mitchell at half-past midnight. Extremities numb from the razor wind, a final ripping downhill into the insatiable maw of the night. Spoke'n Hostel shone like a lighthouse in the distance. Yet to ensure we didn't pass our only service opportunity for fifty miles in either direction, a troop of volunteers waited on the road to flag us down. Eric and I stumbled into a rec room warm with body heat. A spread of pasta and bread, fruit and chocolate bars, juice and coffee laid magnificently before us. I pinched full-fingered gloves off with my teeth, stuffing bills into a donation jar before serving myself a mountain of pasta topped with garlicky tomato sauce that smouldered toward the plate's edges like steaming hot lava.

Despite the cozy surroundings, I shivered violently. Cold emanated from my diaphragm in tight, sickening bursts. A volunteer fetched a quilt to wrap me up in, then pressed hot cocoa into my hands. I shut my eyes for a moment, savouring a sensation best described as blessed.

"Thank you," I whispered, willing the shaking to subside.

After a few minutes it did, but not without causing me to wonder what might have happened had I tried to bivy in the mountains. Places like Spoke'n Hostel were few and far between along the TransAmerica Trail. For myself and others passing through—both racers and touring cyclists alike—the hostel provided a much-needed respite, the volunteers engaged in a well-oiled machine of hospitality. Spoke'n Hostel existed as a welcome outpost on the fringes, their dedication to the wayward traveller surpassing every possible expectation.

A volunteer led me to the dormitory after eating. Still caped in a quilt, I was silently ushered to a bottom bunk, the volunteer's quick flash of a headlamp locating a USB outlet. I flopped onto the bunk and plugged in my electronics. Across the aisle, a sleepy head poked from the covers—Rolf. He grinned.

"Didn't think you'd arrive tonight," he whispered. His practical, shaved head matched his clean-shaven face.

"Wasn't sure I'd make it either. See you at breakfast."

Finally, I had caught up with Mr. Moser. I set my alarm for 4:00 a.m., and prepared to join the ranks of shattered, snoring cyclists.

Day Two

JUNE 5, 2017

MITCHELL TO RICHLAND, OREGON

DISTANCE: 187 MILES

RACE MILEAGE: 605 OF 4,264 MILES

I hatched a revised game plan in Mitchell. No longer content to merely finish within twenty-five days, I wanted to race. See my dot at the front of the pack. This new goal had me shoving off blankets to return to the mountain highway with less than three hours of pillow time. Eric slept soundly in a bunk across the dorm as I gathered my belongings and snuck out the door. I felt a hint of guilt for deserting him, but it was time to discover what I was made of. The best way to put my abilities to the test was alone. Since we rode at a similar speed, I assumed Eric and I would meet again, either down the road, or clinking beers in celebration at the finish line in Yorktown. Besides, we'd exchanged numbers—I could always check in with a text.

Things rolled along fine, at first. The day marked the second in a row that I rode alongside Rolf. We took in the Painted Hills rocky slopes in the fresh light of day, chatting amicably as we passed several still-sleepy riders on the ascent to Keys Summit. He rode with an ease and grace that I envied, yet imagined could keep up with, if only I remained focused. Then we began to trend downhill and he picked up speed, ripping around hairpin turns at a breakneck pace I had no ambition in following. Rolf abandoned me once again in his dust shortly after sunrise.

I paused in Dayville to warm up at the general store, but kept my stop brief, pushing on before anyone else pulled into the parking lot. Signs of habitation appeared with increased frequency. Utility lines loped down the highway, and rambling wire fences stitched together the patchwork of farms and ranches. Heat-resistant pines spotted nearby hillsides, while pockets of prickly scrub grew alongside the road. I congratulated myself on staying ahead of the riders I'd passed leaving Mitchell, but still wished I had the mettle to keep up with Rolf and his red raincoat on that last descent.

I should have sought solid food forty-four miles later as I passed through Prairie City, but I craved only liquids. Dust clung to my calves, the insides of my nostrils. The mercury had skyrocketed since Dayville; I reasoned that I needed to ingest something frigid to bring my internal temperature down. Plus, Rolf's dot appeared to be slowing—now was my chance to spring ahead and rejoin him. I stopped to purchase a cold drink, thinking that I could eat later—dig a granola bar from my frame bag once I was back on the road. Unfortunately, the drug store offered nothing appealing. The market next door was even worse. While not my first choice—or even second or third—I grabbed a strawberry milk to avoid wasting more time, and mixed a tablespoon of caffeinated pre-workout powder into a tepid water bottle to counteract the onset of afternoon fatigue as I prepared to set out.

· · ·

I was digging into Dixie Summit, the first major climb after Prairie City, when my stomach rebelled: a breathtaking, atavistic hurt that reared against the sidewall of my gut. Instead of nourishing my body, the strawberry milk appeared to be at war with the pre-workout powder, both sides drawing their weapons to do battle inside my gut. Opposing armies of sharpened crystals and tiny screws pierced my abdominal wall. I buckled in the saddle. Instead of taking in the striking mountain vistas and wooded descents along the Old West Scenic Bike Route, I fought to stay upright, unable to focus on anything other than the pavement scrolling beneath me.

My GPS map indicated three climbs and eighty miles separated me from Baker City, where the terrain flattened out. No wonder Rolf's dot had slowed—the grade shot up to twelve percent. I bled sweat under the midday sun, perspiration prickling my eyes and soaking my socks. Battling cramps and nausea, it took every shard of energy to sustain forward progress. The slimy, too-sweet taste of strawberry milk seeped up from my esophagus to coat the dry cavern of my mouth like a wash of Pepto Bismol. I downed most of my water on the first climb, but failed to rinse the medicinally artificial flavour from my palate. As heat radiated up from the pavement, I panned toward a viewpoint featuring a replica Conestoga wagon—a tribute to the great western migration of settlers—and considered sneaking inside to escape the inferno and allow my stomach to settle. In desperation, I bargained with myself:

Once you reach the summit, you get to rest going down.

Fifteen minutes and you can have another Advil.

Just. Keep. Pedalling.

Trees shot skyward like bars imprisoning me on the highway. My chances of meeting Rolf again decreased by the minute, yet I hoped to stay ahead of two riders with the initials MR and JB. You didn't need to physically see someone to mark them as competition, since the precise location of every racer could be revealed from a glance at the Trackleaders website. I obsessively tapped refresh each time I debated stopping. Sheer dread of being passed by those two mystery riders kept me grinding the pedals, even when my body screamed to dismount and lie down in the woods.

. . .

I arrived at Baker City late in the afternoon, tomato-paste red and thrashed from the trio of climbs under a blistering sun. That morning I set out with the intention to race—what was I thinking? I could barely keep the wheels turning. Thankfully, my cramps had subsided into a manageable discomfort, no worse than moderate period symptoms.

A main street hinted at Baker City's status as a once-bustling centre, brick and stone buildings bearing historic signs and colourful rooftops. As I pedalled past the Geiser Grand Hotel with its watchful clock tower, I reflected on how I'd gained some distance on the others. Solid food remained out of the question, but I knew I'd need calories later. With this in mind, I bought three bananas, two breakfast sandwiches, and a half-gallon of Pepsi at a gas station. After stuffing the provisions into pockets, I sucked up the soda curbside, hoping the sugar would keep me buzzing until I reached my nighttime destination. Then I checked my cellphone.

From the Facebook page, I learned that Andrew Suzuki, the first rider to Baker City, had scratched from the race due to Shermer's Neck—a brutal ailment unique to cyclists where the neck muscles literally give out after extended periods in the aerobars. The rider's head falls to the side, or against his chest, like a newborn baby's. I also received two messages: one from my boyfriend, Tyler, asking me to call him. Another from my mother.

Meaghan, you are doing so well! Can't believe it. We've been watching your dot...

It was a lengthy one. I tried to imagine my mother tapping it out, elbows resting against the cutting board as she took a break from chopping up a garden-fresh salad. She mentioned my father had reviewed the elevation profile and was impressed by how I weathered the back-to-back climbs. Even my most technologically resistant relatives were following along on Trackleaders. At the end of the message, she told me to check my bank account.

A deposit for $1,000 dollars.

The number stared back at me, the sum in my savings account instantly tripled.

I put my phone away, heart full and happy. I decided to thank her as soon as I hopped on the bike, but Tyler called first. We chatted as I pedalled from town.

"Hi babe, how's it going?"

"Not bad, how are things in Saskatoon?"

Tyler and I had spoken every day since I left Canada, our conversations brief, fractured by poor reception, strident wind, or my anxiety of having to be in two places at once. Today was no different. Worse, he only wanted to chitchat, which wasn't what I felt like doing with lingering abdominal pain and decisions still to be made about how far I would ride that evening.

I rolled toward arid countryside as the sun slouched low, listening to the latest antics from the household cats and how he and Josh (our roommate) test ran a pizza recipe. Another bout of nausea hit as Highway 86 sloped up an insidious hill, and I found myself doubled over once again, unable to articulate anything beyond "mm-hmm" and "uh-huh." I had to go.

"Love you, too," I said.

. . .

Tyler and I got together in the spring of 2016 and began cohabiting almost at once. I'd been living with two colleagues from the Masters of Fine Arts in Writing program, but one of them had abruptly packed up to head back to British Columbia, leaving myself and Patrick, the remaining roommate, to wrestle with the decision of renting the extra room, or moving out ourselves. Neither Patrick nor I had solid plans for after our thesis defence. It was serendipitous timing that Tyler, who shared a two-storey place with a few housemates—laidback stoners with big, gracious hearts—had rooms open up. Patrick and I moved in, and another classmate, Nicole, occupied the upstairs office space. Patrick's partner from Montreal arrived for the summer, and then we added two cats to the existing cat and dog. With parents, friends, and siblings arriving every weekend, it was a full house.

We nicknamed our home the "Weird House" because the street address was on Weir Crescent, and the house itself was spruced up with cheap décor from the Halloween store that most of us had worked at for some brief point in time. With a revolving door of roommates and guests, there was always something unusual happening. I enjoyed the companionship of my writing colleagues as we polished our manuscripts and prepared for upcoming defence dates. When the Weird House became crowded, Tyler and I pitched a tent in the garden, sipping mugs of before-work coffee on the back steps as Tyler's snarky Siamese slunk around our ankles.

Others, a gym rat and someone's younger brother, eventually replaced the writers. On weekends, Tyler's friends would arrive to watch the Pay-Per-View UFC fight, chasing their beers with bong hits. I'd hang out to watch a few rounds, but sneak off to read in bed when I had the chance.

While not the life I had imagined, it wasn't bad, either. In fact, I liked my situation enough to decide against moving back to British Columbia. I found a rewarding job as a volunteer coordinator at a student-run health and wellness clinic and took steps toward making Saskatchewan my permanent residence. I still remember the day I switched over my driver's license—not long after I'd successfully defended in the fall of 2016—swapping British Columbia's "Best Place on Earth" motto for an orange Prairie Lily with green text.

"Wow," I said, turning the shiny new card over in my hands. "Guess it's official: I'm from Saskatchewan now!"

Tyler pointed out that I'd lived in the province for over two years—updating my license was no more than a legal formality.

For me, however, it signified a milestone: my choice to leave family and friends behind to pursue a life with Tyler in Saskatoon.

. . .

A full moon hovered like a candle flame over the Powder River. Above sage and scrub brush, the sky darkened from peach to baby blue to wild blackberry. After getting off the phone with Tyler, I scanned the route to learn that Highway 86 continued east into Idaho, running through Richland, Pine, and Copperfield. The communities offered little in the way of services, but my provisions would see me through until morning. Moreover, the hard part—unforgiving heat, ruthless cramps, and far more climbing than I expected—was finally over. I failed to achieve my goal of transforming into a front-of-the-pack racer overnight, but things could be worse—at least I didn't pass out with heatstroke in a ditch. Placated by the river's aria and a luminous moon overhead, I could convalesce; enjoy the quietude of night. Though I didn't know it then, my experience pedalling through the day on an empty stomach hinted at the mental and physical fortitude I would cultivate over the coming weeks. Instead of phoning my mother, I tapped out a quick thank you message, promising to touch base in the morning.

For the first time since Prairie City, my mind felt clear. While I hadn't eaten for hours, the sandwiches in my back pocket and moonlight all around buoyed me with reassurance. Every bend in the river amplified my courage, a conviction in myself; the gnawing stress of being chased finally dissolved with the closing day. At last, I could simply ride. Savour the lonesome freedom of the road as it traced the Powder River toward Idaho's state line.

Day Three

JUNE 6, 2017

RICHLAND, OREGON TO WHITE BIRD, IDAHO

DISTANCE: 180 MILES

RACE MILEAGE: 788 OF 4,264 MILES

I rolled out of Richland after a night at the Hitching Post, a budget motel on Main and First whose tacky neon sign advertised vacancy.

"Thanks, Mom," I said as I keyed open the door the evening before, grateful for her financial blessing and the opportunity to spend an evening of solitary comfort indoors. I leaned my bicycle against the wall and set to showering both self and cycling kit, wringing my jersey, shorts, socks, and sports bra in a towel before draping each item over the shower rod to dry. Then I climbed into bed naked to devour the first of my breakfast sand-wiches, only to pass out minutes later with the lamp on. In the morning, I blasted my still-damp clothes with the blow-dryer before wolfing down the remaining sandwich and two bananas in frantic hunger. While relieved to have my appetite back, depleting my provisions before even hitting the road triggered concern.

Shuttered doors and unlit 5:00 a.m. shop windows dashed any hope of replenishing my supplies before leaving Richland. But then I remembered the stash of protein bars tucked in my frame bag. I'd be fine. Perhaps my successful push through heat and nausea the previous day had left me emboldened—though I vowed to avoid strawberry milk in the future. I kicked out of Richland on Highway 86 in honeyed light, a soundtrack of Johnny Cash strumming "Man in Black" in my earbuds a pitch perfect pairing to the western storefronts and dry expanse of rolling countryside.

. . .

The road belonged to me during those early morning hours. After a quick descent, I cruised east through farmland greenbelts toward Pine and Halfway. I could have counted on one hand the number of vehicles that passed before I arrived in Copperfield, where Highway 86 transitioned into the Hells Canyon Road. My pace dropped off once I reached Snake River, the dividing line between Oregon and Idaho. Beneath a leaden sky, the route followed the southbound flow of blue—dammed to create the Oxbow Reservoir—as canyon walls soared overhead. Every so often, I'd spot a pullout where one might pitch camp, tucked alongside the water's edge.

Conditions were decent—no hills, wind, or extreme temperature fluctuations—but my heart rate wouldn't budge. With few vehicles and no riders in the vicinity, I found myself hypnotized by the gently winding river, my sense of urgency evaporating like early morning dew. Boredom, or mental fatigue, left me drifting—as if my bicycle were a floating cloud I could steer, but not accelerate.

Pick up the pace, I told myself.

This was an opportunity to put easy miles behind me. But my eyes glazed over, mirroring the placid reservoir wedged between valley walls.

It wasn't long before I received a message from Marj, a cycling buddy from Saskatoon.

Hey you! What's going on? Saw your average drop. Windy??!?

Marj had messaged every morning since I'd left Astoria, Oregon. She was usually up early to bike to work or babysit her granddaughter. As the race wore on, I grew to depend on Marj's daily encouragement, and while I didn't always answer, that never deterred the incoming messages.

Today, I tapped out a response.

Nope, good conditions. Just tired, I guess.

My phone buzzed again.

Psh! how many hours of sleep did you get—seven? Hop to it!

I smiled with the recognition she had kept a watchful eye on my whereabouts—though in reality I'd slept less than five hours. Then my phone erupted with a series of messages:

Have you eaten?!?

Idaho is around the corner—you can do it!!

Bob says Hi.

I wasn't hungry, but I tore open the packaging on a protein bar anyway. Hours had passed since my hotel-room breakfast, and I was digging myself deeper into a caloric deficit with every minute on the bike. As I gnawed through the mulchy, too-chewy bar, I saw Marj working at the café, a pan of mouth-watering cinnamon buns rising in the oven and the mixer whirring up something else. I imagined her toggling between Trackleaders and Google Maps, trying to grasp the lay of the land and anticipate what terrain I'd encounter next. She routinely texted weather reports and queried my clothing choices. To describe Marj as cycling obsessed was an understatement. She was a randonneur: someone who thought nothing of putting 600 kilometres behind her on a single weekend ride.

. . .

My first encounter with the sport of randonneuring occurred in 2014. The summer newspaper headlines exploded with the grisly story of a Burnaby cyclist shot near Spences Bridge, British Columbia, during a 600-kilometre brevet. The act of senseless violence not only caught my eye, but enticed me to know more about why someone was riding their bike so far from anywhere in the middle of the night. To this day the incident remains unexplained.

Was it a random attack? Anti-cyclist road rage? Case of mistaken identity—a hunter confusing the rider for a deer?

I was living in Vancouver at the time and considered myself a reasonably seasoned cyclist. I commuted everywhere, volunteered on Bike to Work Day, and had toured far and wide in Canada, the United States, and Mexico— but I'd never encountered the term randonneur before. Unbeknownst to me, there was an entire discipline of ultra-distance cycling where riders undertook extreme distances within a specified time limit. The thought of anyone completing 600 unsupported kilometres in a forty-hour window seemed like an unfathomable feat—who were these tireless superhumans? But as the headlines faded, I filed randonneuring away, forgetting about it for over a year.

The urge to investigate hit me once I'd moved to Saskatoon to begin grad school, on a drive back to my new hometown after visiting friends in Vancouver. It is tempting to claim this thirst for knowledge arrived from the blue, but when I consider it, I realize that I'd been seeking a challenge. I had recently returned from a ten-day cycle tour of Washington's Olympic Peninsula, my first serious foray into cycling after my second knee surgery, several months prior. The upcoming year would be demanding: completing a thesis manuscript, preparing for my defence, and working to pay off the mounting student debt I'd incurred. With everything on the go, there was little chance I'd find the time or finances to blast off on another bicycle tour, though I held out hope that I might be able to escape for shorter stints on weekends. Randonneuring, I'd hoped, would satisfy my craving for distance without disrupting my studies.

From the cramped backseat of a classmate's Honda Civic I discovered on my iPhone a trove of information about the sport of randonneuring. I learned that riders took part in events, known as randonnées or brevets, ranging from 200 to 1,200 kilometres, while passing through pre-determined control points within a set time limit. While speed was not a requirement— an average of around nine miles per hour is all that's needed to achieve a successful finish—stop time was restricted, efficiency prized. There were no winners or losers, only finishers or DNFs (Did Not Finish), and even the most seasoned randonneurs DNF'd occasionally due to inclement weather, mechanical difficulties, or physical ailments.

I also stumbled on the webpage for the Prairie Randonneurs—a Saskatchewan-based club—that provided a local brevet schedule, and practical information about how to prepare for a ride, not to mention such helpful tips as "If your urine is yellow, drink until it is clear," and "Bring lubrication...for vital areas."

While these visceral details might scare off some—recreational cyclists included—they only piqued my interest. The most I'd covered to date in a twenty-four-hour period was 130 miles on a gusting tailwind in Northern Ontario. I needed to know if I could go farther. I emailed the club contact at once, but the season was wrapping up, so I had to wait until the following spring to learn more. In late March 2016, Marj and Bob (another active club member) agreed to meet me for coffee in the Broadway Avenue café where Marj worked, marking the beginning of my mentorship with the *anciens*.

Marj has remained a constant in my life ever since: a tough-as-nails, no-nonsense, no-excuses woman who responded to text messages with lightning speed—and more exclamatory punctuation than *Seinfeld*'s Elaine Benes. She was deceptively innocuous in her baker's apron, strands of a greying bob trailing over Lennon glasses—her appearance belying a decisive, unflinching demeanour: mettle and nerve. Along with Bob—a balding, cheery-eyed grandfather quick to expound his love of endurance cycling to anyone willing to listen—they taught me the basics of pack etiquette, how to pedal through the night, and how to execute brief, efficient refuel stops. Marj could be bossy, cranky, and frustratingly particular about her meal preferences (poached eggs, mashed potatoes, white bread, and zero tolerance for murky diner coffee), but these quirks—and the fact I wormed my way into her good books—only caused my affection for her to grow.

. . .

Back on the road, I meandered south, increasing pace momentarily before dropping off again. It wasn't until I crossed Oxbow Reservoir at Brownlee Dam and passed the highway marker signifying my arrival into Idaho that I perked up: my first state line. One down, nine more to go.

I climbed from the reservoir, relishing the subtle awakening of my senses as I inhaled aromatic sage and bitterbrush perched among the flinty cuts of sand-hued stone. A few miles later, I claimed a table at the Gateway Café for second breakfast. While waiting for the kitchen to fry up my 2,000-plus calorie plate of sausage, eggs, potatoes, and toast, I called my mother.

"You're not far behind Amy," she said.

I hadn't met Amy Lippe, but had heard that she and her brother, Max, were both racing.

"Where are the other lady racers?" I asked. I could have checked myself, but after my million reloads on the Trackleaders page the day prior, I was trying to avoid being sucked down that online rabbit hole again.

"Janie and Simone are flying," she said. "Neither has slept a wink."

While slightly exaggerated, her statement remained true to an extent. Race leaders used their time efficiently, stopping briefly and only when necessary, instead of squandering precious hours, as I did, on sit-down meals and luxurious two-star hotel rooms.

"Jen is behind you, near Baker City. The other women are way back."

We chatted until my meal arrived. Mostly, I complained about how I couldn't seem to pick up the pace that morning.

"Meaghan, whatever you're doing just keep it up," she said. Then added: "Remember to eat your greens."

. . .

I had told my mother about the race during Christmas vacation in Hawaii. She reacted with disbelief, coupled with disgust.

"You are not doing that," she'd said. "Racing across the continent is the absolutely dumbest thing I've ever heard."

I'd hit a nerve. I tried to rally my father to my side, but he wasn't buying my race plans either.

"You're telling me you plan to pedal nearly two hundred miles a day for almost a month?" he said. "How?"

I touted my success in the Swan River 1200, mentioning that I'd purchased a carbon road bike I planned to equip with ultra-lightweight bags.

"Lael Wilcox pedalled two hundred and fifty miles every day," I said.

My father googled her just to confirm I had my facts straight. After I forced him to sit down and watch *Inspired to Ride*, a documentary about the inaugural 2014 edition of the event, he finally conceded that the Trans Am was indeed legit. Accepting his daughter could compete, however, wouldn't come for months.

. . .

I next saw my parents during Easter break. Tyler and I had driven out from Saskatchewan to see their new place in the Okanagan Valley. Eight hundred miles separate Saskatoon from Kelowna. I left before dawn to ride the first 220 miles, with Tyler plucking me from the moonlit Albertan highway once he drove out after work. I arrived in Kelowna with newfound confidence and resolve. In addition, I'd accumulated the proper gear, including a set of lightweight bags, GPS, clipless shoes and pedals, and aerobars. I didn't bring up the time Tyler rescued me from a frozen outhouse during a training ride, or that I hadn't bothered to put batteries in my GPS yet.

My father remained unconvinced until he took my new wheels for a spin.

"Is your speedometer broken?" he'd asked. "It shows I held twenty miles per hour on the flat—that can't be right."

I assured him that my speedometer worked fine.

From that point, he gained an interest in the Trans Am. I wasn't bothered that it took a fast bike—and not my own skill set or competency—to bring my father around. Back in Saskatchewan, I'd call him during training rides for lengthy discussions about recharging options and fuelling strategies. By the time June rolled around, he was nearly as excited about the race kickoff as I was.

My mother, on the other hand, ignored my race preparations, still fuming over my decision to participate. She hated when I rode at night, especially if I was alone. When I first started randonneuring, she tried to make me promise to stay with the group. I told her there was no group—it was each of us, on our own, though sometimes we chose to ride together.

"Quit being smart with me," she'd said. "Why do you insist on putting yourself in peril?

I didn't see a way to bridge the issue. She thought what I was doing was dangerous; I said I didn't care and went on doing it. It wasn't until I departed from Astoria that I won her over, the $1,000 in my bank account indisputable evidence of her support, though she still couldn't grasp what drove me to cross America on my bicycle.

· · ·

As I paid my bill, the server relayed information about the other racers passing through.

"You're hot on the heels of another woman," he said. "She asked when the guys came by. Grabbed a bag of cookies and dashed out to chase them down."

My heart jumped as encouragement mingled with disappointment. I kicked myself for stopping to eat a farmer's breakfast instead of grabbing snacks to go, like Amy. If I ever hoped to catch her, I'd have to smarten up. Take a tip from Marj and quit dilly-dallying.

I hustled out of the café, tossing a leg over my saddle with the familiar efficiency of a ranch hand. I imagined Marj, cheering me on from Saskatoon. My mother watching my dot from her iPad in Kelowna. After hearing about Amy and the others, I zoomed out to see the bigger picture. Suddenly, I no longer felt as though I was alone on the road. Regardless of how many hours or days went by without glimpsing the competition, I was still part of the race. I held this thought as I sped from Oregon alongside the mercurial meanderings of Brownlee Creek, my legs reinvigorated.

Amy was just a few miles away, and I was finally ready for the chase.

. . .

I pedalled through Cambridge, Council, and New Meadows. From the state line, the landscape became greener and more challenging. A couple of passes rose above 4,000 feet, then a sweeping, wooded descent delivered me to Riggins, *Idaho's Whitewater Capital*. Competitive spirit reignited, I welcomed the obstacles. Unfortunately, the near constant up and down prevented me from using my aerobars, which work best on flat terrain. In addition, there were lengthy stretches of bumpy, uneven road surface. By the time I left Riggins along the Salmon River, I had an inkling that my wrists and hands would be paying a toll for the road vibrations at some later point.

Yet these seemed like insignificant things. Rolf had pulled too far ahead to catch that day, but I had Amy within my sights now. I proceeded with confidence, brimming with the swelling pride of self-sufficiency that comes from tackling a challenge solo. I'd surprised myself with my ability to navigate, making only minor errors after that first day of copious backtracking. But though I could follow the route, my more advanced map-deciphering skills remained minimal, my knowledge of upcoming topography hazy, at best.

For instance, I didn't realize the thirty-mile ride from Riggins to the town of White Bird would trend downhill, following the flow of the Salmon River. I assumed I'd be ascending, since White Bird Pass was rumoured to be a doozy. The climb, however, began after—just north of—the town of White Bird. I spent the final hours of the day in a bout of unexpected ease, savouring the crenulated valley walls closing in dramatically around me. A solitary bird of prey—perhaps a hawk—kited overhead in easy, gliding circles. Marj would be proud, I thought, feeling ten times more alert and ready to get at it than I had while responding to her texts that morning.

. . .

It wasn't Marj, but her riding partner Bob who first clued me into the extent of her accomplishments. "Ask about Paris-Brest-Paris sometime," he said. "Ask her how she raced against the clock to make the time cut-off at the finish in 2015."

Marj's extensive history in the sport of ultra-distance cycling has taken her to events throughout Canada, the United States, and Western Europe. She's lined up among thousands of participants in famous grand brevets like London-Edinburgh-London (1,400 kilometres, or 870 miles) and Paris-Brest-Paris (1,200 kilometres, or 746 miles), riding day and night through abysmal weather conditions with minimal sleep.

Of course, Marj didn't tell me any of this, initially. She preferred to keep our conversations focused on immediate matters at hand: the diner menu, weather forecast, or whatever foolish decision I was in danger of making in those early days of randonneuring. Over time—and considerable prying on my part—Marj opened up, and the more I got to know her, the more astonished I became. She trained through both a broken collar bone (against the advice of her physiotherapist) and a scorching sunburn that left her legs leopard-spotted in macabre blisters. Frequently, she was one of the sole female finishers in the long brevets she completed, oftentimes finishing alone, close to the cut-off time, and in the middle of the night. When pressed, she sums up success as the result of *bonne chance* rather than impeccable execution—and points to all the times she failed to reach the finish line—but still, I couldn't help but feel as though I came up short in comparisons of grit.

. . .

I reached White Bird just as daylight slipped away, basted in bug parts and sweat. Though I possessed sufficient energy to continue, White Bird was where my route planning ended. It also marked 788 miles, officially surpassing the Swan River 1200, the longest distance I'd previously sustained at a similar pace. I checked into a motel room intending to scrub off the insects and research the days ahead, then slip out before dawn.

There was only one motel in White Bird. I rang a bell, and a middle-aged woman appeared from a backroom, television laugh track following her footfalls into the reception.

"Only you? Forty bucks," she said.

The motel resembled places I'd longed to check into during previous road trips: rustic and cheap, and well past its heyday. The suspension of general upkeep lent a slightly creepy *Twin Peaks* vibe. The proprietor didn't ask for identification, or even my name. A little dog shadowed us into the room as she showed me around, friendly despite the anonymity. I admired a tacky gold-limned landscape painting of rocky peaks encircled by timber wreaths, and a narrow bathtub squeezed next to the toilet in a bathroom scented with cheap disinfectant. Upon a threadbare carpet a pair of beds were made up with identical quilts featuring burgundy, cream, and green patches. I didn't mention the race, but she knew about the Trans Am because someone had stopped for just two hours of sleep that afternoon and mentioned it. Once alone, I conjured chocolate milk, an assortment of granola bars, and two plastic-wrapped sandwiches from my jersey pockets and scratched out a mental itinerary: eat, bathe, catch up on text messages, research route ahead, then get a good night's sleep.

Only the first two occurred.

My phone didn't have service. Then, just as my muscles were beginning to unwind in the tub, I noticed a patch of tender, spongy flesh on my right Achilles tendon. I poked and prodded at it until I could ascertain that the ache penetrated deep into the tissue. Within minutes, I went from celebrating the discount motel room of my dreams, into a downward spiral that left me curled up in an anxious ball of regret. Day three, and already I was falling to pieces. Why had I thought I could compete at all?

. . .

This wasn't my first struggle with my Achilles tendon—the band of tough, fibrous tissue connecting the calf muscles to the heel bone. Pain had crept into my Achilles during long days in the Prairies on a previous cycle tour across Canada over half a decade ago, the tissue becoming more inflamed with every pedal stroke as I fought tooth and nail against an unrelenting headwind to reach Winnipeg for Canada Day, where I spent the long weekend recuperating on a friend's sofa before continuing east.

More recently, I limped over the finish line of a brevet last summer with my Achilles throbbing so bad, I thought my calf was going to explode. While I pushed through, wincing my way back to Saskatoon instead of forfeiting my first 600-kilometre ride, as payback I spent the following week off the bike. I borrowed Tyler's silver Ford Explorer to drive to work and hobbled around the clinic during my shift. Two weeks later, my body was well on the path to recovery, though mentally I remained shaken: how could my body deteriorate so rapidly?

. . .

In White Bird, I assessed the damage with a gentle touch and a critical eye. I remembered that lowering my seat had helped previously, so I made the adjustment. But with no cell service or Wi-Fi, I remained stifled and scared. Overcome by loneliness, my behaviour became more frantic and disjointed as the night wore on, and the pressure built like an infected cavity inside of me. I needed to take control, I realized, and drafted a list of possible action items:

- *Lower my seat (done!)*
- *Call Marj to find out if she has any recommendations for Achilles pain*
- *Adjust cleat placement*
- *Detour to Missoula: rest day, massage*
- *Make a brace (with what?)*
- *Olive Oil = good for joints*
- *No more standing to pedal on hills*

- *Ice to help swelling*
- *Scratch in Missoula???*

Without cell service, calling Marj wasn't an option, and I found nothing to construct a brace with. Route planning, my original intent, appeared both impossible and pointless. I could probably ice my tendon, though. There wasn't an ice machine at the motel, so I decided to investigate the bar across the street. My mission also provided an excuse to indulge in a beer and speak with someone—anyone—so that I might escape the doom-spiralling racetrack of my thoughts for a few minutes.

I couldn't locate the key. Maybe I didn't receive one—I couldn't remember. I had bigger concerns. As I abandoned my unlocked room to walk through the empty motel parking lot, I inhaled deep, calming breaths, already imagining the cool relief of ice on my aching Achilles and a beer in hand.

The bar, unfortunately, appeared closed, a swarm of insects kamikaze-diving a streetlamp the only discernible sign of life. I hoofed around the building to confirm I wasn't using the wrong entrance before pacing outside the front door, willing it to open. Instead, the neighbourhood dogs took notice, roused from their backyard slumber by the clap of my metal cycling cleats against pavement. I froze, my hands in a knot and the pit in my stomach sinking deeper. I crushed my eyelids closed and creased my brow, harnessing every remaining ounce of self-control to restrain myself from screaming like Detective Kimble in *Kindergarten Cop*, "Shut upppp!"

But the barking only surged toward a crescendo. I walked back to my lonesome motel room in an uproar, every scratching footstep igniting another cacophony of canine mayhem.

Day Four

JUNE 7, 2017

WHITE BIRD, IDAHO TO LOLO, MONTANA

MILEAGE: 175 MILES

RACE MILEAGE: 963 OF 4,264 MILES

I discovered my hands didn't work in the bathroom of the White Bird motel room. A 5:00 a.m. alarm sent me skittering to the toilet, where I fumbled with the tiny bar of soap, too small and too slippery. I couldn't get a grip, but it wasn't the soap. Something was amiss. My fingers wouldn't cooperate—as though someone had wiped off their tactile pads while I'd slept.

Strange, I thought to myself, turning my palms over as bewilderment transitioned into a recognition of grave danger.

When I tried to cup water from the tap to splash my face, my fingers simply refused to come together. I pawed my cheeks, desperately trying to coax feeling into fingertips.

Shit. Shit-shit-shit-shit-*shit*! First my Achilles, then this. After months of training, my victorious arrival at the finish line in Yorktown was vanishing before me.

No, I thought. *This can't be.*

I closed my eyes, imagining the faces of friends and family—sympathetic yet disappointed—when they heard that I had scratched before making it out of Idaho.

My chest hollowed out until all I could feel was a knot, bulging and twisted. Smouldering like the quiet, deadly embers of a fire. I eyed my reflection, hoping to harness some inner she-woman strength, but hardly recognized myself beneath the pillow-creased flesh, sunburnt skin greasier than the wrapper of a McDonald's cheeseburger. A rumbling stomach interrupted my dismal reverie to send me hopscotching over zip ties and miscellaneous tools toward the remaining half-carton of chocolate milk and breakfast sandwich left warming on the bedside table overnight.

I simultaneously ate and dressed, wrestling socks right-side out and hitching my Lycra shorts up over hips between mouthfuls. Sensation returned to my hands within minutes, but the incident left me wary, distrustful of my body. Would I lose feeling again, and if so, would next time be worse? I blamed yesterday's road vibrations for the numbness and hoped for smoother pavement today. My irksome Achilles tendon still hadn't abated either. I popped two Ibuprofen and washed the pills down with pre-workout mix.

After I returned from my failed sojourn to White Bird's only bar last night, I torpedoed into a self-disparaging tailspin that rendered me wide awake, yet functionally useless. I managed to lower my saddle and adjust the cleat placement to reduce strain in my Achilles during the downstroke, but after that I'd become paralyzed. Stiff as a cut of meat on the mattress. Mind ablaze with the white heat of anxiety, dreading the impending dawn. It was anyone's guess how much I'd actually slept, though clearly not long enough.

Now, last night's unarticulated fears found voice in the morning mayhem of the disheveled White Bird motel room. I dashed about in panic, half-packing one thing before plunging my toothbrush into my mouth, then forgetting about it as I became distracted by some other chore. My mind preoccupied by the recent one-two punch of Achilles pain and hand numbness. I should have seen this coming; should have predicted these physical inadequacies. It was absolute lunacy, I chastised myself, to imagine that I would somehow be able to fight my way through pain and fatigue, as if they were no more menacing than the dim-witted bad guys in one of Schwarzenegger's action films that I could fend off with a well-aimed blow.

Take control, I told myself. *Do something—anything.*

Then I spotted it. On the floor next to the television stand an arm warmer snaked from my frame bag—the perfect makeshift brace. I wrapped the affected ankle and stuffed my immobilized foot into a cycling shoe. Better. Much better. Then I pulled the remaining arm warmer on, zipped my jacket, and dashed out the door. The sun was up, and I was behind schedule.

. . .

White Bird is a tiny place, a mere smattering of houses before the punishing climb up White Bird Pass at 4,245 feet. Yet the dappled morning light buoyed my spirits, lending an impression of tranquillity, and soothing my anxieties about kicking off the day with a massive ascent that would surely stress my Achilles. Hopefully the brace would pass the test. I spotted another cyclist as I approached the edge of town, his florescent vest a beacon—Rolf? I hustled to catch up.

"Heeeeeyyyyy!" I shouted.

The man nearly jumped from his saddle.

Matthias turned out to be a Trans Am racer. He rode a titanium Litespeed and had silken, muscle-toned legs (he shaved) and forearms tattooed in a traditional style: bold lines and bright colours. I learned he was from Germany and had bivied in a post office fifteen miles back in an even smaller town, ditching two other riders to get an early start. I grinned on hearing this, as I'd deployed a similar tactic when I abandoned Eric in Mitchell—though I still kept a keen eye on Eric's dot, and cheered his progress.

We dug in for the climb, a steady grind on a defunct highway boasting breath-catching panoramas of an emerald countryside polka-dotted with white and black cattle. The air, dewy and fragrant, ferried pithy, earthen scents from surrounding hills. I rested my hands lightly on the bar hoods, glad that my fingers appeared fine now. I even temporarily forgot about my sore Achilles—until Matthias brought up my makeshift brace.

"Why," he asked, when we paused so I could remove my jacket, "are you only wearing one arm warmer?"

I blushed with embarrassment as I explained that technically, I had two, though one was wrapped around my ankle. "My Achilles has been bugging me, so I decided to brace it with an arm warmer. There's a hostel in Missoula," I added, thinking aloud as I removed the remaining arm warmer and tucked it into a rear pocket.

"Missoula? That's not on route."

"It's not far off," I said, replaying a painful montage of scenes from the Canada Day long weekend when I'd been laid up on a friend's sofa in Winnipeg; the weeks I'd spent babying my injury after that brevet last summer in Saskatoon. "I'm formulating a backup plan. If I have to scratch, at least I have options."

Matthias appraised me, uttering nothing. His glasses and beard stubble conferred a wizened, professorial air, though he couldn't have been much older than me. Why was I telling him this? For the second time that morning, I felt ridiculous. Must I dump my anxieties onto the first poor stranger I meet? I stopped talking, but the words crackled like Pop Rocks in my head: *Missoula, Achilles, scratch.*

. . .

From the summit of White Bird Pass we shot deep into a valley, our descent discouragingly short-lived compared to the time it took to scale the fourteen miles to the top. I watched in admiration as Matthias eased low into his drop bars and bombed out of sight, human and bicycle united in a dynamic partnership of speed.

"That downhill reminded me of Europe," he said, grinning as we reconvened at the bottom.

I laughed. For me, the descent was a far cry from home. I repeated a saying we have in the Prairies: "It's so flat, you can watch your dog run away for three days."

Since leaving Astoria, it had become undeniably clear I lacked both the bike handling skills and confidence to descend quickly. As a participant in an unsupported cross-country road race, however, this wasn't a weakness I wanted to admit, so I mentioned nothing about white knuckling the brake levers as we rolled into Grangeville.

"There's a long haul without services on the way to Lolo," Matthias said, as we entered a gas station convenience store. "Might be our last chance to stock up."

I filled my arms with Snickers bars and sugar-coated candy, a breakfast bagel from the hot plate and bananas for the road, plus more chocolate milk. Day three, yesterday, was where my preliminary route planning ended. I had the ACA maps downloaded on my phone and my trusty eTrex, but hadn't studied either—I just knew to stick to the pink navigational line.

Matthias, on the other hand, might have been a seer. He could detail exactly what was coming. Feeling woefully insufficient, I slunk to the curb with my bagel and began scrolling through maps with the urgency of an undergrad student cramming for midterms.

· · ·

From Grangeville, we traced the Clearwater River toward Lolo Pass. Already, I'd grown to like Matthias. He was forthright and confident, with razor-sharp tan lines and a quiet determination. Besides, his company served as a much-appreciated distraction from the caustic thoughts running rampant in my mind.

At first, we pedalled in the relaxed hues of morning, enjoying partial shade and a cool breeze lifting off the white water. We rolled by a riverside lodge with an adjoining café in Syringa, opting to continue without stopping since our water bottles remained full from our recent refuel stop in Grangeville. Not long after, a road sign warned of a winding highway for the next ninety-nine miles. A kettlebell dropped in my stomach.

"Ninety-nine miles?" I said.

"This is the race's longest ascent," Matthias responded, matter-of-factly. "We'll climb gradually until Lolo Pass, on the Idaho-Montana border."

The numbers turned over in my head again. How had I not known this?

"There's a store, or at least a restaurant, at Lolo Lodge," Matthias added, sensing my concern. "Near the summit. It might be closed by the time we get there though."

I stared hard at the pavement just ahead of my front bike tire, mentally calculating if the contents of my pockets held sufficient caloric value to see me through the following ninety-nine miles into Lolo.

. . .

By midday, temperatures were sweltering. When we weren't wiping away the sweat, Matthias and I chatted alongside each other, falling into single file when a vehicle approached. Then traffic picked up, forcing us to abandon any semblance of conversation. I glanced at my odometer, the numbers hardly moving in the burgeoning heat. By noon, I felt disoriented, the scenery unchanging—river to our right, forest to our left—mile after blazing mile. You would expect someone familiar with riding in the Prairies to be accustomed to repetition, but it got to me. A mad boredom creeping in. I wondered if we were in Oregon, Montana, or Idaho. The grade remained imperceptible, though I sensed my speed lagging, the tedium wearing me down. Sharp pain splintered at my temples, its cause tricky to pinpoint: dehydration or frustration, or perhaps the frightful suspicion we might actually be stuck in time.

Matthias and I continued to squeegee sweat from our brows. The scenery hadn't changed for hours when we pulled onto a gravel patch and abandoning our bicycles to scramble down a rock scree toward the Clearwater River, empty water bottles in hand, seeking relief from stifling heat and the endless trees barring us in on the road to Lolo Pass.

We peeled off our socks and shoes. Left sweat-soaked jerseys on a boulder to dry and wiggled toes the pale, sickly colour of deep-sea worms as we tiptoed into water with legs uncertain, reluctant to commit to movement off the bike. The kinetic energy of surging white water washed away those cloying road odours of car exhaust and tar snakes. I knelt into the torrent and grit my teeth, embracing the stabbing cold and hard rock against my shins. A few feet away, Matthias lowered himself as well, his face contorting, eyes alternately creased shut and blinking wide from the shock.

"Dare you to put your head under," I said.

He flashed an expression of horror. Then dunked. Came up screaming.

"Now you," he said.

I breathed in, imagining a much-younger self, a girl, fearlessly diving into a Pacific kelp bed to swim down to listen for mermaids singing from depths beneath.

I sealed my lips and thrust my face under, the coursing current drowning out my hammering heart.

One, two seconds.

Bolts of light, stars exploded in the back of my retinas—the intertwining of pain and joy. Water crashed overhead as I held my breath in a dare from a shivering, Lycra-clad German.

. . .

Back on the road, I felt rejuvenated. Still slugging through the same dull trees and baking under the sun, but the dip in the river signalled a turning point—an opportunity to hit the reset button and get my vitals back in check. I considered the extremes: the road's monotony in contrast to the silliness of our afternoon dip; summer snow on McKenzie Pass compared to the blistering heat I'd encountered on the eastern side of the Cascade Range. This race, I was learning, would be a lesson in shifting gears. Not entirely different from how my confidence yo-yoed in those pre-race training months in Saskatoon.

. . .

Leading into the Trans Am, I recognized a growing discrepancy in how my confidence levels fluctuated on and off the bike. Riding, I felt empowered: outdoors, breathing lungfuls of fresh air, entirely in control as the miles flew by. But once I arrived home, showered, and changed into my day clothes, I shrank into a smaller, more insecure version of myself. Pestered by lacerating self-doubt; plagued by What If's and visions of disasters waiting to happen. It was astounding how rapidly I swung from surging self-assurance to mind-bending apprehension about the journey ahead.

Other than my boyfriend, family, and a few fellow randonneurs, I didn't tell a soul about the race until a week before flying out to Portland. Even when I brought my bike into the shop for a tune-up, I didn't mention it.

"Going on some long rides this summer?" inquired a mechanic.

"Planning to," I said, unwilling to elaborate.

After a spin class one day in May, my instructor, Tara, asked if I was training for an Ironman Triathlon—the toughest multi-sport endurance race in the books.

"No," I hesitated. "But I am about to race my bike across the continent."

"Get out!" she said, her eyes growing wide with excitement.

I decided to open up about the arduous race: how I planned to pedal from coast to coast, on my own, sleep-deprived and probably malnourished. Tara was excited, herself an ultra-runner who'd amassed a laundry list of accolades, and suggested we pose together for a photo for her Instagram.

"No, I don't think so," I said, suddenly stricken by myriad anxieties that lurked around the edges of my training. Tara asked why not, and I admitted the truth: fear of failure. I was hesitant to share my race plans because I was petrified of failing miserably. Worse, I didn't want defeat to define how other people remembered me.

Tara convinced me otherwise.

"Listen," she said. "You are doing it—that is enough. Think of the commitment just to train for something like that. I've done dozens of races. Shit happens. No one is guaranteed to finish. Sometimes, it's out of your hands. What matters is getting your ass to the starting line."

Her words echoed in my head all afternoon. I was the only one putting pressure on myself, I realized. Nobody else was. My friends and family would celebrate my successes, but they would not judge my shortcomings— that was on me alone. It was as if I'd been stripped of a too-tight sports bra and could finally inhale fully. On the other side of fear was freedom.

After the conversation with Tara, I began telling people about the epic ride I had slated for June.

. . .

When Matthias and I reached the turnoff for Lolo Lodge late that afternoon, there was no question about whether we would stop. Under cover of mighty evergreens, vacationers milled among cozy-looking wood cabins and a rustic main building. Amenities were clearly open, and I exhaled relief: we would eat, replenish supplies, and refill our water bottles from an actual faucet.

That was when I noticed a barefoot brunette pushing her bicycle toward us.

It was Trans Am racer Simone Bailey.

"I'm out," she told us. "Hot foot."

Matthias and I both expressed our sincere condolences. Hot foot, in case you were wondering, is a condition where the nerves in the foot become damaged and the foot burns in searing pain when pressure is applied.

"It is what it is," she shrugged.

I couldn't take my eyes off Simone. Shoeless, skin on her lips and cheeks flaking like fish food, white mesh top stained Dijon-yellow under the armpits. Beautifully annihilated. Simone arrived at Lolo Lodge barely able to walk. After imbibing a cocktail or two on the patio, she came to terms with her injury and decided to call it.

"What are you going to do now?" I asked.

"Don't worry about me," she reassured us. The alcohol seemed to be having the desired effect of reducing pain perception. "I'm gonna hitch to Missoula. Take a bus from there."

Simone also passed her roll of KT Tape off to me with instructions on how to brace my Achilles before continuing toward the highway.

"Can I pay you?" I offered, knowing how expensive this stuff was.

"Nah. I'm just happy it's going to good use."

After we parted ways with Simone, Matthias and I resupplied at the lodge's general store—more accurately described as a refrigerator-lined shack. Sandwiches approaching expiry dates were accompanied by iced Starbucks mochas on the steps. I taped my Achilles, relieved to get rid of the sweaty sleeve at last. By the time we returned to the highway, Simone was gone. The sun had dropped below the treeline, but the summit was finally in sight.

I experienced a strange serenity for those final few miles of the climb. Something to do with meeting Simone. I couldn't shake our encounter: seeing her trudging barefoot uphill, totally nonchalant about throwing in the towel. To this day, that heroic vision of Simone remains etched into my memory. The following year, she would return to the start line. In 2018, she rode to the finish.

. . .

Matthias and I arrived in Lolo after midnight. The long descent from the summit passed easily, requiring little more on our part than the effort of staying upright. Every once in a while, softly-lit log homes set among pines partially revealed themselves in the distance. The two of us lost ourselves in our stories as we glided downhill: tales of friends, post-secondary institutions, and home. With no prior knowledge of each other, any topic was fair game. We spoke in revering awe about ultra-cyclist Amanda Coker's recent feat of smashing the annual milage record, and traded knowledge from previous race finishers' blogs we had read, wondering where they slept and what thoughts spun through their heads as they faced challenges impossible to imagine from the outset. After hours of silky darkness, the haloed lights of Lolo left us momentarily stunned.

The day had tested my resilience. It was also uplifting to realize, in contrast to Simone, I wasn't in nearly as rough shape. Which explains why Matthias had looked at me so incredulously when I confessed my fears of scratching, while simultaneously powering up White Bird Pass. I reassessed the pain in my Achilles as manageable—comparable to what every other racer was experiencing on some level by this stage. Now, if only I could reign in those runaway thoughts.

Thankfully, my insecurities were swept aside as I prepared to ransack the gas station, feet happily planted on *terra firma* once again. Among the aisles of high-carb snack items and canned vegetables, I had a reckoning. The sight of all my favourite treats—pepperoni sticks, cheese puffs, pre-packaged mini-donuts, and a rainbow's selection of candy—stirring within me such intense joy, I knew this was exactly where I should be. I would not be departing the race yet. While our brush with Simone had served as a living reminder of just how precarious one's time was, I parted ways feeling more determined than ever. As I placed items into a basket (who shops at a gas station with a basket?) I received a text from my mother:

See you're riding with MR. How goes it?

MR, I wondered. Who is MR?

Then it hit me: I didn't know his name. I'd spent the entire day—seventeen hours, to be precise—with Matthias and either he hadn't mentioned it, or, and this was the more likely case, I simply didn't remember.

Feeling strong! I texted back. *Can you do me a huge favour and tell me MR's full name?*

Matthias Rau.

I was still puzzling over how I'd committed such an enormous social faux pas when Matthias himself rounded the aisle.

"Wanna share a beer?" he said, sheepishly clasping a tall can.

He didn't need to ask twice. I thought back to last night and how hopeless I'd felt during my retreat from the bar with only the local dog population for company. Now, it was approaching 1:00 o'clock. I was bone tired. Yet among aisles of nutrient-deficient junk food, I had discovered my happy place. More importantly, my body proved fit to ride another day.

That alone was reason to celebrate.

Day Five

Matthias and I slept in a budget hotel room one block from the gas station in Lolo. Not a beer I've had since compares to that well-deserved can of mediocre pale ale, which we poured into glass tumblers before taking turns in the shower. Six hours later we were back at the same gas station, stockpiling snacks for the day ahead. I was learning firsthand that the event was, as 2015 race winner Jesse Carlsson once said, just as much "an eating contest across America" as a bike race. I counted my blessings that aside from that painful fiasco with strawberry milk, my stomach seemed to be rising to the challenge.

From Lolo we followed the paved Bitterroot Trail, enjoying the opportunity to warm up our legs away from traffic. Not far along, we were joined by a cyclist who greeted us by both first and last names.

"I'm Roger. No, don't stop," he said. "I wouldn't want to hold you up. Keep riding and we'll do the interview."

"Interview?" asked Matthias.

If we'd had cell reception yesterday, we would have noticed Roger posting video clips with racers on the Trans Am Facebook Page. Now, it was our turn.

"I'll ride alongside and you can say a few words," Roger said. "Who's first?"

I volunteered, beaming into Roger's camera. "I'm stoked to be here in the Trans Am!" I said. Gratitude—just to stay in the game after that scare with my Achilles—pouring out.

Matthias remained more subdued. "I'm kind of enjoying the ride," he said, eyes squinting sleep from behind glasses; cracked lips plastered with a waxy, protective balm. His fatigue was as striking as mine twenty-four hours prior, when we first bumped into each other in White Bird.

. . .

From Lolo, we maintained our course along the Bitterroot until merging onto Highway 93 toward Chief Joseph Pass. According to Matthias, the pass marked our first crossing of the Continental Divide, the point from which water flows west to the Pacific Ocean, and east to the Atlantic. This mini-lesson in geography was delivered between stats on average gradients and important refuel waypoints.

"You really didn't know this?" he asked.

I radiated the same puppy-dog happy grin as during Roger's interview. So long as we stayed on route, I did not care—I was just thrilled to ride.

But one thing bothered me: how did Roger know where to find us? Then I remembered our dots. He could see where we slept, what time we rolled out, even our speed leaving Lolo.

I wondered what my boyfriend, Tyler, would think. He hadn't messaged yet that day, but I guessed he would have checked the Tracker. I sent him a quick text while I had service, in case he had weird feelings about his girlfriend sharing a hotel room with a stranger who went by the initials MR.

. . .

I met Tyler working at a Halloween store in the final year of my studies in Saskatoon. He wore glasses, his hair trimmed short in a clean-cut 1950s style. We bonded over mutual appreciation of throwback comedies—*Ferris Bueller's Day Off, Bill & Ted's Excellent Adventure*—quoting the cheesier lines of Schwarzenegger's classic bodybuilding documentary, *Pumping Iron*. Tyler was ten inches taller, but liked to be the little spoon, which I found endearing. We had disparate upbringings—him in rural Manitoba and small-town Saskatchewan, me in Surrey's suburbs, neighbouring Vancouver—and looking back, not much in common. What we shared was an emotional compatibility; a sense of "I'll be there for you," that brought us together during that frigid Prairie winter.

While Tyler wasn't much of a cyclist, he whole-heartedly supported my long-distance endeavours. Before my first ride with the Prairie Randonneurs, he ventured to Walmart alongside me, carrying the basket as I ticked items off my list: high-vis vest, powdered Gatorade, granola bars. At 6:00 a.m. the following morning, he dropped me at the starting location—a Husky gas station on the north end of town—and at 6:00 p.m., he dutifully picked me up, treating me to a vermicelli bowl at our favourite Vietnamese place on the drive home as I gushed about the 200-kilometre return trip to Biggar, a town of 2,161 inhabitants whose tongue-in-cheek motto is "New York is Big, but this is Biggar."

There were other things, however, that looked like red flags. I was nearly a decade older than him, and as I mentioned, we had grown up in very different worlds. Try as I might, oftentimes I just couldn't wrap my head around where Tyler was coming from. Aside from scanning articles on his phone, he didn't enjoy reading. Didn't own a bookshelf, or have a favourite author. This should have given me pause. How could I, a freshly minted Masters in Fine Arts in Writing graduate, relate to someone who had no appreciation for the worlds that existed within the written page? Instead, I told myself our differences would bring us together.

The biggest issue wasn't the reading thing, but something more substantive: Tyler dreamed of the day we would settle down and have a family. Grow roots just as his parents had done, and his high school friends were now doing. I, on the other hand, wasn't sure what I wanted. While not dead set against marriage and children, I also questioned whether, with all the energy I was putting into defending my thesis, and then establishing myself in a new job at the clinic, this was the time.

. . .

Ranches pitching with waves of bottle-blue lupins gave way to long-needled pines and towering Douglas firs as we gained elevation. My breath became laboured, each gulping inhalation searing my lungs. I was burning matches, fast. I lowered my effort, but unfortunately also lost sight of Matthias on the final miles of the climb up Chief Joseph Pass. Despite the groggy interview, he still had more kick in his legs. I wasn't worried though: we'd meet again, or maybe we wouldn't. Either way, I'd be fine. Still, I experienced a tug of disappointment not to find him waiting at the summit.

I continued alone, flying downhill toward Wisdom, one eye glued to the route on my eTrex. In 2016, race leader Sarah Hammond detoured seventy-five miles off course near Chief Joseph Pass, losing her advantage. I certainly couldn't afford to get lost if I wanted to stay in the race—or if I wanted to see Matthias again—so I cut my speed and proceeded with caution, content to enjoy ranks of conifers, the dark seam of a waterway gushing far below.

The year Sarah Hammond owned the lead for the first five days coincided with the year Lael Wilcox pulled ahead to take the win from rider Steffen Streich in the final hours. Equally exciting, that year three women—Lael, Sarah, and Janie Hayes—landed top ten finishes. Janie had returned to race this year, and was moving up the ranking daily. We met briefly during the wee hours of the pre-ride boozefest at Fort George Brewery in Astoria. I congratulated her on a stellar 2016 performance and asked about her favourite state.

Janie threw back her head like a giddy mare in response, waist-length hair swinging around a lean, tanned neck. "Every state is amazing. You're going to love everything!" she said in a Texan accent so sweet and encouraging, I almost believed her.

Now, with Janie moving through the top ten, I wondered if this might be the second year in a row a woman nabbed a podium position. While female participation remained a small minority—not just in the Trans Am, but in all ultra-cycling events—those who did compete proved women could excel in endurance athletics. As to why female participation hovers so low—only 13 of 131 competitors in the 2017 Trans Am identified as female, about ten percent—a few possible explanations spring to my mind, including responsibilities associated with motherhood and the reluctance to leave young children for extended periods, feelings of vulnerability on the road, and income disparities posing barriers to access.

The possibility for women to challenge their male counterparts was undeniably a draw to the sport for me—a tomboy by nature—despite being far from ready to compete at the pointy end myself. Self-supported ultra-distance cycling differs from traditional bicycle racing in that the focus broadens to include endurance and efficiency, rather than favouring raw strength and speed. Mental stamina, including the ability to maintain focus and wisely manage time off the bike, becomes as much a contributor to success as riding time. A slower rider who can "keep calm and carry on" may finish ahead of a rider who paces poorly or takes frequent breaks.

I believed my proficiency in randonneuring and cycle touring gave me an edge, including a familiarity with fuelling on the road, camping in unusual places, and keeping my bike in decent working order. What I wasn't accustomed to was night riding and sleep deprivation. Would my body handle the sustained rigours of pedalling day after day with only four hours of rest? I couldn't say. But that afternoon, I still felt good.

. . .

Wind tore through Wisdom, Montana. It chewed flags to streamers but did little to hinder mosquitoes. An entire shelf in the gas station was dedicated to bug spray labelled "Big Hole Cologne"—Big Hole being the name of the river that transects town. I bumped into Matthias en route to Wisdom, and now he chuckled as I snapped a photo of the handwritten sign, though neither of us were laughing as we were chased from our picnic table lunch by a scourge of bloodthirsty mosquitoes.

We hit the road, deli-meat sandwiches in hand, tearing off doughy bites while pedalling just fast enough to stay ahead of the swarm that buzzed louder than a chainsaw at our heels. Luckily, the breeze had our backs—in my imagination a cartoon cloud face whistling wind through pursed lips—and we flew through effortless, easy miles.

Endless pasture, distant peaks—Montana lived up to its name: Big Sky Country. Occasionally, a ghost town. A solitary log home puffing smoke from a stone chimney. Clouds gloomed dark overhead, mirroring snow-capped mountain ranges in shades of periwinkle and grey. But rain was not forecast, so we relaxed, leaning into the bars to listen to dancing sweet grass, as we gazed down the double solid line of a highway that was ours alone for miles and miles and miles.

. . .

It wasn't until after I returned home from the race that I spoke openly to Tyler about my anxieties regarding our shared future: that I couldn't imagine raising children, and while I enjoyed my life in Saskatoon, I wasn't ready to commit to making the city my forever home.

Tyler was disappointed, but put on a brave face, saying we could revisit the topic again in a few months, when perhaps my thinking would have changed.

I said sure, we could put that conversation on hold.

His sisters were both in the glow of pregnancy that summer, and perhaps he hoped that witnessing their transition to motherhood might result in a change of heart on my part. But as their bellies ballooned, the reluctance only gripped me tighter, a cold hand at my heart. Looking back, I wish I had stuck to my guns. Dug a little deeper. Carried on until my thoughts unwound, and I discovered words to articulate the uncertainties pinging around inside me like bumper carts.

There are details we just can't see, though in retrospect appear so obvious. I never felt as though I had the information: what if I found my ideal job, house, and friend circle—would I change my tune? Would the stability of a husband, family, and a mortgage suddenly become more enticing? On the other hand, some things we just know. Feelings that arrive from within, eluding explanation. It is up to us to listen. I wish I had known myself better when I started dating Tyler. I wish I possessed the courage to speak my truth from the start.

. . .

At 1:00 a.m., Matthias and I rolled up to a McDonald's Drive-Thru in Dillon, Montana, and ordered two breakfast sandwiches apiece, milkshakes and fries. Liberated from polite mannerisms and rituals, the act of eating becomes primal: an overwhelming urgency to vanquish the hunger. English muffins oozed ketchup on the curb between outstretched legs as we sucked milkshakes through tiny straws in frantic, gulping bursts. Between mouthfuls of breakfast patty, I caught my reflection in a floor-to-ceiling window: grimy, sunscreen-clogged pores and a bloodied gash on my shin from where I stumbled during an inelegant dismount to pee in a ditch. After hours of tunnelling through the darkness, my exhaustion was total, all-encompassing. I silenced a call from Tyler, unable to contemplate non-essential communication.

I was ready to pass out on the curb—sandwich wrappers balled under my head for a cushion—when Matthias jabbed my ribcage with a straw, suggesting we check into the neighbouring Motel 6. Within white walls, white sheets, and white towels that I left graffitied with grease and grime, I felt even more ruined. The once-clean space was instantly tarnished by our filthy presence, and the sweet-sour body odours that impregnated our close-fitting kit. Still, the motel room signified a minor victory. A bed apiece, and the luxury of space—room to stretch and sprawl. I fell asleep face down in a pillow. One hand arched overhead, the opposite knee tucked towards an elbow.

Sometime later, my eyes flew open. A door slamming, retreating foot-steps, then the unmistakable *click, click-click-click* of a freewheel in motion. I shoved off covers and hurled our door wide to inspect the second-floor balcony, first left toward exit stairs, then right, blood ringing in my ears.

"What are you doing?" Matthias asked. Without glasses, he resembled a mole, squinting as balcony light flooded the room.

"Thought I heard someone. A racer leaving." Maybe Rolf or Amy.

I stepped outside to peer over the railing. The parking lot remained as still as an album cover. Did I dream it? But I didn't have time to dwell on before the chilled night air forced me back into bed, tumbling into sleep faster than I had flung off the covers.

Day Six

JUNE 9, 2017

DILLON TO ENNIS, MONTANA

DISTANCE: 65 MILES

RACE MILEAGE: 1,219 OF 4,264 MILES

Matthias poked fun at my late-night apparitions during our diner breakfast the following morning, before we hit the pavement for Ennis.

"It might have been someone," I responded in my defence.

"Sure," he said, cocking an eyebrow before tipping a sugar packet into his coffee. "But what would you do—chase'em down in your pyjamas?"

As I struggled to de-foil a creamer, I could no longer deny that my body was atrophying. Fatigue outpaced recovery. I walked a precariously thin line between scratching and surviving, and it only took a moment of critical consideration to realize that I wasn't in any shape to chase other racers. All of my contact points suffered from low-grade pain. Not serious enough to raise alarm bells, but present enough to be a nuisance and distraction. On top of that, the unsettling hand numbness I had first experienced in the White Bird Motel room was back, albeit to a less debilitating degree. While my Achilles pain had stabilized, it had not abated, and even after I retired the makeshift arm warmer brace, I faithfully continued to wrap my ankle with the blue

KT Tape Simone had passed on. At any moment, it seemed I might blow up spectacularly.

Overall, Matthias fared better, though a staunch German disposition may have masked the true extent of his suffering.

"Guess I just wanted to know who it was," I shrugged.

Last night Rolf's dot was in Dillon—now, gone. Did he sneak out before anyone awoke? It didn't matter, I supposed. Today, same as yesterday, the day before. Pedal, eat, and pedal some more.

I was, however, beginning to appreciate Matthias as company. Level-headed and determined, but also delightfully silly—quick to make good-natured fun of my quirks, and the oddities of small-town American life. We both planned to finish within twenty-five days, though our strategies for achieving this goal couldn't have been more different. In his jersey pocket, Matthias kept a series of laminated elevation graphs, mapped out with researched essential services and proposed daily end points. In contrast, I woke each day hoping to knock off another 186 miles. Strangely, our approaches proved compatible. We travelled at a similar pace, our personalities gelled, and our breaks timed up like clockwork. Sharing the cost of motel rooms simply made sense. Plus, we had plenty to chat about, from past cycle tours to the intricacies of our individual packing schemes.

Today marked our third day together. While Matthias and I talked about the route ahead, we never discussed whether we'd continue side by side, our friendship tenuous—another hour in each other's company more possibility than guarantee. Matthias could blast out of sight any second, and I might not see him again in this lifetime.

. . .

Matthias and I caught Rolf twenty miles from Dillon in Twin Rivers, a town where the wind left screen doors swinging off their hinges and dogs cowering under porches. I smiled on seeing the familiar red raincoat, a quick giveaway to his identity, as he hoisted himself from a catnap in a weedy, dried-up ditch.

Unlike Matthias and most of the male riders I'd encountered, Rolf remained clean-shaven, his lack of facial hair emphasizing the tired creases around his eyes. I wondered when he found time for self-grooming.

"I am so happy to see you," he said, his expression caught between relief and hopelessness. Eyes red-veined and tormented.

We pulled off the road as Rolf recounted his anguishing experience over the previous two days. "The wind has been horrendous," he said, shaking his head. "An absolute nightmare."

While Matthias and I were flying high on a tailwind from Wisdom, Rolf was less than sixty miles ahead, battling a vicious headwind. After Rolf passed through, the wind reversed direction. In consequence, Matthias and I had been gaining ground until Twin Rivers, when Rolf hopped off his bike to nap.

The broken figure we encountered now appeared entirely different from the cheerful man I'd met keeping company with the Flower Lady on the bridge over the Willamette River in Oregon. In his desperation I detected something of myself—a flashback to that lonely night in White Bird. Instead of surfing the anticipated swell of victory for having finally caught him, I wanted only to relieve his pain. I scrambled through billowing grass to wrap Rolf in a hug.

"C'mon," I said. "Let's get going."

. . .

Rolf's circumstances reminded me not only of my low point in White Bird, but how the fatigue and pain that seemed insurmountable only forty-eight hours prior appeared normalized now. My body didn't necessarily feel better, but systems had stabilized, accepting the constant state of discomfort, exhaustion, and hunger as a new normal, despite it not being normal at all.

This "new normal" had comparisons in my relationship with Tyler. How I dodged his questions about our shared future and remained guarded about mentioning my ex (or any other guy) in front of him, were indications of bigger issues. But like my faltering body in the Trans Am, I accepted these circumstances as my new normal. In the thick of it we wear blinders. It is easier to ignore those nagging doubts or niggling pains than deal with them—though there will be repercussions at some point. There always are.

. . .

The three of us made painstakingly slow progress in the wind. Grasses in surrounding fields bowed low in surrender under threat of an overcast sky; small, leafy trees and bushes snapped back and forth with whiplash force. Dust particles wedged into my eyes, my sunglasses offering only a degree of protection against the swirling current of air around me. I felt luckier than ever to have pedalled through yesterday with such ease. Now, it felt as though we were attempting to swim through a turbulent sea: most of our energy spent simply keeping our heads above water. Forward progress felt like a secondary, near-impossible feat.

Yet the three of us remained cheerful, happy in each other's company and the opportunity to brave the elements together. On a roadside pit stop in Virginia City, a former gold rush boomtown now home to less than 200 souls, we stopped for pie.

"Why are we doing this?" I asked, half-laughing as I glanced out the diner window to assess whether my bike was at risk of toppling over in the wind.

"Because it's there!" enthused Rolf.

His mood had improved. I cocked my head in curiosity, inviting him to go on.

"All my life, I have enjoyed epic, month-long adventures. Mountaineering, trekking—Switzerland has no shortage of options. But that is not possible anymore." He patted his kneecaps with both hands. "And you know where broken knees go for an encore?"

"Ultra-cycling!" I said.

He nodded, pleased that I had made the connection. I'd mentioned my own knee issues to Rolf during the ride out of Mitchell: two ACL surgeries, three complete tears. My shoddy knees had ended both my snowboarding and roller derby careers, and while I knew that physiotherapy and a third surgery offered hope for improvement, to tell the truth, I was scared. Better to stick with cycling, a low-impact activity that didn't invite the risky scenarios that had gotten me into trouble previously.

"What about you?" Rolf asked Matthias.

Matthias had been bitten by the cycling bug a few years ago. After a DNF in Montenegro during the Transcontinental Race, he surprised himself with a strong finish in the TransAtlantic Way, a 1,550-mile self-supported race tracing Ireland's craggy coastline in expectedly abysmal weather conditions.

"The TransAtlantic Way was difficult, no doubt, but making it to the finish boosted my confidence—I realized that I actually could race competitively. I've always wanted to visit America, and I heard the TransAmerica Trail has spectacular scenery. I enjoy training and preparing for big challenges, so naturally, I signed up."

Like me, Matthias was also a randonneur. In addition to the early-season brevets, he'd adhered to a strict training regime, while also dedicating time to research the route—the resulting product being his set of laminated cue cards.

It was my turn. Again, I glanced toward the window.

"I just wanted to test my limits," I offered.

Rolf's ruddy, wind-burnt cheeks stretched into a smile. "I think you got your wish."

. . .

The beer was cold in Ennis, Montana. That's the highest praise I can give to a place offering a choice between Bud or Bud Light. It was three o'clock in the afternoon. Rolf and Matthias sat opposite me in a booth in the back of a bar, lecturing me meticulously on the importance of Lycra care: "Of course, all zippers must be zipped tightly before you put the wash in, otherwise they will snag on the delicate fabric!" All three of us were dressed in the firefighter red and highlighter yellow of raincoats as our cycling clothes tumbled dry on low heat at the neighbouring laundromat.

Outside, the wind picked up momentum until it rose to a howl—a gale-force wrecking ball strewing carnage down the highway, toppling construction cones in its wake.

A few hours after encountering Rolf, all three of us reached our limits. Following a harrowing descent through a crosswind into Ennis, we literally stopped in our tracks heading east toward West Yellowstone, grinding to a halt the moment we eased off the pedals. I gazed into open range, imagining ourselves hard-luck heroes in a John Wayne film, sagebrush bouncing past our tires. According to Matthias's laminated cue cards, the following eighty-mile stretch to Yellowstone National Park lacked much in the way of services, and at our current pace, we wouldn't arrive before morning. Rolf checked his own set of laminated cue cards and confirmed this. Instead of toughing it out, we backtracked to check into a motel in Ennis. We'd eat, launder our clothes, and rest, then hit the road under the guise of darkness, when hopefully the wind would have died down. While both Matthias and Rolf regarded the act of machine drying one's kit to be in violation of some sacred cyclists' code, they agreed to grant an exception—just this once—so that we could get our laundry over and done with while we wolfed down our meal.

I reached for another slice of deluxe pizza. The fatty, curling edges of bacon and pepperoni sent my taste buds into watering anticipation before the food even touched my lips. Perhaps I was under the pizza's spell—or maybe the glorious, instantaneous intoxication of cheap draft beer was to blame—but I wasn't overly disappointed by our seventy-mile day. My quadriceps burned with exhaustion from fighting the wind; my back and shoulders ached as though I'd been shovelling wet snow for the past eight hours instead of simply riding my bicycle. For once, the preservation of long-term health outweighed the short-term benefits of accumulating mileage. The Trans Am Bike Race would not be lost or won in a day. Besides, the leaders were too far ahead to catch—we might as well make the best of an opportunity handed to us. Heads bowed close and pint glasses in hand, Rolf, Matthias, and I discussed preparations for our late-night rollout with the hushed tones of insiders, international agents engaged in espionage.

"Hey," Rolf turned to me. "Thanks for the hug back there in Twin Rivers. I needed it."

"Anytime."

For the moment, we had banded together: Three Musketeers plotting a midnight siege on the highway.

Day Seven

JUNE 10, 2017

ENNIS, MONTANA TO MORAN, WYOMING

DISTANCE 170 MILES

RACE MILEAGE: 1,389 OF 4,264 MILES

Shivers hijacked my body before I escaped the motel room in Ennis. Despite the reassuring back-and-forth of German chatter between Matthias and Rolf, I was ill at ease. Wide awake but gut-sick to be heading onto the highway at such an unfathomable hour as midnight.

We packed and left. The dry, cool air raked my throat. I was glad for the three-dollar puffy jacket I scored at a thrift store on the walk back from the bar, just hours prior. In an effort to remain as lightweight as possible, I hadn't packed a warm jacket, only a merino base layer, arm sleeves, and a raincoat. Rookie mistake. As I'd already learned on the freezing ride into Mitchell, temperatures plummeted at high elevations, particularly at night. The puffy jacket was a lucky find—a layer of appreciated insulation as the route crept further into the Rocky Mountains—and came in useful the very night I purchased it as we kicked it out of Ennis.

A winding, deserted highway pitched us toward Yellowstone National Park. While the wind had backed off, it still carried a punch. The jacket should have kept me toasty, yet my jaw chattered like a pair of those creepy, windup teeth, frequently gag gifted at retirement parties. I suspected that I shivered not due to air temperature, but an internal malaise: a metabolic failure brought on by accumulative exertion, or low blood sugar. I mentioned nothing to the others, holding out hope that my body would sort itself out as we pushed through the endless gloom. My focus narrowed to the quiet notes of movement: the hiss of wind through spokes, and sandpaper sounds of the gritty road surface. Rolf and Matthias's blinking rear lights shrank in the distance as they pulled farther ahead, and I thought back to a night ride one year prior.

. . .

I completed my first 600-kilometre brevet in July 2016. Alongside Prairie Randonneurs Marj and Bob, I'd ridden west from Saskatoon toward the Alberta border, stealing brief interludes of air-conditioned comfort inside Subway restaurants as the weather alternated between sweltering heat and torrential downpour. By midnight, we had covered just over 300 kilometres (186 miles). Next up: Kerrobert, a blip-on-the-map town where Marj and Bob's partners waited with their vehicles. The plan was for us to hunker down for an hour or so of sleep in the back seats before heading on to Kindersley, Rosetown, and eventually the Husky gas station in Saskatoon where we'd departed. The brevet marked my longest ride to date, and the first time I would pedal most of the night.

The three of us rode staggered on the wide shoulder as we approached Kerrobert, watchful for potholes, glass, and the edge of the bone-rattling rumble strip. Beams from our bike lights swayed to the hitch of our hips as we stood to pedal inclines, giving our tenders parts momentary relief before settling back into the saddle. Grain elevators loomed like ancient monoliths on the horizon, but we remained oblivious to everything outside the scope of our lights. I was shattered mentally, yet simultaneously amazed by my body's resiliency. After dark, I entered a calm, borderline catatonic state.

Thoughts seemingly exterior to flesh and bone.

But when an engine roared in the distance, I was jarred back to the reality of my own body. My shoulders arched to meet my ears as the vehicle careened toward us like a jet fighter preparing for takeoff, and my heart was trampolining against my diaphragm. Just as I prepared to hit the ditch, vehicle tires squealed to a halt. I glanced over my shoulder, only to become blinded by close-range headlights. The vehicle followed for a few beats, then pulled up alongside. I heard the whirr of an electric window, and I glanced over to see a pickup truck, the passenger's side door scabbed with rust.

"Hey!" shouted the driver. "What the hell are you doing out here?"

Two men, short hair—no distinguishing features. My chest cinched tighter.

"What does it look like?" said Marj. Her voice cracked, like my Grandma Hackinen's used to, when she spoke. "We're riding our bikes."

"I didn't know what the hell you were," said the driver. "Nobody is expecting bikers this time of night. You might cause an accident."

His anger was palpable. I still couldn't make out a face, but recognized his aggression; a thirst for blame. I hunched low over my handlebars and willed myself invisible.

"Did you not see our lights?" asked Bob. "Or our reflective vests?"

"If I saw something unusual at night," added Marj, "I'd slow down."

Oh, please don't, Marj, I thought to myself. *This is not the time.*

The passenger and driver exchanged words.

"What's the problem, then?" asked Marj, growing impatient with this prolonged interrogation. "If you could see us, and we're riding on the road shoulder anyway, tell me what exactly is your problem?"

"You should be more careful," said the passenger, his tone more threatening than cautionary.

My heart rate slackened as the vehicle pulled away.

"Idiots," muttered Marj.

As the night of my first 600-kilometre brevet wore on, Bob entertained me with memories of his time as a roadworks engineer, explaining various composition types and treating me to a scintillating history of provincial highway expansion. Marj lagged a few bike lengths behind—she had heard these stories before. At one point, Marj veered onto a pullout and curled up like a cat in a pocket of afternoon sunshine. She appeared so at ease, not to mention immune to the blood-thirsty mosquitoes buzzing around my neck. I envied her.

"Wake up, sleepyhead," Bob said after a few minutes. "Time to roll."

The tide of fatigue had come for me as well, my legs increasingly resistant to my brain's admonishments to move. Shoulders winched tight from hours without shifting position. Less than fifteen miles separated us from Kerrobert, but our pace continued to drop—it could be dawn before our arrival. Marj fell back again. Bob and I stopped, scouring the pitchy night.

"I think I see her," he said.

We waited as her light warbled closer.

"I might go ahead," I said, when she rejoined. "That okay?"

"Sure," said Bob. "Know where you're going?"

"Gas station in Kerrobert."

"Right. It'll be on your left."

So, I went. Claiming independence with every pedal stroke.

What drove me to split from Marj and Bob on that interminable night in Saskatchewan? I didn't realize until I was on my own, their lights dissolving as I entered a marsh. A slinking mist enveloped me, the choir of frogs burping louder every minute. Before I dwelt on my fears—the possibility of being hassled by another hostile driver—I morphed back to a past time, a younger, fearless version of myself playing hide-and-seek during a warm summer night in a friend's backyard and relishing the transgressive, otherworldly thrill of experiencing a familiar setting without light. That excitement hadn't vanished, I realized. Stepping into night remained an act of faith, where objects appeared off-kilter, sometimes scary. But in letting your eyes adjust, you recognized the fences and molehills were the same as in daylight. Darkness invites risk, but also adventure. My phone buzzed with a text from Marj's husband, John:

Heard you're leading the pack! I have a sleeping bag with your name on it and snacks. Red Bull or coffee for morning—take your pick. Call if you get lost.

I grinned, tucking my phone back into the handlebar bag. The northern lights had come out and flickers of emerald swayed in and out of focus like giant ribbons of bull kelp in an invisible tide. I admired the strange light dance, feeling as though I was right where I should be. Ten miles to go.

. . .

Rolf and Matthias waited at a pullout, the high vis strips on their jackets intermittently glowing like a pair of distant lighthouses under a thicket of darkly woven trees. Seeing them put me at ease in a way I hadn't expected. My chills had worn off, and while I wasn't concerned about nighttime harassment—I'd hardly seen a vehicle in hours—the wind remained formidable, clawing at fences and awakening fields into a soughing concerto of grasses. Illogical as it may sound, I feared we might never reach Yellowstone, as far flung in the encompassing darkness as a remote, unexplored galaxy. Alongside Rolf and Matthias, I felt reassured that if I were to hang in eternal cosmic limbo, at least I would not suffer alone.

After we regrouped, it took a moment to realize our trio had grown to four.

We had been joined by Lochie, an Aussie kid who I'd heard through social media channels had lost his money and identification in Portland. Lochie's dynamo hub—a battery built into the front wheel that could be recharged by pedalling—had died, and he hadn't been able to charge his lights. He scrambled to latch on to our nighttime convoy the moment he spotted our approaching lights.

"I was sleeping in a tractor tire in a field over there," he said, waving toward the void.

We chatted among ourselves, swapping stories of struggles and small joys. Lochie had experienced a similar dilemma leaving Ennis, though continued, despite the wind.

Truthfully, I found Lochie abrasive, and slightly annoying. Perhaps it was the floppy hair that obscured his face, or an Australian accent so strong, I could barely comprehend his words as English. More likely, my irritation sprang from the fact that Lochie seemed to do so well, despite plunging headfirst into situations he was clearly unprepared for—as evidenced by becoming stranded in a tractor tire halfway to nowhere. At the same time, I recognized I was being hypocritical: I was the one, after all, who'd skimped on packing a warm jacket in some ill-conceived attempt to cut back on grams. Lochie was simply coping with unforeseen circumstances the best he could—the same as everyone else.

Dawn seeped light into the landscape, pencilling in spindly trees and brushing a distant horizon in soft pastels. As we approached West Yellowstone, my mouth watered in anticipation of breakfast: pancake stacks gooey with syrup, tender morsels of sausage on the tip of my fork, and coffee refills as far as the eye could see.

. . .

Rolf, Matthias, and I blasted through Yellowstone National Park, released from under the wind's thumb at long last. Our midnight start paid off. Since emerging from the cloak of darkness, we had been knocking down miles— plus, we ditched Lochie after a pancake breakfast in West Yellowstone. He wasn't such a bad kid after all, I'd decided, yet remained guarded over my companionship with Matthias and Rolf. The three of us had gelled so easily—a fourth would complicate everything, and only result in further dithering at stops.

Upon entering the National Park, we encountered a fresh set of challenges, namely frigid temperatures and a perilous road bearing a torrent of impatiently maneuvered rental RVs. I witnessed little of the geothermal activity and jaw-dropping scenery that Yellowstone was famous for, instead honing my focus on the space between the thin white line and the road's edge. Stakes were high. I rode with trepidation, posture stiffening as I channelled my focus into claiming a small sliver between passing motorists and a sheer drop to my right. A day later, racer John Egbers would veer a little too far over to avoid being clipped by a motorist's mirror. He abandoned the 2017 race after breaking his wrist.

On top of my rattled nerves, fatigue poisoned my veins with sleeping sickness. An insidious chill worked its way into both hands and feet, slithering from calves to thighs before penetrating my ribcage. How did I expect to ride night and day without it taking a monumental toll on my already-failing body? Reducing the pace was not an option. After nightfall, temperatures in the park plummeted—snow skirted the road's edge already—and we would need to descend to lower elevations if we wanted to camp. I kicked into the pedals, determined not to let Rolf and Matthias drop me, or worse, give Lochie an opportunity to catch up.

After a couple hours of hard riding, we agreed to a break. Pulling gas station sub sandwiches from our back pockets, we trekked along a boardwalk to lunch in view of a massive, steaming geyser. Amid a swarm of camera-clad tourists, not one of us snapped a photo, though Matthias asked someone to record the three of us singing "For He's a Jolly Good Fellow," for a friend's birthday.

Months later, Matthias would send me that clip. Out of the blue. Only twelve seconds long, shot from the waist up. I stand between him and Rolf, straw hair poking from cycling cap and the geyser's sulphuric liquid seething into a tumultuous river behind us. We swing deli-meat sandwiches on mayonnaise-smeared bread to the tune; only Matthias knows all the words. My voice rings a pitch squeakier than I'd imagined. We look cold. At the last line we pause for a beat, then rush out, "and so say all of us," before erupting in glorious, head-thrown-back laughter.

· · ·

The day of the midnight start from Ennis closed with the Grand Tetons caught in sunset's afterglow behind us. I kept glancing back, bewitched by some celestial magic. Captivated by the shifting hues, I craned my head to catch one last glimmer of light piercing an indigo sky long after the sun had fallen. It struck me also how I'd grown from that anxious first-time night rider of the Prairies. Over the course of a year, I'd learned to feel my way in the dark; find comfort in the night's solace.

That being said, I was pleased our day would end shortly after nightfall when we acquired the last two rooms at the Hatchet Lodge in Moran, a tiny community at the base of Togwotee Pass, a climb that would launch us into Wyoming.

According to the Tracker, Lochie remained somewhere in the park, miles back, but another pair of cyclists had arrived at the lodge—the Osborns, an All-American father-son team composed of Adam, a stocky, muscular Navy Seal (Osborn Junior), and Greg, a sinewy ultra-marathon runner (Osborn Senior). The Osborns were racing as a pair, a category competing under a slightly different ruleset than the general classification: unlike solo racers, pairs could draft, and offer each other assistance. In contrast, solo racers were permitted to ride with others, but had to remain entirely self-sufficient. That meant no drafting, as well as refusing help from another racer, even if it was for something as trivial as borrowing a tire lever. Being busted could result in an asterisk next to one's finishing time, or worse, a DQ—disqualification. Of course, an event of such magnitude was difficult to oversee, and therefore the race's integrity relied far more heavily on the collective honesty of its participants than external monitoring. From my experience, the vast majority of competitors held themselves to an extremely high standard in regard to self-sufficiency, despite the fact that no one was looking over our shoulders to ensure fair play.

We fell into easy conversation with the Osborns, all five of us happy-tired, dazed by the stupendous light show of sunset to crown another long day. My neck and shoulders unkinked as I absorbed the fireplace glow, studying sun-bleached antlers suspended on polished wood beams. A waitress caught me in the act of swapping our empty ketchup bottle for a full one on a table kitty-corner to ours.

"Why didn't you tell me so I could refill it?" she sassed, tapping the empty bottle against a denim-clad thigh. Her knee-high cowboy boots clipped the floorboards as she returned plates to the kitchen.

Rolf and Matthias chuckled while I shrugged under her admonishments, garnet red from sunburn and embarrassment as I shoved another ketchup-oozing mouthful down the hatch. My mouth was too jammed with fries and beef patty to explain our time-crunched circumstances and how, after pedalling from midnight to nightfall, I had no time to wait around for condiment refills.

Day Eight

JUNE 11, 2017

MORAN, WYOMING TO JEFFREY CITY, WYOMING

DISTANCE: 199 MILES

RACE MILEAGE: 1,588 OF 4,264 MILES

Terror first sank its iron teeth into me during the slippery descent from Tog-wotee Pass. Until that point in the race, I'd experienced the gamut of emotions from elation to lethargy, to anxious concern over a growing list of physical ailments, but never deep-seated fear. Nothing yet translated to that harrowing, roller coaster leap of the stomach—the injection of adrenaline which hijacked my nervous system as I navigated over a high mountain pass in blowing snow.

The climb up Togwotee began the moment Matthias, Rolf, and I rolled out of Hatchet Lodge in Moran that morning. Our legs warmed up as temperatures cooled off, eyes on the lookout for glints of movement within the woods around us. Yet we saw neither grizzly nor moose, only roadside patches of snow and ice in increasing diameters. By the time we crested the summit at 9,658 feet, the ground was buried beneath a white sheet, the same flaky precipitation tumbling down overhead. My heart pounded not from the exertion of climbing, but with rising dread as the consequences of the deteriorating weather conditions finally sank in.

"I've never ridden this bike in snow," I admitted when we stopped to layer up for the descent at the elevation marker. I pedalled my winter bike—a $50 mountain bike with studded tires whose gruesome spikes resembled a medieval torture device—from November to March on Saskatoon's snow-rutted streets. But never my sleek carbon road bike, Epona.

"Same as riding in the rain," assured Rolf as he donned a reflective vest. "Take it easy on the corners."

"Nothing to worry about," echoed Matthias. "But don't go slamming the brakes."

The three of us set off, me bringing up the rear. An inch of snow dusted the roadway. My chest constricted. On my winter bike in flat Saskatoon, I wouldn't have given the frosty surface a second thought, but on top of Togwotee Pass the sight of my front wheel knifing through powder accelerated the shakiness of fear.

Nothing to worry about, I reminded myself, blinking fat, fluffy flakes from my eyes. *Absolutely nothing to worry about.*

But my instincts spoke differently. Within seconds, I locked into a rigid, upright, posture. Throat clenched; hands clamped to handlebar hoods. Squinting into the snow, which quickly transitioned to lashing rain as we lost elevation. The road turned slick and slippery. Water washed down the mountain in snaking rivulets that I tried to avoid with my skinny road tires as nightmarish thoughts about losing control of my bicycle and crashing over the guardrail escalated to code-red panic. Every muscle tensed in cold horror, the sound of rubber slashing through streaming water more unnerving than a blizzard. What on earth was I doing? Wouldn't it be safer to walk?

But that would have taken a lifetime.

I got down, eventually. Focused on the road ahead rather than my ratcheting fear, numb fingertips, and discomfort of a soggy bottom. At a general store where Matthias and Rolf had waited for me, we warmed our hands against paper cups of hot chocolate, wringing out gloves and watching the droplets fly as we snapped jackets shellacked in rain.

"That wasn't so terrible," said Rolf. "But where are your pants?"

Instead of rain pants, I had opted for ultra-light rain chaps, which boasted not only waterproofing, but exceptional visibility: neon yellow with reflective strips. Without a rear fender, unfortunately, I discovered the chaps (which only covered the front of my legs) were next to useless. Rolf and Matthias chuckled at the sight of me in such a ridiculous-looking getup—a twisted interpretation of the Western motif that influenced the architecture and décor of these small towns. I couldn't help but laugh at my ill-advised gear choice as well. A fitting symbol for my inexperience in this whole long-distance bike racing thing.

By the time our extremities had regained sensation, the cloudburst had passed. The Osborns overtook us as we straddled our bicycles: Osborn Junior hammering the pedals in the lead, calf muscles like grenades, and Osborn Senior stuck on the back, tucked in to make the most of the draft. While I didn't relish the thought of sniffing someone's bum all day—and drafting was prohibited for solo racers anyways—I must admit, I did envy their accelerated pace. Additionally, I wondered about their team dynamics. Whose idea was it to race across America? Did they share the burden of pulling in the front? The Osborns also conjured memories of a family bike trip of my own, a father-daughter journey seven years prior.

. . .

In 2010, I bicycle toured across Canada. I didn't yet own a road bike, favouring a hybrid with flat mountain-bike style handlebars and a sturdy frame to which I affixed a pair of canary yellow panniers and a tent. In late May, I set off from where I was living with my parents in Surrey, British Columbia. First to Vancouver Island to dip my toe in Victoria's harbour, ceremoniously beginning my journey at the far Pacific before heading east toward the Atlantic off of Newfoundland's distant coast.

Because my departure aligned with a holiday long weekend, my father accompanied me for those first days on Vancouver Island. He returned home once we'd made our tour to the harbour and enjoyed a celebratory round of beer in one of Victoria's English-style pubs, while I continued east toward British Columbia's Interior alone. My father was unable to resist the call of the road for long, however, and hopped an overnight Greyhound to join me in the Kootenays. I met him before sunup at the bus depot in Nelson, where he had liberated his bicycle from the cardboard travelling box and assembled it before I'd even contemplated my first cup of coffee. His early morning fervour—hands, mouth, and body out of sync in uncontained excitement as he described the places we would soon travel together, towns he had zipped through on his motorbike before I was even born—remains etched in my memory. He must have driven the other passengers nuts as he chatted away about his upcoming journey while everyone was trying to rest.

We crossed the Rockies together, winding up Highway 3 toward Crowsnest Pass in the worst weather imaginable. Rain that beat harder than any bass-heavy club track, soupy fog, and havoc-wreaking hail that forced us to duck for cover under the nearest barn awning or fir tree. Regardless, he approached every day as a treat, a chance to witness epically more than his daily rush hour commute. Each bakery an opportunity to indulge; every roadside map or interpretive stop an occasion to uncover another layer of meaning. Never complaining about rain that left our socks perma-wet, or the not-so-scenic spots where we sometimes stealth camped, half-flooded gravel pits or mucky fields. I followed his lead, slipping bread bags over my feet to ward off the damp as I sought thin slices of pleasure—moments of spontaneity and humour—during those dreary days of thigh-crushing climbs.

Once, while cycling with my father during that Trans-Canada tour, we were rained out of a campsite near Frank, Alberta. I'd just swapped my cycling shorts for pyjamas—my only remaining semi-dry clothing— and made up my mind not to leave the tent until the following morning, once the weather was forecast to improve. My heart sank when my father unzipped the vestibule flap to inform me of the evacuation notice posted on the outhouse door: the river was flooding.

"Where will we go?" I wailed, unable to refrain from melodrama in my weakened state.

"Tonight, we'll get a motel room."

I shoved everything into stuff sacks, back into panniers. Rode off wearing my pyjamas, no longer caring. Precipitation rolled down my face like the tears welling up inside. I gave into the encroaching misery: to me, it felt like the end of days. Our bike lights were not enough in the oppressive darkness. We stopped at the first roadside motel we encountered, sun-bleached postcards from the movie *Brokeback Mountain*—it must have been filmed in Alberta—in the lobby. I stood kitty-corner to the postcard carousel in the tight space, afraid I might tarnish the souvenirs if I inched any closer. Devoid of psychological bandwidth, my feet wavered like a balloon on a string. My vacant mind checked out as my father filled in the necessary paperwork and handed over his credit card.

Once inside our room, my father marched straight to the bathroom. He plugged the drain in the bathtub, turned on the faucet, and suggested I hop in to warm up. Water sent pins and needles through my toes and blotched the skin on my chest and legs with misshapen Valentine's Day hearts. Outside, I heard the door to our room click shut, then silence. I sank deeper, cradled by ceramic. Awash in gratitude and serenity, my face and knees were the only islands protruding from the surface as the water's warmth nourished every cell, rejuvenating my inner psyche.

I can't say how much time passed before the bathroom door cracked open. A beer can rolled across the tile floor, clinking to a halt against the tub. Then a shout: "Cheers!"

"Thank you!" I called back, thumbing the tab as I leaned back to sip my Kokanee beer.

Outside, the crinkle of a bag, a handful of potato chips crushed in a palm: first course of a gas station feast. I raised my can again, savouring the refrigerator-chilled aluminum against my lips. The antidote to my misery as simple as a hot soak, a cold beer, and the promise of greasy calories.

. . .

Wyoming's colour intensified after rainfall—rock hues a deeper rust, grasses shamrock green. Rainbows threw arcs over Highway 287, the double solid line glistening brighter than the sun. Like the highway, the sky-world remained divided as well: the northeast a precipitation-stained cement-grey, the southwest a whimsical harbour blue sheltering a flotilla of sail-white clouds. I gazed around in the wonderful calm of being present. Comfortably dry. Assured my cycling companions were down the highway—I'd reunite with them at the next gas station.

Hours passed as I rode alone, mesmerized by miles of dude ranches intermittently pierced by spurs of fiery red rock. Wind River Basin's largely unoccupied landscape provided welcome relief from the tourist havoc of Yellowstone Park the day prior, the frenzied descent through flurries and downpour from Togwotee Pass. In Wyoming's semi-arid high country, I discovered room to breathe, and began to appreciate the vastness of the Great Plains as America's least populous state lived up to its claim.

At some point, I spied a hint of movement: a solitary antelope to my right, lifting its pronged head above a plume of grass. I grinned at the swish of a powdery white tail, bounding down the hillside. Then, I stood to pop the pedals in my own springy antelope emulation.

For the rest of the day, I hopped from my seat every single time I spotted an antelope. Committing to the silliness—a promise not to take myself too seriously.

. . .

I pushed my heart rate on those final flattish miles to Lander, Wyoming, wiping sweat from my brow as I approached the sprawling town, red hills rearing in the distance. Lander boasted a wide main street with several laundromats, motels, and gas stations. I spied my companions' bicycles outside a Pit Stop convenience store. Rolf knelt by his bike, fiddling with his drivetrain.

He had changed out of his familiar red raincoat into a similarly red jersey, adorned with a massive Swiss cross.

"My chain was dirty," he said. "So, I put a new one on. What," he continued, "you don't change your chain when it gets dirty?"

"Uh, no." I just squirted more lube and wiped the chain with a roadside rag, if I was lucky enough to find one that hadn't previously been used for something too disgusting.

"Shame on you," he chided, grinning.

A joke, I realized. Unaccustomed to his brand of subtle Swiss humour.

Rolf explained: "I brought a spare one with me. I change my chain every couple thousand miles, and figured I'd do it now while I was waiting around."

"I'll hurry," I said, struck by guilt for delaying our progress.

"No problem. Our friend Matthias is in the bathroom anyway."

I dashed into the store to stock up on provisions: deli sandwiches, more granola bars, and a king-sized sweet tea to guzzle on the curb. Salt stains crept up my armpits and thighs like tide marks. When Matthias returned from the toilet, Rolf launched his plan. The wind had been shifting. For the next twelve hours, it would be directly at our backs.

"This is our chance. If we push hard and ride through the night, we can overtake the group ahead."

"Amy Lippe," I whispered, remembering how she had passed through the same restaurant-cum-convenience store as me a few days ago, moments before I arrived and indulged in a longer break while she pedalled out of sight. I still didn't know what Amy looked like, but imagined a larger-than-life Wonder Woman dressed in red, gold, and blue, her mass of flaxen hair a character unto itself. I was spot-on about the hair, it turned out.

"Yes, Amy," confirmed Rolf. "Also, Anton Lindberg, Jack Peterson, and the Brit, Brian Welsh."

But we would need to ride without stopping until we reached Rawlins—130 miles away. Over the past few days, my ambition had shifted from competitive advancement, to mere survival. I worried that dialing the intensity up another notch would push me past my breaking point. Our trio was well-rested after last night's sleep at Hatchet Lodge, true, but pedal another ten to twelve hours? I wasn't sure. From the look on Matthias's face, he shared my concern. Rolf spoke convincingly, however, appealing to our sense of adventure and the opportunity to catch the competition off-guard.

"We might not get a setup like this again," Rolf said, wrapped up in a frisson of excitement. "Think how surprised they will be when they wake in the morning and check the Tracker, only to discover that we are fifty miles ahead!"

We hopped back on the bikes before rejecting or committing to Rolf's plan. I wondered if he would continue without me and Matthias, or if Matthias would go ahead with Rolf if I decided I wasn't up for it. Would this be our goodbye?

The three of us passed the Osborns' bicycles outside a grocery store as we left Lander. Perhaps it was my imagination, but our pace picked up. Miles rolled by faster than I could tally them as I pedalled alongside Rolf and Matthias, swapping exclamations of awe and wonder about the surrounding red rock. Optimistic that we may actually succeed in Rolf's wild scheme of overtaking Amy's group under shadow of night.

. . .

After the flood forced me and my father from the riverside campsite in Alberta, the weather improved. Furthermore, I gained some perspective: farmers lost crops; herds of livestock were washed downstream. I didn't have it so rough after all.

In Medicine Hat, Alberta, my father received an email requesting his presence back at the office. This spurred a quest to put on as many miles as possible in the interim. We raced past flax fields in dusky blue and miles of golden wheat. We rode into blossoming sunrise with a gentle wind at our backs; toward nightfall my father rode with a six-pack of beer on his back rack. The even prairie terrain accompanied by a slight tailwind made for ideal cycling conditions. We pedalled with determination and a sense of purpose, relieved to have escaped the worst of the rain and keen to see where the road would unfurl.

We reached Regina—the city from which my father's flight would depart—in sizzling afternoon heat. Odours snaked from garbage bins and alleyways, the remainder of takeout meals and spilled Big Gulps merging into a sweet, treacly mess. The plane wasn't scheduled to leave for another few hours, but he needed to track down a cardboard box to package his bicycle before the shops closed. A whirlwind tour of Saskatchewan's capital culminated in the grand effort of hauling a bike-sized box across the city. My father dismantled and packed his rig in the basement suite of my Regina host, a cinema attendant and aspiring roller girl named Kyla with hair the colour of peacock feathers. Our farewell at the terminal was brief, since Kyla was waiting in her mud-coloured Toyota Corolla.

"Well, that was fun!" my father said. "Thanks for dragging your old man along."

"Anytime." Although I was sure it was more him coaxing my tired bones halfway across the country, and not the other way around.

We hugged, then he turned to lug his box toward the oversize baggage check.

. . .

Matthias and I rolled into Jeffrey City just as the golden hour came to a close. We spotted Rolf's bicycle parked in front of Split Rock Bar, a brick and wood building bedecked with Christmas lights; neon beer signs illuminated the windows. Aside from an automotive shop, Split Rock appeared to be the only business with scheduled hours of operation in the dusty ghost town— definitely not a city, as its name suggested. Despite our earlier discussion about pushing on, when I stepped into the barroom to find Rolf guarding three pint glasses, I knew we'd be calling it a day. I settled into the stool next to him while trying to avoid eye contact with a taxidermied stag head presiding over the bar.

"Nothing like a refreshing beer after a hard day's work," Rolf announced as he raised his glass, a hint of mischief in his eye. "And you wouldn't believe—it's even local!"

"No Bud?" I responded, feigning disappointment.

The need to unwind hit me hard. Fatigue and relief piled on with every minute out of the saddle. Without realizing it, I had nearly drained my glass before Matthias pulled up a stool next to me.

Despite the promising start from Lander, I had soon faded. Though I hated to admit it, there was no way I could summon the energy to chase Amy and the others into nightfall. But no one cared about that other plan anymore. Instead, we recapped the events of earlier race days. Fuelled by alcohol, I found humour in moments of fear, courage in retrospect. We joked about distracted motorhome drivers in Yellowstone, the treacherous descent from Togwotee Pass. Scary moments were beaten down like a video game boss, for the time being.

Matthias offered up a five-dollar bill for single-serving bags of chips when the bartender regretfully informed us the kitchen had closed. We opened them all at once, shovelling in salty handfuls between gulps of round two beers.

I circled back to that feast of chips with my father in an Alberta motel room. During those two weeks of cycling in Western Canada, he taught me so much, from cultivating resiliency in dire conditions, to using bread bags to shield your feet from precipitation (I've since upgraded to Gore-Tex shoe covers). My father gifted me a way of seeing—unfazed by difficulty, around every corner an opportunity—a chance to see what was possible. Armed with these lessons seven years later, I found myself crossing another country, with a different set of companions schooling me in a curriculum of safe descents and midnight starts; puritanical laundering regimes and the maintenance of crisp tan lines.

A toothless representative from a table of card-playing locals asked our names. Worn denim and mud-caked boots identified him as a rancher. We told the locals about the race and the toothless rancher deposited a quarter in the jukebox. Telltale twangy guitars of a country song sprang to life. He proposed a dance, but I demurred, telling him (truthfully) that my legs were kaput.

"You know who this is?" he asked.

"Hank Williams?" guessed Matthias.

"Close."

"Hank Williams Jr?"

"Very close—Hank Three," he said, before two-stepping across the red-and-white checked floor to the toilet. None other than the Osborns replaced him, the father-son team laying down their cycling caps with mirrored expressions of relief. We ordered yet another round—liquid carbohydrates sufficing for proper food—swapping gossip about other racers: who was leading, who was back in Idaho.

"You guys hear they closed the pass?" asked Adam, the younger Osborn.

"When?" I asked.

"Not long after we crossed."

I wondered if I knew anyone—Eric, or maybe DBR—stuck on the Yellowstone side of Togwotee. I hoped they were holed up near a fireplace, at least.

As for us and the Osborns, our shenanigans landed us in the basement of a local church that night. Guided by moonlight along a residential road that crumbled to sand, we shouldered our bikes for the final few hundred feet, eventually bumping into our destination, the side door unlocked. On my way back from the bathroom tap, I noticed a glow from the room where Matthias was supposed to be sleeping and poked my head inside.

"How did you guess Hank Williams?" I asked, emboldened in my tipsy state.

Matthias looked up. "Hank Williams is the only country singer I know."

"Oh," I said.

Then I glanced around: socks, arm warmers, and tools scattered across the floor; precious laminated elevation graphs flung like a deck of cards toward a corner. Matthias had apparently detonated the contents of his frame bag in some ill-conceived attempt to reorganize, and now sat among the wreckage.

"You're drunk, amigo," I said, booting an errant water bottle toward him. "Go to bed."

Then I wandered off to stare at the ceiling in my sleeping nook down the hall, head spinning with liquor, amused by the irony of admonishing someone else for being intoxicated.

Day Nine

JUNE 12, 2017

JEFFREY CITY, WYOMING, TO SARATOGA, WYOMING

DISTANCE: 105 MILES

RACE MILEAGE: 1,693 OF 4,264 MILES

I was the first to leave Jeffrey City. Without even a granola bar in my frame bag, I took off at daybreak, before hunger or the tentacles of a hangover could poke their way in. Balancing on a knife's edge of nausea, I felt strangely euphoric, legs sure and sturdy, rhythmically propelling me toward Muddy Gap, where I would end my fast with a service station breakfast.

It was stupid, I knew, to continue without eating, especially after beer and chips for dinner the night before. But less than thirty miles separated the church in Jeffrey City from Muddy Gap. To beg food from the others was not only a breach of race rules regarding self-sufficiency, but would reveal my poor planning, and invite unwanted scrutiny of my decision making. I would survive. Overhead, squatting clouds flushed apricot and plum as the sun's early morning ferocity flared. I felt my heart quicken with excitement as I advanced into an open landscape marked by clutches of rasping grass and grazing antelope.

But by Muddy Gap, my stomach quaked. A headache had crept in, and I popped two Ibuprofens while waiting for a beef burrito to thaw in the service station microwave. As I laid the mushy burrito, coffee, and an assortment of plastic-wrapped snacks on an outdoor picnic table, I congratulated myself on being first. For once, I could relax knowing Matthias and Rolf were behind me. It took a good fifteen minutes for them to roll in, and though I was ready to set off myself, I went back for a coffee refill.

"Today will be difficult," announced Rolf. "The wind is no longer with us."

At that moment, the breeze didn't appear to approach menacing. Every so often a rogue gust flung a napkin across the lot, but I hadn't noticed a shift during the ride from Jeffrey City. A quick glance at the route, however, revealed a straight shot south to Rawlins before zigzagging southeast into Colorado. According to Rolf, the wind would also be advancing from the south.

"We should go," said Rolf. He spoke with gravitas. I wondered where Amy was now. Somewhere ahead, I assumed. If only we had stuck to the Rolf's original plan instead of withering at nightfall—we could be in the lead.

. . .

By Walcott, Wyoming, the wind had broken me. Dust devils whizzed past pickup trucks while mutton-chopped drivers lined up to pay at a gas station where corn dogs were advertised 2-for-1. I bought a litre of chocolate milk and braced myself for a sandstorm before trudging across the unpaved lot, eyes shielded by my forearm, in search of a shady, wind-sheltered corner to rest.

Since Muddy Gap my pace had dropped. It took less than an hour for the wind to find us, awoken like an angry watchdog, unable to give up its guard. My body submitted as though to a sickness, an earache advancing to soft tissue and bone as the wind's howl waxed and waned, consistently from the south. Nothing in my arsenal of distractions—music, podcasts, even visualizations of finish-line success—provided relief. I felt like I was pedalling with my brakes on, but of course, my brakes were fine. It was simply the wind slowing me down. After lunch, an hour past Rawlins, the route veered south again. I paused at a pullout to confirm the turn on my GPS, hoping I'd made a navigational error—there was no way a person could ride into this. But indeed, the route turned due south. I checked the distance to the next resupply in Saratoga: twenty miles. Twenty wind-in-your-face, choking-on-dust, miles.

I stared at the GPS map. Air surged around me; tree trunks listed like the masts of sailboats in rough seas. I ran my tongue over my lower lip, feeling cracks like broken eggshells, recoiling at the bitter tang of sunscreen. Suddenly, I was tearing up, upset about the weather's unbearable cruelty, and frustrated beyond measure by my own inability to cope. Rather than hardening my resolve and buckling down—as my father would have done—I unravelled.

Matthias pulled alongside as I was turning Epona around.

"What's up?" he asked.

I told him I was done—I'd had it. "I'm going back to that gas station we passed in Walcott to wait this out," I said, wiping dusty tear lines with the heel of my glove.

"Sure," he replied, oblivious to my theatrics. "I'm out of M&M's."

Now, on the dilapidated stoop of a boarded-up trailer (a restaurant in a former life) Matthias joined me: family-sized bag of peanut M&M's stuffed into his jersey pocket, two hands clutching an absurd gallon-cup of fountain soda for maximal comedic effect—he got a kick out of super-sized American portions—and an absurd, jocular grin stretched across his face. Sheltered by the trailer, we eased off our shoes and conversed in groans, taking an inventory of aches and pains as we pointed to body parts—raw soles, ballooning knees, my numb fingers, and achy Achilles—that hurt the most.

We also discussed how, while our bodily grievances were racking up, Rolf appeared stronger than ever.

"It's not going to last," Matthias lamented, as though he were speaking of a doomed romance. "He's too good for us, and he knows it."

I laughed in agreement. Matthias was right: while Rolf seemed to enjoy our company, it would be only a matter of time before the Hamster, as we had secretly begun calling him—a moniker derived from his ability to spin his legs like a contented hamster in the wheel—would dump me and Matthias as abruptly as he had joined us in Twin Rivers, Montana.

Minutes passed before Matthias asked if I was rested enough to go, to which I responded that I planned to wait until nightfall, when hopefully the wind would die down.

"You can't stay here," he said simply.

My gut instinct was to protest—*Just watch me!*—but as I eyed the gas station lot, I recognized he was right. Without shade—other than where we were sitting on the nail-ridden steps—I would overheat or go crazy if I stayed put another six to eight hours.

Yet the thought of returning to face the elements on the highway brought me close to tears once again, jaw trembling as I drained the dregs of my chocolate milk.

"Get yourself together," I muttered. "You live in the Prairies, Goddammit. You're supposed to be used to this."

I flashed back to the day the three of us called it quits in Ennis, Montana. While we holed up in a motel room, others had pushed on. We had paid for our pizza and beer not only in cash, but the precious currency of time. The three of us had been pedalling in the wakes of those who had pressed on ever since. If I wanted to stay in the game—and continue to ride with my current cycling companions—I could not afford to waste another minute. Rolf was pulling further ahead as we spoke, sights likely set on catching Amy's group.

Matthias hoisted himself from the stoop and limped toward his bicycle. I watched him fiddle with his GPS unit for a moment. With deliberation, he threw a leg over the saddle, releasing a groan. He was tired—tired of riding, but also tired of waiting for me.

"One mile at a time," he said, threading his fingertips through the holes of a glove.

I reached for my shoes feeling so, so weary.

. . .

Three hours later, Matthias and I arrived in Saratoga to check into a motel room. Rolf joined us after a second lunch, or early dinner, from one of the main street restaurants. Not yet five o'clock, but we were all destroyed—even Rolf. Across the street was a Kum & Go, a twenty-four-hour gas station convenience store whose name invited a slew of juvenile jokes. We would eat both supper and midnight breakfast there, aiming, as we did in Ennis, to duck out under cover of darkness and evade the wind.

I crumpled into bed, grateful for thick blankets to cocoon my fatigue and incubate my wasted body until I metamorphosized into an actual human again. Those twenty miles from Walcott were the toughest I'd ever covered. I feared I would never arrive. Conversing with Matthias proved impossible over the turbulence. We rode alone through tumbling hills and fields of wind-whipped green, muscles strained and taut as they fought for every foot of pavement. Time no longer progressed linearly, but in some roundabout way I can only describe as dream time—looping and repeating, refusing to move quickly or signify any promise of release. Desperate for sympathy, reassurance, or simply recognition that my little dot was moving, I phoned my mother. But the gale roared with such vehemence that she couldn't make out a word I uttered into my earbud microphone. I hung up. If there'd been any semblance of shelter, I would have stopped—succumbed to exhaustion instead of plowing myself further into the ground.

Now, secure in a budget motel room shared with two other riders, I was glad that I didn't give in. The struggle had been worth it: I'd arrived in Saratoga at long last. I dozed off in lamplight while Matthias repaired a tire that had mysteriously gone flat, unbothered by his quiet cussing, or the scrape of plastic against aluminum as he pried rubber from rim before tweezing out a miniscule shard of glass with practiced, surgical precision.

Through all of that, I remained elsewhere.

Day Ten

JUNE 13, 2017

SARATOGA, WYOMING, TO KREMMLING, COLORADO

DISTANCE: 149 MILES

RACE MILEAGE: 1,842 OF 4,264 MILES

The three of us rolled out of Saratoga at midnight, intent on crossing the Wyoming-Colorado state border before breakfast.

Initially, our late-night departure provided a much-needed respite from the wind that had sapped our energy the previous day. But we found ourselves in another world of trouble when temperatures dipped below freezing as we climbed higher into remote ranch land, gaining elevation none of us had accounted for. Ice chips clinked in our water bottles; frost scratched the grass like discarded tinsel. Even with my puffy jacket, I didn't possess sufficient clothing to weather the sub-zero temperatures. The possibility of black ice left me anxious. Around us, everything was leaden. Not a drop of moonlight, lonely as a dead galaxy, except for the beams where our bike lights shone bright. I turned to Rolf, who I'd been riding alongside.

"Where's Matthias?"

We glided to a halt. Not a car, or even indication of a dwelling, for hours. Squinting back in the direction from which we had come, there were no signs of light. No cell service either, so we weren't able to check our friend's location on the Tracker.

The two of us continued at a slower pace, turning to quiet conversation to distract ourselves from the crisp night. Matthias would surely catch up. I enjoyed listening to Rolf, who spoke in ponderous, curiosity-driven sentences, delivered in a tone just audible over the whir of our spokes. I learned of a deep love for his two cats, his long-standing passion for mountaineering and outdoor expeditions.

He also described how, after a heartbreak coincided with a layoff from work, he had dedicated the last two years to training and competing in ultra-endurance cycling events: the Tour Divide and Route 66 Race in the United States, Tour Aotearoa in New Zealand, and now returning to America for the Trans Am Bike Race.

"I figured I might as well do one more before heading back to the cubicle," he said.

In addition to shifting my attention from the chill creeping through my layers, listening to Rolf's obsession with cycling reassured me I wasn't alone in my desire to traverse increasingly longer distances at speed.

"What about you?" he asked. "You're not a student anymore. What does your life look like?"

I told him about Tyler and the Weird House. The revolving door of roommates, our ragtag troupe of pets. Offhandedly, I divulged that I had a completed manuscript I hoped to publish.

"You never mentioned you were a writer," responded Rolf.

"Oh, I'm not."

"But you have a degree in writing?"

"Sure. But I work as a coordinator of the volunteers at a clinic. I don't get paid to write."

"What about this manuscript?" he said. "Sounds like something I'd read. But you said it's unpublished?"

On my writing mentor's recommendation, I'd sent the manuscript—a travel memoir about my first two-wheeled escapade down the Pacific Coast with my sister—to a Vancouver-based publisher she was connected with. Eight months later, I received a kindly-worded rejection letter.

"I should put in another round of revisions. Shoot it out to other publishing houses," I mused.

"Your work—does that involve writing?"

"It's more of a hands-on job."

As one of two paid office staff, I ensured shifts flowed smoothly, which mostly entailed putting out small fires. I enjoyed getting to know the regular volunteers and clients, and sent a ridiculous number of emails, mostly requests for criminal record checks and confirmation of new volunteer orientation dates—not exactly what you'd call creative writing.

"Good to hear you're contributing to the community and helping others. But I still don't understand," he paused, catching his breath as we crept up the final feet of a climb. "If you're a writer, why aren't you trying to get your work out there? Why aren't you writing? What exactly did you go to school for?"

"It's complicated," I said. "I'd like to write, yes. Absolutely, I'd love to publish my manuscript. But I've got other things on the go. It's not that easy."

We had reached the apex. A paling sky hinted toward daybreak; the time for talk was over. As we gained speed on the descent into Cowdrey—just across the Wyoming-Colorado state line—the exposed skin on my face burned from the wind's attack. The fast-moving air was stunningly cold. My thighs felt raw under Lycra; my fingers entirely numb, though I still managed to yank the brakes as I cornered. I also worried about Matthias. Where was he? I feared the worst—a crash, or mechanical he couldn't deal with—but didn't dare vocalize these thoughts.

We were, after all, solo racers. According to the rules, there wasn't much I could do.

. . .

Rolf and I pulled over at our first opportunity at the post office in Cowdrey, where we had an unexpected reunion with the Osborns. Inside the dim foyer, all four of us huddled tight, struggling to eject words from chattering jaws, fists stuffed in armpits until sensation returned to our extremities. Matthias turned up ten miles down the road at the diner where we eventually stopped for breakfast. A flat had delayed him, Rolf and I already too far ahead to notice. As Matthias regaled the four of us—the Osborns plus Rolf and I—with the story of replacing his tube in frigid nighttime temperatures using only the faint glimmer of his failing headlamp, I couldn't help but wonder what might have occurred had it been me. My hands had deteriorated over the last few days. I doubted I could manoeuvre a tire lever, let alone summon the strength to pry a whole tire off, after my recent loss of fine motor skills—especially with the cold factored in. The alarming truth was if it had happened to me, I might have scratched.

. . .

Tin-roofed houses and a ripping crosswind welcomed us to Colorado. Overhead, the bluest sky I had ever seen. Just to maintain a straight course I had to lean in, heave my weight behind my right shoulder to combat the fifty-mile-an-hour gusts threatening to toss my bicycle into traffic. Coupled with the fierce glare of early-morning sun, the circumstances felt hairy, to put it mildly. Yet Rolf, who had been at my side all day, made pedalling look effortless. After breakfast Matthias rode with us for a while, but soon fell off, drifting back further until he disappeared behind a slow bend in the road. Concerned—and hoping to avoid ditching him twice in one morning—I checked in with a text.

Think I'm going to bivy in a ditch, he responded. *Can't go on. Don't wait up.*

C'mon, you can do it! I replied. *A few more miles and the wind dies down.*

The last part was a lie. I had figured if he could just get back on the bike, he might establish enough momentum to keep going.

I can't.

As I continued to ride alongside Rolf, I racked my brain for words to spark Matthias's motivation. This was the first hint of a crack in his imperturbable composure, and I found myself at a loss for what to do. All my cheery phrases of encouragement rang hollow. The Trans Am Bike Race was tough; we were all struggling. Still, I wished I had come up with something, especially since Matthias always seemed to possess just the right sentiment to bring me back from the brink.

Before long, I found myself with heavy eyelids as well. I relaxed my grip, slouching toward the bars before a particularly violent gust snapped me upright, body braced against the wind. I knew I was in deep waters. With traffic streaming by, there was little room for error—the consequences of letting my guard down were potentially fatal. I told Rolf to go ahead, and then sussed out a spot in the low ditch grass to nap. Alarm set for just ten minutes.

I awoke to my ringer and an avalanche of pain: an explosion detonated in my quads, tumbling down into my knees, calves, Achilles, the very soles of my feet. My head throbbed. I took two Ibuprofen. To my surprise, Rolf was waiting at the next pullout.

"I'm not going to drop you," he said, voice sincere with promise.

But I gassed out as the wind continued its offensive. Within a few minutes, Rolf had drifted from sight. For the first time in days, I was well and truly alone.

. . .

Rolf pedalled off just as the route loped into wilderness. Open countryside gave way to towering green conifers and shrubby deciduous trees closing off the surrounding views. I plugged along, thankful to be rising up a grade which, combined with the thickening treeline, lessened the wind's blow.

I had no clue how long this climb would last. Rolf and Matthias would have known. They had kept me informed of the route, from upcoming terrain to major resupply centres, both with their trusty cue cards. But it didn't bother me I was no longer privy to this information. I'd arrive, eventually. I wondered, however, if I would ever see either Matthias or Rolf again. It would be a lonely ride to Yorktown on my own.

Though I'd temporarily escaped the wind, and the Ibuprofen had silenced the worst of my aches, I could not outrun drowsiness. My chin tipped forward, as if in expectation of an imaginary pillow, as the muscles on my neck relaxed with fatigue. Then some pebble or skidding debris under my wheel would snap me alert. I'd fling my head back, surprised to find myself staring at snow-capped mountains instead of the road directly in front of my wheel, or the filth that marred my previously white handlebar tape. When I reached the summit, a road sign informed me I had climbed Willow Creek Pass, reaching the not inconsequential elevation of 9,659 feet.

I geared up for the descent like a sleepwalker, tugging my raincoat and leg warmers on in a daze. Thankfully, the speedy downhill perked my senses: I imagined myself a pilot in the cockpit of a low-flying plane, relishing the effortless fluidity of motion as I sped down into the woods. I lost elevation quickly, and as soon as sunlight warmed my back, I pulled over for an overdue nap under a pine tree, not bothering to remove my helmet or set an alarm. Before I passed out, I dry-swallowed a caffeine pill, struggling to work the chalky pellet down my throat, but too out of sorts to fetch a water bottle from my bike frame.

· · ·

My father is an expert napper. He can sleep anywhere: on a rocky beach, dining room chair, or in the driver's seat of a parked car. During our time cycling together across Canada, he frequently vanished during breaks. I would walk into a grocery store or restroom, and return to our bicycles to discover him missing. Vanished. After waiting around for a few minutes, I would start searching, annoyance growing by the minute. He'd eventually turn up in some quiet corner, tucked out of the wind in a grassy hollow with a book over his eyes.

Not wanting to wake him, I would grab my journal and settle into a spot of my own until he rose, and we could hit the road again. Sometimes, I gave him a hard time about sleeping at every conceivable opportunity.

"Wait until you're my age," was his response. "You'll understand."

Perhaps I'd finally put my body through sufficient toil to appreciate the sacred art of napping.

. . .

The caffeine pill did not have the desired impact. Following another catnap, I stopped in Hot Sulphur Springs around three o'clock, moody and delirious with fatigue. Matchstick trees along the river's edge whipped in the wind. I decided to get a hotel room. Already, I missed the company of the guys, but looked forward to claiming an entire space to myself—I could lounge around completely naked and finally return Tyler's calls. Besides, my reserves were tapped. I reasoned it made little sense to keep going at such a dismal pace, especially with frequent sleep breaks factored in.

But first, I needed to eat. I pointed my wheels toward a bustling snack shack on the side of the highway, only to be intercepted by a pair of Québécois touring cyclists.

"You are doing fantastic!" they said, aware of not only the race, but my position as lead Canadian—a fact I had been oblivious to until then. "It must be exciting to be crossing the country so fast!"

"Guess so," I said. Had I been feeling better, I might have recounted the excitement of our recent night rides, or how the landscape transformed far faster than I could keep up. But the headwind had sapped me. Looking back, I made for a terrible ambassador for the sport: half-awake and listless, unable to drum up even the slightest inkling of enthusiasm.

The couple picked up on my internal grief, however, and responded with kindness, plying me with granola bars to ease my suffering.

"*Bon courage!*" they said, mounting their loaded touring bicycles to blast off in the direction I had just come, riding high on the northwest tailwind.

At the snack shack, I ordered french fries and rocky road ice cream—comfort food. I ripped open one of their granola bars while I waited at a red picnic table, googling nearby hotels and imagining my body's instant surrender to the hot springs from which the town received its name. When my order came up, I began to cram food into my face like an unselfconscious toddler in a highchair (I really wish I'd had a bib). Matthias arrived just as I was licking the dark, sticky rivulets of melted ice cream from where they had drizzled down my forearm. After a wash of momentary relief for our reunion, I announced my intentions to overnight in Sulphur Hot Springs.

"I'm done," I declared, mimicking words I'd spoken during my meltdown in Walcott just the day before, too tired to conjure tears this time. "I'll score a hotel room here and move on in the morning."

"I didn't chase down your dot to have you call it quits on me, Hackinen. You're really going to let the Hamster get away this easily?"

He leaned his bike against the picnic table opposite mine and lined up at the snack shack. My mind was made up by the time he returned. "Fine," I said. "Finish your ice cream and we'll go."

. . .

Back on the road, my mood improved. Suddenly, everything snapped into sharper focus. I concentrated on shifting power to my legs, as though I were racing from the grip of fatigue, visualized as a mischievous, crooked-eyed troll still haunting the picnic table in Hot Sulphur Springs. The wind and accompanying ache in my shoulders remained constant, but I enjoyed myself regardless. We pedalled alongside the surge of the great Colorado River, peering over the guardrail to take in a powerful waterway crushing everything in its path. Then the route led us between pleasant fields, a countryside straight from a crayon box: red farmhouses, green pastures, and brilliant blue sky.

We fought the breeze gallantly until Kremmling, the last dust-bowl town until the road climbed into the resort community of Silverthorne at the base of Hoosier Pass. A hotel advertising free breakfast and a pool lured us in. Despite the premature end to the day, we reasoned it only made sense, seeing as we'd hit the pavement at midnight.

Matthias and I ditched our bicycles in the room and slung our shower-washed cycling shorts over the backs of chairs to dry before heading out on foot into the shoulder of the day. Ambling along Park Avenue in search of dinner, it was as though a weight had been cast aside. I was out on parole, freed from torturously chafing Lycra and a routine of self-inflicted suffering. Body cleansed and spirit lifted from a quick dip in the pool—nearly as good as hot springs. With most of our food procured from gas stations and slated for immediate curbside consumption, the simple act of consciously choosing a restaurant became a novelty.

Evening light waxed low and golden. Charmed by rusty wagon wheels and Old West storefronts, I submitted to the urge to spin round for a second glimpse of tourist kitsch—a bejewelled cowboy hat or pair of shotgun-print oven mitts—in shop windows. Matthias made fine company: unhurried and content to wander.

We seated ourselves at a booth inside the most Western-looking saloon we could find, pointing out the stone fireplace and bull horns mounted over the bar. Matthias and I almost passed for normal people—two work colleagues in town for a conference—though our cycling cleats and mirrored expressions of desperate anticipation every time a server emerged from the kitchen gave away our true identities.

. . .

My memories of previous touring experiences are filled with evenings like the one in Kremmling: a few hours out of the saddle to explore an unknown place before bed. The difference between those trips and the Trans Am was that scales were now tipped in favour of time on the bike. Lingering moments in small towns and picturesque camp spots significantly diminished, accompanied by feelings of guilt for staying put while others remained in motion.

In Kremmling, however, I shook off the guilt for a night. I simply did not care. While my driving goal remained to test my limits, it felt more important to take a time out to hit the reset button. Forget about the pressures of racing for an evening. Even if that meant calling it an early day, and wasting precious time walking the main drag to find a restaurant we wanted to dine in.

. . .

Matthias and I strolled back to our hotel on the edge of town after dinner, satiated by grass-fed beef burgers and·dozens of crispy, thick-cut fries. I reflected on the previous twenty-four hours: our trio still dredging sleep from eye creases as we stocked up at the Saratoga Kum & Go in Wyoming, our frigid nighttime mountain crossing into Colorado, and Matthias and I chasing the gushing Colorado River toward Hoosier Pass. Continuing on from Sulphur Hot Springs had proven to be the right decision, and I remained grateful to Matthias for not letting me convince myself otherwise.

As we made our way back from the restaurant in Kremmling, the underbellies of clouds bubbled salmon pink; marmalade streaks radiated from the setting sun. Fatigue set in as my fairy-tale evening as a tourist came to a close. A gust tore through an abandoned lot, prompting us to pick up our feet, fists balled into pockets to combat the alpine chill. Silhouettes of distant mountains rimmed the horizon, and closer, the lit-up exterior of our hotel, beckoning us to sleep.

Day Eleven

JUNE 14, 2017

KREMMLING TO PUEBLO, COLORADO

DISTANCE: 208 MILES

RACE MILEAGE: 2,050 OF 4,264 MILES

By daybreak, our carefree evening in Kremmling had faded like a dream. Last night's crumpled meal receipts on the bedside tables were the only reminder of the brief break in routine which had transpired. We dressed in our newly laundered kit without fanfare or remark, neither of us quite warmed up enough for conversation. I grinned on discovering that, despite the early hour, the front desk attendant had kindly left the dining room unlocked. Matthias and I helped ourselves to self-serve coffee and Raisin Bran, the two of us pocketing bananas for the road and packets of peanut butter to be slathered on future gas station fare. Heading toward Silverthorne, the air felt thinner. I wasn't sure if it was because, at over 7,000 feet, we were in among the snow-capped peaks—sailing along at over a mile high—or perhaps we were simply so far from anywhere, my lungs hadn't yet adjusted to the unpolluted alpine environment. Whichever, my body responded with delight, as though I'd sprung wings to effortlessly glide past sparkling lakes rimmed by well-kept vacation homes, and pines flawless in their perfect symmetry, like beauty pageant contestants.

I remained anxious about navigating the larger centre of Silverthorne, however. The touring cyclists outside of the snack shack in Hot Sulphur Springs had uttered caution, describing their struggle through busy streets and close encounters with traffic. Luckily, the GPS track steered Matthias and me onto a separated bike path, curtailing those traffic problems. We continued along the peaceful Dillon Reservoir side by side, our front wheels slicing through air like scalpels as we discussed the Osborn's race tactics. After spending the night at another hotel in Kremmling, they had leapt ahead. I accused the father-son pair of taking the more direct but busier Colorado State Route 9 instead of tracing the windy country roads around a lake as the GPS track had indicated.

"We had to U-turn to get on the right road," I reminded Matthias. "They probably missed the turn completely."

"Or, they could have woken up earlier and worked efficiently," said Matthias, not buying into my entirely unsupported conspiracy theory.

It was only a short segment the Osborns would have bypassed, and I had no actual proof they missed the turn—I was merely annoyed they had vaulted in front of us. Now, we had slipped to the middle of the racing pack, trailing behind Rolf, the Osborns, and Amy.

. . .

Tyler told me that his mother, a five-foot-nothing, take-no-crap-from-nobody woman with jet black hair and an aptitude for Texas Hold'em, had been fervidly dotwatching the race and noticed that Matthias and I were often in proximity.

That German guy is hot on her heels! she had messaged Tyler one evening. *Tell Meaghan to get moving before he catches her.*

She didn't realize Matthias and I were not competing, but keeping company.

When Tyler recounted this anecdote over the phone, I laughed. My amusement shifted to discomfort, however, as I realized my life was under the microscope: my precise whereabouts accessible to anyone with an internet connection. Before the race, I'd never considered the invasive aspect of having a location tracker clipped to my bike. While wearing the Spot device was necessary to maintain integrity in such a sprawling field of competitors, it was also disconcerting to have my every movement broadcast, available for others to interpret as they wished.

· · ·

Despite my desire to close the gap between us and the Osborns, Matthias and I pulled over at a bike shop in Frisco—between Silverthorne and the ski resort town of Breckenridge—so Matthias could pick up new tubes and replace an unreliable bike pump. A second stop for cappuccinos and pastries followed, neither of us able to resist a European-style café offering courtyard seating and an actual espresso machine. The weak gas station coffee wasn't cutting it. Gearing up to commence our attack on Hoosier Pass—the highest point on the Trans America Trail route at 11,542 feet—we reasoned a fortified dose of caffeine was in order.

We paid for our drinks separately. Seated across the table from Matthias, I recognized that he was no longer another dude in Lycra, but a friend. Someone who inspired me to dig deep, and dragged me from my lows with his pragmatic, no-fuss attitude. Our comradery was unique, forged under strenuous circumstances with minimal intrusion from the worlds we had left behind to pursue the Trans Am Bike Race.

· · ·

Between work and training, friendship was something I had missed out on in the months building toward the race. My writing colleagues had long since moved out of the Weird House, and incoming roommates were not individuals I could discuss narrative arcs or favourite authors with. After work and training, I couldn't summon the energy to make plans with my own friends circle, yet somehow accompanied Tyler to obligatory family dinners and the birthday get-togethers of his chums. While I didn't begrudge any of this—waking to the smell of bacon sizzling in the pan at his parents' place, or laughing over Bulldog Margaritas on rooftop patios—I longed for time with friends of my own, without Tyler as the middleman.

As soon as I rolled out from Astoria, however, it was as though I'd entered an alternate reality, my previous life a dream that became more pixelated as the days wore on until it was little more than an indistinct blur, something that once was. Thoughts of Tyler—as well as of work, friends, and Saskatoon—inhabited my mind less as fatigue and sleep deprivation kicked in, nearly all of my brain space diverted to focus on the immediate task at hand. I guessed that Tyler would probably feel insecure about my growing friendship with an unknown man, but I pushed these musings aside. I wasn't physically attracted to Matthias, and with a long-term girlfriend back in Freiburg, he was as unavailable as I was.

. . .

From Breckenridge we climbed. First on bike lanes past souvenir shops and nouveau rustic restaurants that offered whiffs of stone-oven pizzas and edamame appetizers, then into the real estate of winter cabins. Higher and still higher, one leg rhythmically followed by the other; gulping air as we pushed the pedals. I swore I felt the chill of the snow that decorated the Rocky Mountain peaks encircling us. Matthias rode ahead, vanishing on switchbacks until I rounded a corner and he reappeared in my sightline. With a training base of Black Forest climbs, he was at least somewhat prepared for Hoosier Pass. In contrast, most of my preparation had been flatland miles; I was lucky to gain 400 feet of elevation on a full day in the saddle. And while I had previous experience as a touring cyclist, with laden-down panniers and a heavy bike, scaling mountains was something I grimly accepted rather than enjoyed.

Climbing Hoosier Pass, however, I glimpsed what summit-hungry road cyclists must live for as I began to revel in the thrill of the challenge, the combination of mental effort and physical exertion. Every corner offered a fresh view, a visual cue I was one step closer in an exhilarating chase to the finish, with Matthias as my motivation coach.

I danced on the pedals before shifting back to the seat, relishing the surrounding greenery, a wild wood that opened up to expansive glimpses of the Rockies—mountains that kissed the sky. The grade remained steady but rarely steep, a kindness which made it possible for me to hang onto Matthias, though I kept my distance enough to avoid suspicion of drafting.

Even now, I can hear Matthias's laboured breath. Recall the lemon-yellow stripes marking the back of his jersey as I chased him up the mountain slope.

. . .

We rolled into Pueblo, Colorado, at 2:00 a.m., another long haul behind us. During the day, I had snapped photos of an elevation sign at Hoosier Pass that marked the summit of the Rockies and the monstrous club sandwich I devoured for lunch in Hartsel. Later, after we left the foothills behind us and entered the windswept plains, I watched the Osborns' dots pull further ahead on my iPhone screen as Matthias, fixing his third flat in as many days, swore that his new pump proved as useless as his last.

The minutes dragged on the outskirts of Pueblo as we pulled closer to our nighttime destination, streetlamps humming atomic tangerine. As we ghosted into town, I noticed a street sign reading "Good Night Boulevard," and exhaled into a silence so all-encompassing, it was as though the entire world had fallen asleep. I smiled inwardly, counting door knockers on single-storey homes as I imagined all those strangers tucked in next to loved ones or animals—and then Matthias and I, saying goodnight to saddle sores, knee aches, and headaches. Goodnight to these husks we called bodies and the ceaseless endeavour of forward momentum, another 200-mile day in the books. Goodnight, goodnight. Goodnight as we collapse into two ragged heaps in some dive hotel room, stiff mattresses, and a twenty-four-hour reception.

Long after I returned to the Canadian Prairies, it would be these unremarkable glimpses of America that remained stuck with me—imprinted into the back of my retinas. The makings of a scrapbook from photos I didn't take, yet able to conjure the road-worn ache of fleeting adventure in the briefest blink of an eye.

Day Twelve

JUNE 15, 2017

PUEBLO, COLORADO TO LEOTI, KANSAS

DISTANCE: 188 MILES

RACE MILEAGE: 2,238 OF 4,264 MILES

The day unfurled lazily before us. Hot before I knew what time it was; hot before the sun awoke. The road was an arrow's shot through a pancake-flat landscape, past lopsided barns and sagging fences. We were shrouded in car exhaust as we left Pueblo, heat waves as we entered the Colorado plains, with every mile, a setting more closely resembling Saskatchewan's scorched prairie. Except in America, massive penitentiaries accompanied crops of wheat and corn.

By mid-morning, the wind had shifted decisively against us. Drought marked the inside of our cheeks and back of our throats as conspicuously as it afflicted the dust-bowl landscape, the heat-flattened earth. It was always too far to the next refuel point; temperatures in the shade never cool enough to reset our inner thermostats. But we soldiered on, pausing at every small town for pie or ice cream.

At one stop, a gas station attendant informed us about a wild event called the Trans Am Bike Race. "Those racers are ripping through here at twenty miles an hour, riding twenty hours a day," he exclaimed, boasting how he personally had supplied a dozen of these heroic, cross-continental cyclists.

I didn't have it in me to tell him we were also racing, lest he laugh in our faces. Matthias and I were averaging closer to twenty kilometres an hour (twelve miles per hour) and stopping for any excuse we could cook up.

Instead, I asked for the restroom key and trudged off to dunk my head in the sink. The coolness evaporated within minutes, my hair as dry as straw before we even got moving. Adding insult to injury, a touring cyclist with double the gear who had been leapfrogging us since we left Pueblo that morning passed us again. Despite our efforts, we couldn't overtake him until dinner time, when he stopped for the day in Sheridan Lake, and we continued on to cross the border into Kansas.

· · ·

As Matthias and I plugged away, I thought of ultra-cyclist and race organizer Mike Hall, a down-to-earth UK cyclist responsible for popularizing this style of self-supported bikepack racing. Mike spoke eloquently and passionately about the sport of ultra-cycling, remaining an unpretentious ambassador despite his abundance of record-setting rides.

"Nothing that's worth anything is ever easy," he once said.

I repeated this mantra while slogging through the barren Kansas countryside—as my eyes traced golden, hypnotic fields of wind-stirred wheat—but also remembered there remained much that separated accomplished elite endurance athletes like Mike Hall from myself. There was no way Mike would have frittered the day away, stopping at every opportunity for lemon meringue pie or cherry tarts. No, once set to motion, Mike remained that way. He had won the inaugural World Cycle Race in 2012, the inaugural edition of the Trans Am Bike Race in 2014, the Tour Divide mountain bike race in 2013 and 2016, in addition to a handful of twenty-four-hour events. I envisioned Mike as depicted in the Trans Am documentary, *Inspired to Ride*: body tight and aerodynamic, every muscle honed on the road ahead except for his hands, resting lightly on the aerobars, tapping out an easy rhythm. This image encapsulates much of what I'd come to know about Mike as a dedicated, hyper-focused individual who appeared utterly at home on the road.

Tragically, Mike died in a road collision during the Indian Pacific Wheel Race, a self-supported bike race across Australia, on March 31, 2017. A vehicle hit him in the early hours of the morning, only a few days out from the finish at the Sydney Opera House. He died on impact. The reality of his death surged in the backwaters of my brain. A reminder of the unanticipated, potentially fatal consequences of riding alongside vehicle traffic.

. . .

Dusk fell. Matthias and I kept rolling, our pace creeping up as the temperature became more comfortable. We were on a busier road—Kansas Highway 96. A knot of anxiety tightened in my chest as pickup trucks approached from behind, their sudden headlights illuminating the asphalt ahead far brighter than the beam of Epona's single front light. With a narrow shoulder, I straddled the white line, attempting to strike a balance between veering into the ditch and making myself a target for approaching traffic. I imagined the metallic lick of blood; saw my head cracked open like a watermelon on the cement. I regretted my decision to skimp on packing a reflective vest, reasoning my highlighter-yellow rain jacket with high visibility piping would double as both my reflective garment, and protection against the elements.

But I did not want to wear a non breathable rain jacket on a warm Kansas night. Looking back, I should have put it on—ridden with the jacket unzipped, flapping at my waist. Thankfully, Matthias donned his reflective vest and paced behind me for once. With the flat, unobstructed terrain, vehicles should have been able to see our blinking lights, and his hyper-bright vest, from half a mile off.

. . .

The Indian Pacific Wheel Race was called off after Mike Hall's death. The tragedy sent shock waves through the global cycling community—from race participants to dotwatchers to aspiring cyclists—Mike had left his mark on the sport of endurance cycling. His sudden departure was an incomprehensible thing to imagine.

Folks chimed in from all corners on social media, however. Some pointed fingers, saying cyclists shouldn't have been routed on such a busy stretch of road or riding after dark; others believed the driver was negligent, probably glued to his phone instead of minding the road. Many voiced their grief, doubling down on efforts to "#BeMoreMike" and keep his adventurous spirit alive. An inquiry into the circumstances of Mike's death began, but nothing could change the reality that a phenomenal athlete who had become a hero to many was gone. I never met Mike Hall, but after watching *Inspired to Ride*, I count myself as someone influenced by his legacy.

Coincidentally, Mike and I also share the same initials. On Trackleaders, Trans Am course record holders are displayed alongside current racers: LW in pink for Lael Wilcox, the female record holder; MH in blue for Mike Hall, the male record holder (as of 2017). During the first days of my race, I often confused Mike Hall's blue MH dot for my pink MH dot, wondering how I passed so many riders during the preceding hours. The bewilderment didn't last long, of course. I quickly learned to pick out my dot from the centre of the pack, somewhere behind Janie and Amy's pink dots, engulfed in a sea of blue.

Mike crossed the finish line of the Trans Am in 17 days, 16 hours, and 17 minutes. A full week faster than it would eventually take me to reach Yorktown.

. . .

In addition to my anxiety about the vehicle traffic, fears about my failing body once again mounted during the night ride on Kansas Highway 96. This time, it was my legs—my quadriceps, specifically. They simply gave out after we crossed the Kansas state line, no longer able to generate power. I shifted focus to my hips, swallowing one Ibuprofen, and then another. But the status of my quads remained static: they were as useless to me now as my neon yellow rain chaps.

Perhaps my time was up. After all those trials in the mountains and skirmishes against headwinds, I'd finally hit my limit. The realization arrived without panic or fear. Like Simone Bailey back in Idaho, I simply accepted there was no juice left to squeeze from this overused body.

I held off on telling Matthias. It is a well-known adage in randonneuring to avoid making critical decisions—like throwing in the towel—at nighttime. Only when fed and rested should one make the call. If I woke tomorrow still feeling as though sacks of bricks had replaced my legs, I would consider my options. But just then, we had a hotel room in Leoti waiting. Ten miles down the road. There was nothing to do except spin, spin, spin.

The group riding out of Portland on the 120 mile pre-ride to the race start in Astoria

*The author's road bike, a Cannondale Synapse named Epona,
complete with bikepacking gear at the start of the pre-ride in Astoria*

*The manager of a gas station supplies Meaghan with free provisions
near Corvallis, Oregon*

A quick break on a deserted road near Wisdom, Montana

Enjoying Big Sky Country near Ennis, Montana

Selfie with riders Rolf Moser and Matthias Rau near Virginia City, Montana

Among red rock and wide open spaces in Wyoming's Wind River Basin

Crossing the Continental Divide in Yellowstone
National Park, Wyoming

Summiting Hoosier Pass, Colorado:
the highest pass on the Trans Am Bike Race

Matthias consults his information cue cards in Missouri

The finish line at Yorktown Victory Monument, Virginia (l to r): Matthias Rau, Rolf Moser, Meaghan Hackinen, Brian Welsh, Nuno Lopez

Day Thirteen

JUNE 16, 2017

LEOTI TO NICKERSON, KANSAS

DISTANCE: 213 MILES

RACE MILEAGE: 2,451 OF 4,264 MILES

We met racer Brian Welsh for the second time in the entranceway of a gas station in Scott City, Kansas, twenty-five razor-straight miles due east from where the two of us had overnighted in Leoti. Brian shuffled through the automated sliding doors—shoeless and sunburned—with the mechanical stiffness of C-3PO in need of head-to-toe lubrication the precise moment Matthias and I stepped outside bearing armfuls of salty snacks and chilled drinks.

"Nice to see you guys again," he said, squinting through scuffed eyeglasses. His forced grin revealed several missing teeth.

"He looks alive," I said to Matthias once we settled into a shady spot around the corner.

Matthias nodded in agreement. "Surprisingly so."

An hour prior, we had spotted Brian for the first time that day, sleeping in a ditch under the scalding 9:00 a.m. sunshine. We knew at once who he was—for a week, we'd been tracking the Brit. Brian must have tuned into the sound of our freewheels, because on approach he poked his white-tufted head from the grass like a baby ostrich in search of its mother. We pulled over to discover a groggy, incoherent rider on the verge of sunstroke.

"Heat's a bugger," he had said.

Since coming down from the Rockies, we had been riding into a furnace. The road glimmered with mirages; fields crackled with dry wheat. We checked the Brit had water in his bottles before abandoning him, blinking on the roadside in a sleepy, heat-weary daze.

· · ·

Outside the Scott City gas station, I cracked two bottles of Gatorade.

"Drink up," I said, handing one to Matthias. "This is magic juice."

Gatorade, I had discovered just that morning, was the cure-all for my leg problems—better than any wonder drug pedalled on late-night infomercials—resurrecting lifeless quadriceps with its sodium-dense liquid. Suddenly, I couldn't get enough of it.

Matthias obliged and broke off half a king-sized Snickers bar in return. A few seconds later I glanced up from snacking to witness the Brit pedalling away, back pockets bulging comically with gummies, electronic cables, and extra layers.

"Are you kidding me?" I asked.

An hour ago, the guy couldn't string together two sentences. Now, he was leaving us in his dust.

· · ·

The Brit maintained a lead during the heat of the day, even during the buggy hour around sunset, when we rode tight-lipped to keep winged insects out. But later, as Matthias and I threaded through a mosquito-ridden swamp, we found him asleep on the bank of another ditch, the Union Jack emblazoned on his jersey giving away his identity.

"You think we should check on him?" I said, easing off the pedals.

"Nah. He looks comfortable."

An itch pricked my forearm. The drone of blood-thirsty mosquitoes was closing in. I swatted my bicep, squashing several into pulpy oblivion before kicking up my heels in hasty retreat, the sound of beating wings like a fleet of tiny helicopters in my ears.

I sensed we had not seen the last of Brian Welsh, however. A hardened fifty-something-year-old, he possessed what is oft-referred to as "old-man strength," which, coupled with an ability to sleep pretty much anywhere, made for strong competition. Henceforth, Matthias and I no longer called him the Brit, but the Tough Ol' British Bastard, a nickname bestowed with both affection and admiration for our steadfast Trans Am competitor. Later, we would learn that Brian was an accomplished triathlete who earned a living as an endurance coach.

. . .

My grandmother, Marie Hackinen, introduced me to the concept that a person could stretch her limits past those of comfort—the notion of endurance, essentially. Grandma Hackinen, my father's mother, was widowed by the time I entered kindergarten, which freed her schedule to babysit for my younger sister, Alisha, and me. She was a no-nonsense woman with muscular thighs, greying curls, and glasses with thick, wide lenses.

Overall, I enjoyed our afternoons with Grandma Hackinen, though there were significant differences between her care and that of my parents. My mother and father painted clear boundaries around whatever activity we would undertake, establishing how long we could expect to be engaged for, and what we would eat for lunch. With Grandma Hackinen, no such blueprint existed.

On a typical day, our trio would venture out in gumboots, Grandma Hackinen shouldering an ancient army green MEC backpack that bore raincoats, Band-Aids, and a tied-off bread bag stuffed with trail mix. We meandered through nearby woods and meadows, walking for hours as we explored train tracks or earthen paths shaded by new-leaf alders, littered with horse dung. These walks were a brilliant source of discovery and excitement for me: the critters, vegetation, and strange things we might find if we followed creek beds or animal tracks. The problem, however, was that Alisha and I encountered our perceived limits of exhaustion prior to the arrival at whatever turnaround point our guide had in mind. From a very young age, I remember being possessed by fear that I might never make it back home. Would my parents come looking? How would they even know where to begin?

Tantrums and meltdowns ensued. Grandma Hackinen stood stoically by, rarely crouching to meet our blotchy, crimson faces and fitful tears. In her practical blue windbreaker and trousers with their multitude of pockets, she reasoned with us, explaining how we only thought we were too tired to go on. That if we stopped now, we would miss out on whatever surprise or treat awaited: a thicket of Saskatoon berry bushes, or a friendly horse we might whisper sweetly to while proffering handfuls of grass, or perhaps a few wormy apples pilfered from a nearby tree. Sometimes, she bribed us with the promise of Danish butter cookies that came from a navy-blue tin, though usually, it was her unrelenting patience that won out.

Alisha and I plucked ourselves from the ground and continued, dragging our heels until moods improved. We would always arrive home, knees caked in dirt, sometimes waterlogged after being caught in a downpour, and famished enough to devour whatever microwaved concoction was placed in front of us—Grandma Hackinen was not known for her culinary skills.

While I can't say I delighted in every moment of those adventure walks, I became more at ease once I recognized I was not going to perish in the wilderness. I came to appreciate them more as I aged into adolescence, and realized I could out-play my classmates, and spend an entire day at the ski hill without concern for fatigue or hunger.

. . .

Matthias and I continued into the Kansas night. We were closing in on Newton Bike Shop and hoped to reach the famed Oasis in the Grass Desert before calling it quits.

"Only one hundred miles to go," I chirped.

Matthias's silence indicated my optimism was misplaced. Still, we had cycled halfway across the continent—surely we could push a few more miles to Newton before sleeping.

Newton Bike Shop is one of the few places to have your bike serviced on the TransAmerica Trail. Though not quite the geographic halfway point—that we passed yesterday in Pueblo, according to one of Matthias's handy cue cards—or an official race stop, the shop had gained a reputation as a haven for Trans Am racers, providing twenty-four-hour bike service, hot meals, and a pillow to rest a weary head. From the Tracker, we saw that Rolf, Amy, and two others had arrived.

Want me to save you pizza? Rolf texted.

Yes! I answered. Then I turned to Matthias to share how I imagined our arrival in Newton: The Three Musketeers squeezed onto a sofa, alternating between slices of pizza and sips of beer as we regaled one another with our tales. I would finally meet Amy, and get those annoying creaks in my bike worked out.

"And sleep," said Matthias. "Don't forget the most important thing!"

. . .

My energy faded as the night wore on, despite a steady ingestion of Gatorade, coupled with caffeine tablets. Matthias followed suit, our pace plunging toward single digits by midnight. Every so often a small town interrupted dark country roads, a handful of lit-up front porches and a church. Funny sort of sightseeing, I thought to myself, perking up to observe the brief smattering of houses, a few streetlights radiating gracious brightness into the chasm of night.

"I take back what I stated earlier about 'only one hundred miles,'" I said, recalculating the distance to Newton. Despite steady progress, we weren't moving as fast as I'd anticipated.

"A century is a long way if you're crawling," he concurred with a small smile.

After a particularly drawn-out stretch between towns, my vision began to tunnel, the pavement's edge softening and converging with the night like the darkened outline of an old-fashioned portrait. I saw less and less, my aperture narrowing; focus diminishing with each sleep-weary blink. Magical thinking, I realized, would not get us to Newton—and only sustained hard work would see us through to the finish line in Yorktown. How could I have been so foolishly optimistic?

Forty-five miles from Newton, we rolled into the medium-sized town of Nickerson. Matthias and I had long quit talking, but remained in proximity, our bike lights illuminating the road in tandem. Despite deserted 2:00 a.m. streets, my ears echoed with sound: a muffled crash and fall that I imagined, in my fatigued state, to be blood's spurting rush through arteries with each contraction of my heart. The flow mimicked the rhythmic rise and tumble of distant crashing waves, and I visualized myself adrift in an ocean current as I floated through Nickerson, less grounded to reality every minute. Barely turning the pedals. I gazed up at ethereal boulevard trees, enchanted by our surroundings, the repeating pattern of limbs and trunks an intricately woven brocade. Thick branches gold-limned with streetlight glow.

There was no way I could cover the remaining forty-five miles to Newton; I would be lucky to pedal a further forty-five seconds. I recalled the promise I'd made to myself—only ride if I could keep my wits sharp—to avoid dangerous situations like last year's Swan River 1200, when I hallucinated golden fries and spaceships. One look at Matthias's blank expression told me he would soon be unfit to continue as well.

We pulled alongside a city park. East of the Rockies, "city park" refers to any green space with basic amenities, regardless of whether it's in a genuine city or a town boasting twenty citizens. This one featured a soccer field, a grove of tall trees, and an unlocked restroom. A perfect spot to rest. Once our reserves were topped up, we could continue toward Newton.

"Here?" I suggested, pointing toward grass.

"Sure," said Matthias, tipping his bike against a nearby bench. He heaved the word out in a sigh. His eyes were two thin, grimacing slits behind glasses; his neck and arms gleaming slick with sweat that hadn't yet evaporated.

The night remained warm and muggy. We unrolled our bivy bags as ground sheets on the fresh-cut grass and clumped unused clothing into makeshift pillows. A web of stars glimmered overheard. Grateful for the absence of biting insects, we sprawled atop Gore-Tex and Lycra—clad in the day's clammy cycling kit—alarm set to sound in two hours.

Day Fourteen

JUNE 17, 2017

NICKERSON TO CASSODAY, KANSAS

DISTANCE: 82 MILES

RACE MILEAGE: 2,540 OF 4,264 MILES

I woke up from my second nap that day to the gentle whirr of a ceiling fan. The time on my phone read 3:00 p.m.— I'd slept five hours in a bottom dorm bunk at Newton Bike Shop, fifty miles from where we'd had our first 2:00 a.m. nap in Nickerson. I staggered into the kitchen to discover Matthias sipping coffee with none other than white-haired Brian Welsh—the Tough Ol' British Bastard.

"G'morning, love," said Brian, looking spry. A far cry from the man passed out in the ditch twenty-four hours ago.

"When did you get here?" I asked, leaning in for a hug. Our appearance in Newton felt monumental: a moment to put friendly rivalries aside and celebrate. If you reached Newton, chances were that you'd arrive at the finish. I experienced a sudden pang of guilt for referring to Brian as a bastard, even though his nickname had been borne from admiration.

"Rolled in just after you," he said. "This shop is a fine place, isn't it?"

"Beats sleeping in ditches," I teased.

"Best sleep of my life last night."

"Surrounded by mosquitoes big enough to lasso?"

"Bugs don't bother me, love," he replied with a cheeky grin. "They only go after ones like you with sweet blood."

I shook my head and made a face at Matthias: what was up with this guy? Was he a British Superman with iron flesh impervious to insects? Matthias shrugged, looking equally bewildered.

. . .

When I was ten, my grandmother cycled across Canada. At seventy-one, she held the title of being the oldest of approximately fifty athletes completing the coast-to-coast van-supported tour. In early June, the group departed Vancouver Island, and came through the Lower Mainland the following day. Alisha and I bounced up and down with homemade signs as cyclists in bright Lycra passed by. I stood tall with the pride of seeing my grandmother among the others, knowing that it was only the beginning of an incomprehensibly arduous journey. I had never been outside of British Columbia then, but every classroom I'd set foot in displayed an enormous wall map of Canada's provinces and territories, providing the appropriate impression of national grandeur.

Grandma Hackinen grinned when she caught sight of us. She pulled over for hugs and photos before taking off, her quick wave vanishing into the sprawling peloton. Her stop was so brief, she didn't even praise our signs. But later, she would write: postcards from Kamloops, Winnipeg, Wawa, and Halifax. Her teacher's cursive filled the blank space with descriptions of topography, habits of other riders, and places of interest. Alisha and I looked up these faraway locales in our atlas, imagining our Grandma Hackinen's days in the saddle, her unflinching resolve in the face of challenging climbs or inclement weather.

Trouble was, no one at school believed me. Not my classmates, nor my teacher. I came home in tears one day after my teacher accused me of spreading lies. "No one rides a bicycle across Canada," she had said, *tsk-tsking* my outrageous claim. "Especially not an elderly woman. Isn't possible. Maybe she's travelling by motorhome?"

I brought one of the postcards in the next day, as well as a note from my mother that verified my claims about my globetrotting grandmother's whereabouts. My teacher examined both and shrugged. I had hoped to be vindicated, but was left disheartened by the teacher's lack of interest: if someone tells you their seventy-one-year-old grandmother is pedalling across the world's second largest nation, doesn't that warrant greater enthusiasm than mere acknowledgement?

. . .

As Brian, Matthias, and I munched breakfast burritos paired with fistfuls of conveniently sliced fruit, Matthias informed me that our bikes had been worked on while we napped—scrubbed factory-clean and tuned up, brake pads and chains replaced.

"Our kit should be dry soon," Brian added, before marching toward the shower, outfitted in loaner baggy shorts and college sports team T-shirt like we had all slept in while our own clothes received a much-needed laundering.

I remained disappointed that our plan to arrive in Newton during the night—when we could have slept on schedule, hitting the road at first light—hadn't panned out. Instead, Matthias and I crawled in from Nickerson that morning, the 2:00 a.m. nap insufficient to convince our legs they had rested. We just missed Rolf, who set out twenty minutes before our arrival. I wondered why he didn't wait—what had happened to "I'm not going to drop you"?—but at the same time understood his urgency. Rolf gained eighty miles as we slept in the dorm, though at least our bikes were now in tip-top shape. Plus, we'd eaten something that didn't necessitate the removal of plastic wrap.

After breakfast, Matthias and I settled onto the sofa, cradling hot mugs of coffee with remarkably clean hands as we relished a brief respite from racing—the small luxury of creature comforts. With Brian out of earshot, we concocted a plan: stock up on snacks and pedal through the night, stopping to snag shuteye in another city park, should that be necessary.

"Want to keep riding together?" I asked.

So far, we had taken it day by day, never discussing our race future. But in Newton, as we schemed about overtaking the Hamster and re-establishing our lead on the Tough Ol' British Bastard, it seemed like a topic warranting discussion.

"Sure, I only find you slightly annoying," he teased.

I grinned, reassured he was joking by the glint in his eye, and slapped his thigh: "Till Yorktown do us part!"

After five hours on the dorm room mattress, I felt more alive than I had in days, ready to throw everything into the second half of the race. Our journey no longer felt like a never-ending slog, but a mythic and noble saga whose conclusion had yet to be written. If Matthias and I could maintain a consistent pace, there was still hope we might finish within our mutual goal of under twenty-five days.

. . .

I moved in with Grandma Hackinen after a year's stint in Southeast Asia in my early twenties. When I returned home, broke and regretting my arrival during a dreary West Coast winter, my parents informed me that my grandmother was experiencing a concerning degree of memory loss. She was also recovering from a nasty fall that had left her with a fractured vertebra, among other injuries, and while her physician had recently deemed her fit to return to independent living, another person in the house would provide a welcome safeguard. Since she shunned outside help from "do-gooding strangers," I became the obvious choice for a roommate.

This was fine by me. After twelve months of stumbling between Full Moon parties on tropical islands and steamy noodle stalls in bustling metropolises, the last thing I wanted was to be confined at my parents' home in Surrey. At least my grandmother lived close to a SkyTrain station in Burnaby, more central to Vancouver's nightclubs, and the North Shore ski hill where I found work. Plus, I had neither money in my savings account, nor an actionable plan for the future. My parents lent me their aging cardinal-red minivan and I moved in with my grandmother, returning home for a night or two on weekends.

Grandma Hackinen had shrunk since I last saw her. Her spine arched into a question mark, so she had to raise her head to make eye contact, brushing wayward curls from her brow with an unsteady hand. Though her short-term memory was shot, she could tell you about digging sloughs in Richmond as a teenager, or picking strawberries for meager wages on the neighbouring farm. I slept on the living room sofa just outside my grandmother's bedroom—close enough to hear her snore—comforted by sun-bleached walls hung with gaudy seashell décor, the piano my father had learned to play as a child, and the soft, tired scent of ancient furniture. A neighbour came by with dinner when I was visiting my parents or working an evening shift, pretending that she had cooked too much, and would my grandmother please do her the favour of eating the leftovers so good food didn't go to waste?

I lived with Grandma Hackinen on and off for eighteen months. Slow ambles around the block replaced the adventure walks of my youth. Sometimes, our excursions took us no farther than the backyard picnic table, whose peeling red paint matched the colour of apples the overhanging tree—now gnarled in age—once produced.

During her final few months, my grandmother spent most of her time in bed. Instead of hunching over the cluttered kitchen table with her notepad or a hardcover library book, she would recline in her down sleeping bag—warmer than a comforter, she claimed—eyes lidded but awake. I would narrate my shift at the ski hill, describing fresh snow in tree boughs, friendly chickadees, and nighttime views of Vancouver's twinkling lights from the chairlift. Under lamplight, her wrinkles softened. I watched the corners of her lips turn up in pleasure as she took in the scenes I painted, relishing the opportunity to experience second-hand the sights and sounds of those same mountains she had once guided novice hikers through, when her legs were as nimble as a mountain goat's.

My grandmother has been gone over a decade now. She never knew me as a cyclist, but my family assures me she would have been proud. I trace my passion for travel and endurance sports back to her, a legacy imparted over time together. From her, I learned the value of curiosity; the rewards reaped by those who dare to explore. I learned to trust my body, and with that trust enabled my legs to carry me farther and farther from home.

. . .

Matthias and I departed Newton full of promise, ushered across Kansas plains by an easy wind. As we rode toward Missouri, the landscape became more undulating. The road gently curved up and down—hills! Well, not exactly, but compared to the uncompromising flatness of the past few days, any change in grade could be mistaken for a slope. Then I remembered what Matthias had told me regarding the upcoming terrain: we were entering the Ozarks.

"We'll accumulate several thousand feet of vertical gain a day," he stated, pointing to the tiny zigzags on Missouri's laminated card.

Now, we appeared to be closing in on the foothills. While I had no doubt regarding the formidable challenge the Ozark Mountains presented, I took pleasure in these breezy, easy warmup climbs.

Engrossed in the terrain's changing curvature, I failed to notice storm clouds building to the north. The cement-toned conglomeration expanded—a darkening, portentous brew of clouds patched over a distant horizon—then turned black. My stomach knotted when I realized that this ominous mass was reeling directly for us.

The sky opened within minutes. Lightning ignited the horizon like Canada Day fireworks as rain cascaded down on the dry fields. My self-preservation instincts took over just as quickly, and as the first fat droplets splatted against our forearms, I was already directing Matthias to follow me down a rutted path toward a farmhouse where I hoped to find shelter. Our knock was met by a slim woman behind a mesh screen who extended an invitation to wait out the weather in the carport, a semi-enclosed structure that housed, in addition to a pickup truck and quad, an assortment of farm implements. Though not yet 7:00 p.m., daylight had vanished, the storm's dense cloud cover blocking the sun. Raindrops came down like gunfire. I grabbed my bike light to snoop around, encountering hay mounds and open boxes of giant hypodermic needles meant for injecting livestock amid the orbiting dust.

I felt helpless. With reduced visibility and lightning, I knew we wouldn't be safe on the road, but a grimy carport full of enormous needles didn't appear like a brilliant place to remain either. During a lull in the rain, the farmwife came over to invite us inside, an offer I did not hesitate for a moment in accepting. After removing our mucked-up cycling cleats, Matthias and I introduced ourselves properly to the woman and her husband, both wispy-haired and in their golden years. We explained the circumstances of our arrival at their doorstep—our participation in the Trans Am Bike Race—over a muted television news broadcast, interrupted every few minutes by another spine-straightening crack of lightning. I no longer recall their names, but the husband was a sturdy man, dressed in denim and plaid, and nearly deaf; the wife appeared frail, her floral dress a pale pink and cream, temples and ankles displaying the same curlicues of lilac veins.

"Why don't you sleep upstairs?" asked the wife. "There's a guest room, but the bed's unmade. I haven't been able to get upstairs since my stroke."

She cast her eyes toward the staircase, then back to us.

"Sheets and pillows should be laid out. I'll make oatmeal in the morning."

"I guess we're not going anywhere in a thunderstorm," I said, thinking aloud. "And even though outside assistance isn't permitted, I suppose it's fine as it's not premeditated."

"What was that?" she asked.

"Nothing," I said, realizing that most people would not comprehend the specificity of bike race rules. "Thank you for the kind offer. We'd love to stay."

"But we won't be here at breakfast," Matthias piped in. "Because it's a race, you know, and we have to keep moving."

The upstairs room turned out to be a cluttered space, storing boxes of old photographs and cuts of fabric. A massive watercolour of a tiger featured as the centrepiece over the bed. But the room proved more than sufficient for overnighting, boasting a king-sized bed, antique lamps, and plenty of bedding. Despite the torrential downpour, Matthias and I harboured hopes of salvaging our mission to ride through the night. We tucked into bed with his phone between us, alarm set to chime every two hours to reassess conditions and make tracks as soon as the storm let up.

. . .

At 2:00 a.m., Matthias and I lumbered downstairs for the third time to check the weather. We swung the back door open to find rain coming down in streaks of silver that ricocheted from the path to splatter our ankles.

The two of us trudged back upstairs. Matthias checked his phone before setting another two-hour timer. "Did you read the post on the Facebook page?" he asked. "There's a rider down."

I reached for my phone to see what he was talking about. Someone had been hit. Police pulled over the racer in his wake for questioning, and that person—who happened to be Lochie, the Aussie kid we had met en route to West Yellowstone—had posted about the incident: *I think it was Eric Fishbein.*

My breath arrived in tight bursts. It couldn't be. I glanced toward Matthias, then back to my phone. "How did the cops know it was a racer?" I said. "Might have been any guy on a bike."

"Eric's tracking device stopped. I just checked. But maybe he's just hiding out from the storm."

I flashed back to Eric, the two of us at a barbershop in Astoria, carried away with excitement as he described the upcoming race to the woman buzzing his head. I still owed him twenty dollars. Eric and I had also exchanged phone numbers that day. If I sent him a text and he responded, I would know everything was fine.

I typed quickly, the need for reassurance manifested in fingertips: *Hey Eric! How's the ride?*

Then I set my phone on the nightstand. No use worrying about something that might be hearsay—a mix-up. Still, I wondered. Where was Eric headed; had the storm that marooned us in a farmhouse reached as far west as Leoti?

Two hours later, the alarm buzzed again. Matthias walked downstairs to investigate the weather while I checked my phone. No response from Eric. Still storming. Cocooned in silky darkness, we drifted back into the ether of our dreams, untouched by rain lashing against the windowpanes.

In the morning, the race director confirmed the news: Eric Fishbein was dead.

Day Fifteen

JUNE 18, 2017

CASSODAY, KANSAS TO GOLDEN CITY, MISSOURI

DISTANCE: 190 MILES

RACE MILEAGE: 2,730 OF 4,264 MILES

Matthias and I left the farmhouse just after daybreak. The downpour had slowed to a trickle, but after schlepping our bikes through a slough of sloppy puddles, our legs were spackled with muck by the time we reached the highway. It didn't matter, anyway. Wet feet, filthy shorts—who cares? After hearing the news about Eric, none of this mattered. What was I even doing here? I wondered. What was the point?

We pushed on. Through grey weather matching the nondescript countryside and our moods. Or perhaps I have simply blanked this part of the TransAmerica Trail from memory—it's hard to say.

I felt numb, as if the wires linking mind and body had been disconnected. My heart continued beating as sure as my legs spun, but mentally, I remained lifeless. Adrift in a fog that made the act of connecting thoughts a painstaking chore, the task of rational consideration an impossibility.

. . .

Around 10:00 a.m., I called for a stop, "Just a fiver."

We had arrived at a small city park with a picnic table. The landscape screamed with green from the recent downpour, slender grasses and bushy shrubs eye-poppingly vital. As Matthias and I dislodged yesterday's gas station snacks from pockets, a touring cyclist heading the opposite direction pulled up, her bike frame saddled with enormous panniers, helmet dangling by its chinstrap from the handlebars. She greeted us with a broad smile, her cheerful disposition in stark contrast to our own dire expressions. We discussed the storm, which we had all managed to wait out indoors.

"Well, you can't predict the weather, can you? Every day an adventure!" she crowed.

Matthias and I nodded, alternating mouthfuls of carbs between mumbled replies. A few minutes later, we watched her continue west, the steady, measured cadence of her pedals vanishing over a rise in the terrain.

"She seems to be having an enjoyable time," Matthias observed.

"I'm excited for her," I said flatly, though I meant it. I just found it difficult to summon my usual enthusiasm that day.

Several minutes passed before either of us spoke again.

"This really sucks," said Matthias. He held his phone, presumably open to the Trans Am Facebook Page where people were sharing their grief.

"It really, really sucks," I echoed.

How could this even happen? How could the person I had been drinking beer alongside in Astoria be deceased? It didn't seem real. Surely someone would come along to yank my arm and tell me this had been an obscene joke, or nightmare.

"I just," I stammered, "I just don't know what to do."

"I wonder about his family. Did Eric have kids?"

"Three. I think they're grown up. Not that it makes this easier," I said. I remembered something else: "He was planning to visit an aunt on the East Coast after the race. He hadn't seen her for years."

"Damn."

"I ditched him that morning in Mitchell," I said. A confession. "I figured we'd run into each other down the road. Maybe share a beer in Yorktown." I thought back to Mike's rooftop in Astoria, sitting next to Eric as we sipped the dregs of our porter and watched the sky explode with sunset, while he reassured me that I was enough.

Matthias's features softened. "You couldn't have known."

"I just took off. Never said goodbye."

I still hadn't cried, but knew I would. I perceived that at some point, my emotions would explode like one of Yellowstone's geysers, and I'd burst open to cry uncontrollably.

. . .

I have never been a religious person. Yet, I appreciate there is much I do not know. The afterlife is one of those things.

If life after death exists, I like to imagine that it is in spirit form: the possibility of a soul untethered from our cumbersome human bodies.

During those last weeks of Grandma Hackinen's life on earth, I imagined her transcending into the spirit realm as her body and mind incrementally powered down. While she lay in bed, body motionless inside her sleeping bag, I would look around the dim room and picture her vaporized spirit filling the surrounding space, testing the unfamiliar waters of life outside the body as it peered down from the ceiling, or skated along the floorboards before returning to its familiar human haunt in time for another slow exhalation of breath.

Now, I imagine my grandmother's spirit free to wander. In a high breeze, she moves where she pleases, revisiting mountains once trekked in the Andes and the Himalayas, scenic byways she cycled across Canada. I envision her in a gust of wind at my back, cheering, "Go, Meaghan, go-go-go-go-go!"

. . .

The road became hillier as Matthias and I pedalled toward Missouri. The scent of budding floral undergrowth replaced the breakfast-cereal smell of wheat. A cool, overcast day proved excellent for cycling, and we made decent time. For once, there was not a breath of wind. I didn't respond to texts from Tyler or my mother and avoided social media, though I monitored the Trans Am Facebook Page for updates about the circumstances of Eric's passing.

Unlike Mike Hall's death during the Indian Pacific Wheel Rim Race, the Trans Am had not been called off. Race organizers issued a statement, offering condolences to Eric's family and support to those still on the road:

"To all racers, please know we're all pedaling together wherever we're sitting. Let your loved ones know where you are and what you plan to do. Some will keep pedaling, some will go home. We urge all to take the time to find the quickest path to healing."

Over the following days, a handful of riders would pull out of the race, citing the loss of a friend and fellow racer as a reason to return home to safety, family, and loved ones. Others put grief to words, vocalizing emotions in a vocabulary of loss that I had yet to acquire. Dotwatchers chimed in with condolences and messages of support for everyone reeling in the wake of the Eric's sudden death.

Few details of the actual incident were forthcoming: Eric had been struck from behind at 10:10 p.m., eight miles east of Leoti, Kansas, on a flat, straight section of highway. The storm hadn't travelled that far west, and I assumed Eric had been riding with lights, and the high-vis vest he'd worn while we pedalled through the Ochoco Mountains into Mitchell on day two.

Thinking about Eric's passing, I also questioned if I was I putting myself at serious risk by being here. The quixotic delirium I had been living in, motivated by the ideals of self-sufficiency and relentless forward progress, lost its hold. Instead, I was forced to reckon with the realities of racing: was the potential cost—death—a price I was willing to pay to participate in this transcontinental quest?

Yet people died in traffic accidents all the time. Any mode of transportation—be it car, plane, train, or bicycle—had associated risks. Just because someone I knew personally had died in a crash didn't increase the likelihood I would suffer the same fate.

Still, my neck hairs quivered as I recalled the frightening vulnerability I experienced on that same stretch of Kansas Highway 96, when Matthias and I pedalled toward Leoti after sunset. I wondered how many more times I would find myself in similar circumstances, fearful that I may be invisible to approaching traffic.

. . .

When the route shifted to quiet roads, Matthias and I rode side by side, trading stories of Eric and sharing our brief memories of him from Astoria. I told Matthias about the pre-race beers on Mike's rooftop, and how Eric and I lingered for the sunset after others returned to their last-minute packing.

"That night, Eric sent me off with confidence," I said. "He wasn't worried about me; said I was strong enough to make it to Yorktown on my own. Since he thought I could do it, I decided I might as well believe in myself too."

I swallowed, unable to continue speaking. Blood flooded my face; my throat constricted.

"And look at you now, Hackinen," Matthias said, meeting my eye. "You're doing it."

"Guess so," I replied, smiling weakly in return.

Inside, a maelstrom of emotion pulsed in my chest. But still, I did not cry.

Day Sixteen

JUNE 19, 2017

GOLDEN TO HOUSTON, MISSOURI

DISTANCE: 152 MILES

RACE MILEAGE: 2,882 OF 4,264 MILES

Missouri rollers replaced the pan-flat plains of Kansas. At first glimpse, I registered excitement in the change of scenery. Pastoral hillsides promised shade from oppressive heat; towering elms invited afternoon catnaps. But the gentle contours transformed into something vehement and challenging, and before we knew it, Matthias and I were careening along a roller coaster of unforgivingly steep climbs chased by nail-biting descents.

There, the reality of Eric's death sunk in.

Anger boiled up as I attacked a grade, heaving my weight into pedals. I sucked air in rapid, violent bursts. Fighting for every vertical foot with pistoning knees, forearms taut against the bars. Inside, a cauldron of pain.

I was mad.

Mad at the driver who hit Eric, and pissed at the rider, Lochie, who broadcast the news on social media before police confirmed his death.

Exhaustion set in by the time I reached the hill's apex. After regaining my breath, I looked up to discover an even bigger set of rollers dauntingly laid out ahead. This was only the beginning, I realized, eyes misting over as frustration and fatigue gave way to sadness. Hands twitching on the bars, flexing and trembling as if sparked by a low-level electrical current.

I once heard if you're going to cry during a race, don't waste time—do it on the bike. So, I rode it out, easing off the pedals to coast downhill, creating space for the anguish to boil over.

Since receiving the news, I had replayed memories of Eric: meeting him during the pre-ride from Portland; strolling back to our host's apartment along the Astoria waterfront after a long evening of revelry; racing around in search of Lithium batteries for our Spots; and traversing the mountains to arrive at Mitchell's Spoke'n Hostel after midnight. Now, descending an emerald slope that promised to spit me out at the base of a seemingly infinite series of longer, steeper, and more taxing climbs, the tragedy became genuine. I gushed all the way to the bottom, a hot mess of tears, spittle, and hiccups. I felt terrible—as though someone had reached down my throat and wrenched my insides out. Never had I lost someone so abruptly. I also recognized my grief remained incomparable to that of Eric's family and friends.

I continued up, and then down again. Up, and then down. Looping the reel of memories to eke out every detail, remember each word spoken between us. Trying to make solid those few moments we had together and guard them against the ravages of time. For hours, I retreated inside myself, oblivious to anything other than gradient as I grunted up punchy slopes and released my grief on ripping descents, where the rush of wind brushed away my tears.

. . .

We reached Ash Grove, Missouri, to find a dotwatcher waiting with Little Debbie's cinnamon rolls and Gatorade. My head throbbed from crying so hard; the backs of my eyes ached. But I felt closer to whole, more human than zombie. Matthias said nothing, so I couldn't judge if he had witnessed me fall apart.

"How are you holding up?" asked Wendy, the volunteer host of a local community-run hostel. In other circumstances, I imagine she would be a bubbling spring of enthusiasm and good cheer.

"I've been talking to the racers coming through," she continued in a sombre tone. "Everyone is struggling with the news. It's so sad."

We stood, heads bowed, until Wendy reached her arms around Matthias and me, bringing us close in a circular embrace. My chest rose and fell as I prepared for another bout of tears, but they didn't come. Perhaps I was all cried out. Instead, I experienced something else: the warmth of two unfamiliar hands against my spine and a kindling in my heart as we shared both connection and sadness.

We chatted a while longer, Wendy filling us in on the latest race news. The Americans were leading the ranks, with Evan Deutsch closing in on Yorktown, Jon Lester and Janie Hayes hot on his wheels. Our conversation provided a welcome break from the rollers, which only promised to become more brutal as we continued east, as well as a heartfelt reminder of how close the long-distance cycling community was. To have a total stranger greet me with condolences and snacks was something I had not prepared for. The Trans Am was less a contest against competitors, I realized, than a band of dreamers bound by the same intrepid spirit. Eric personified this: a fit yet ostensibly ordinary sixty-one-year-old taking leave from work to discover if he was capable of the extraordinary.

Wendy gave us each a white plastic flower to carry to Yorktown, in memory of Eric. I pierced the wire stem through a zip tie on my handlebars, placing the artificial blossom in clear sight. If Eric was watching, he'd know I remembered. That our briefest of friendships would not soon be forgotten.

Day Seventeen

JUNE 20, 20177

HOUSTON, MISSOURI TO CHESTER, ILLINOIS

DISTANCE: 178 MILES

RACE MILEAGE: 3,060 OF 4,264 MILES

My mood continued to deteriorate as the Missouri rollers kept coming. The landscape failed to inspire like the impressive panoramas of the west, views that forced me from the saddle to snap a photo. Missouri sounds a lot like misery, I decided: backroads bordered by swamp or dense woods, humid and thick with the syrupy rot of roadkill. A sour wind. This was not fun—it was hard work, slavishly pedalling sawtooth hills from sunup to midnight. To make matters worse, I feared I was losing it: in a dip between hills, I thought I'd caught a glimpse of a swamp monster. Dark and ghoulish, it slunk like a panther through the dim underbrush, its inky fur sloughing off chunks of muck and grime. I imagined wickedly sharp canine teeth and massive paws that made a sucking noise as they rose from the boggy ground. What was this creature? And more importantly, did I even see it at all—or was it merely a trick of the light and an overly active imagination?

I turned my attention to the firm—equally dismal—realities at hand instead. My average had fallen below six miles per hour on climbs, so I nudged my bike computer's speed sensor out of place to avoid the disheartenment of seeing my snail's pace in numerical form. I just wanted to cross the state line. But why, I wondered, did I believe I'd fare better in Illinois? Because of some Sufjan Stevens song, "Come On, Feel the Illinoise"? It made no sense.

A self-imposed isolation only made matters worse. I had continued to avoid messages from my mother, afraid she had learned of the recent tragedy and would try to convince me to scratch like so many others. I still received daily encouragement from Marj, for which I remained grateful, amazed by her tireless eye and long-distance zeal. Then there was Tyler.

I couldn't get away with ignoring his calls much longer. Finally, we talked. He complained about the silly office politics that mar any workplace and voiced frustration over our roommate's dog, who upchucked all over the basement carpet—not for the first time. I listened, trying to be sympathetic. Letting him unload. But inwardly, I wanted to scream. To stand tall, look him in the eye (impossible, I knew, with several thousand miles between us) and tell him to get over himself. Look at the bigger picture. Didn't he realize that none of his stupid, trivial qualms and inconveniences mattered? Instead, I grit my teeth. I understood full well that being reminded of the grand scheme of things wasn't what he wanted to hear from me. During a conversational lull, I mentioned Eric's death.

"Oh," he said, his voice shifting toward surprise. "Are you okay?"

"I don't know," I answered. "I only met him in Astoria. But still, he's gone."

Static filled the void between us. I was struggling to remember what, if anything, I had mentioned to Tyler about Eric, when he resumed venting his workplace frustrations. After we said goodbye ten minutes later, I felt more detached from him than ever.

. . .

Matthias and I pulled over at a gas station in Eminence to refuel. The muggy air clung to my skin and stunk of grass clippings laced with something decrepit. Two close passes by inconsiderate drivers had amplified an already low mood, and I staggered through the automatic glass doors feeling ornery and disenchanted. I shuffled among convenience store aisles, wincing in pain as I collected an armful of ready-made sandwiches, Hostess Donettes, cola-bottle candies, and extra-strength Ibuprofen. I hated the thought of consuming this crap, speculating that a nutrient-poor diet only aggravated my aches and pains, inhibiting my body's ability to recover. But with an insatiable hunger and limited dining options, I didn't have much choice. We ate under an air-conditioning vent by a window, a cool sanctuary from the smothering humidity outdoors, the faux-wood table quickly obliterated under packaging and condiment wrappers.

"I feel somewhat guilty," confessed Matthias. "Just look at all this waste."

Back in Germany, Matthias co-owned a fair-trade organic clothing store. He shopped locally and didn't need a reminder to bring his reusable bag.

"Get used to it," I responded, flicking a balled-up straw wrapper toward him.

I cracked open the bottle of Ibuprofen and offered one to Matthias. When he declined, I shrugged and swallowed both pills. My knees were killing me. The absurd amount of climbing had punished my joints. Ibuprofen would help. I also decided to raise my seat a few millimetres in an attempt to alleviate some of the strain, though I worried the adjustment might also exacerbate the pain in my Achilles. Wait and see, I supposed.

"Sorry. I'm not feeling it today," I said, flopping my upper body onto the mound of trash we had accumulated. Gone was my usual optimistic determination. I shoved empty drink bottles aside to lay a cheek against the table's cool surface. "Roadkill turtles, endless hills, and, you know—Eric. Guess the race is just over for me."

"Thinking of quitting?" he asked.

"No," I answered. "Just sick of it all."

Matthias had also been struggling, tackling each climb more wearily than the last, the bags under his eyes etched like moon craters from sleep deprivation. We maintained the same pace, though often rode separately during daylight hours, regrouping at dinner to keep each other company after dark. I never mentioned the swamp monster though.

"I'm in too deep to scratch now, but I just can't imagine things like they were before," I continued. "The wild beauty of the west, breathtaking views around every turn—the romance of adventure. That's all over, for me at least."

He appraised me before speaking. "You don't really think that, do you?" he said, peering concernedly through his glasses.

"Whatever," I shrugged. "We should get going."

We shovelled our waste into the trash bin and headed back outside. The muggy air hit me like a wall—as deadly and uninhabitable as the toxic atmosphere of Mars threatening to suffocate Schwarzenegger's character Douglas Quaid in the 1990s sci-fi action film *Total Recall*, leaving him bug-eyed and fighting for breath. I wanted to turn on my heels and dive back under the cool breeze of the air conditioning vent. Instead, I shuffled forward, drawing air in slow, measured breaths. A little girl with pigtails, fountain drink in hand, trailed us through the sliding glass doors. Then, for no apparent reason, she released her drink onto the sidewalk, drenching Matthias's calves with fruity red splash.

"Daddy, I dropped it!" she said.

The father looked from her to the fizzy puddle, and then to Matthias, trying to piece together what happened.

"Really?" he replied, in a tone as doubtful as his expression.

Matthias stifled laughter as the girl dutifully apologized. But the moment the father and pigtailed daughter disappeared into a rusted-out pickup truck, the two of us erupted into chest-heaving, stomach-clenching hysterics.

"Daddy, I dropped it!" we said, impersonating the little girl's utter surprise—as if the soda had sprung from her hands like a cricket. We cackled in delight, slapping our thighs and stomping the pavement until our voices became hoarse and only rasping wheezes escaped our lips.

"See," said Matthias, after we recovered from our silliness. "Don't give up hope yet."

I understood his angle. Anything might happen. Though the odds were tilted against us—we had lost far too much time to the stormy night and ensuing hills, it was exceedingly unlikely that we'd reach our precious goal of a sub-twenty-five-day finish—I could choose to loaf in a pile of my own rubbish and mourn the passing of glory days, or soldier on, like my hero Schwarzenegger, fighting through adversity until the bitter end. Comparatively, my role was definitely easier: instead of risking my life like Douglas Quaid to uncover corruption on a hostile Martian planet, I had only to remain present and engaged with the world around me—though hopefully it wouldn't always come at some poor kid's expense.

"Okay," I promised, "I'll try to have a good time."

"Good," he nodded. "And who knows, perhaps romance and thrilling adventure are still ahead." He winged an arm expansively toward the road.

"Doubt it," I replied, diverting my eyes and huffing air through my nose as though his suggestion was utterly preposterous.

I knew the romance he referred to better described the pleasure and excitement of experiencing something new rather than the notion of amorous love. Yet his words stuck. What would a romance with Matthias be like? A small part of me was curious to find out.

I held this thought until I realized I was blushing. Hopefully Matthias hadn't noticed. In a panic to draw attention away from my ruby-red face, I snatched a water bottle from its cage, extended an arm, and let the bottle crash to the sidewalk.

We fell to stitches all over again.

. . .

Matthias and I crossed the Mississippi River marking the border between misery—I mean, Missouri—and Chester, Illinois, at 12:00 a.m. Midnight marked the hour in which I could no longer ignore the manacles of sleep, my body systems powering down in preparation for total shutdown. Worse than simply a case of diminishing returns—the wheels entirely fell off the wagon.

In fairy-tale terminology, I transformed into a pumpkin.

Since we weren't planning to ride farther than Chester, I accepted my reduced strength and took comfort in wheels hugging asphalt and jersey pockets stuffed like Christmas stockings with snacks. We had resupplied our junk food cache at a gas station before the bridge, grateful for America's bustling twenty-four-hour economy. As I fought to tie a chocolate milk carton to my aerobars, Matthias approached me.

"Nice work, Hackinen!" he said. He bore the expression of a little boy, bright-eyed and gleeful, shins and forearms spackled with the same insect collage that graced my own filthy limbs. I imagined him as a child in Germany, dressed in lederhosen at some village fair. Ridiculous. I couldn't help but smile back. He shot his arms in the air and strode toward me, coming in for a high-five.

I released the bungee cord I'd been fiddling with and turned to face him, raising my arms to meet his. But instead of clapping our palms off one another, we interlaced our fingers and lowered our hands to chest level. His palms were warm. Larger than mine, though similarly grimy. I realized then how I missed being touched. That shared hug with Wendy yesterday marked the first human contact since Newton Bike Shop's congratulatory back slaps.

"Three states left to go," I announced, releasing him.

"Yes!" Matthias replied, still grinning. "Plus, Illinois will be quick. We should be in Kentucky by tomorrow."

Not bothering to have looked ahead, I took his word for it.

· · ·

I found myself mesmerized by the oily depths of the Mississippi River; fragments of streetlight reflected in the breadth of inhospitable darkness. Chester's claim to fame as "Home of Popeye," meant that a brass statue of the fictional character ushered us over the bridge. In reality, it was Popeye the Sailor Man's creator, Elzie Segar, who hailed from Chester, though this particularity wasn't brought to my attention until later. Matthias and I dug in for a quick climb from the bridge before rolling through town in search of the Fraternal Order of Eagles, an establishment rumoured to house travelling cyclists in a bunkhouse on their property.

Chester's sleepy avenues bathed in streetlight proved easy to navigate, and before long we located the Fraternal Order of Eagles. The inconspicuous brick building, adorned with an outdoor signboard and flag, resembled an American equivalent to the Royal Canadian Legion. I wondered if they had any sort of membership requirement. Member or not, we needed to track down the bunkhouse, so after securing our bicycles to a railing we marched in, our form-fitting Lycra and tap-toed cycling cleats indubitably labelling us as outsiders.

Thankfully, we were greeted by deserted pool tables and an empty dance floor. The heads of a few late-night stragglers in the dining room turned to follow our path toward the bar's neon beer logos, where we hoped to inquire about accommodations.

"What'll it be?" asked the bartender, a woman of about fifty with pigtails resembling those of the little girl who spilled her drink earlier. She leaned across the bar to wipe down the surface with a rag.

Matthias and I locked eyes: "Beer."

Two glasses of draft were placed in front of us. Closing in on 1:00 a.m., the prudent course of action would have been to seek slumber. But for the first time since Eric's death, I felt good. The Ibuprofen, or raising my seat height, had relieved some pain from my knees; the satisfaction of safely arriving at our destination contributed to my uptick in mood. As Matthias and I clinked our glasses together, I snapped back to that original tallboy we split between glass tumblers in a Lolo motel room. I could barely remember his name then. Now, I couldn't imagine a day without him.

It was Matthias who had helped me through the last few days. I thought back to my recent phone conversation with Tyler and the disappointment that lingered. I had expected more from him, somehow—but it seemed like the gap between us only grew deeper with distance. It wasn't his fault. Tyler wasn't present to witness the daily challenges I faced off against, and he had never met Eric. There was no way he could comprehend what I was going through.

In Matthias, however, I found comfort. The race, coping with loss and grief—we were in this together, our shared circumstances the basis of a unique understanding, despite the newness of our acquaintance. Since leaving Newton, I felt as though Matthias remained my only handhold in a world of uncertainty and discomfort. I took another slug of beer, emptying the glass, then peeked over at Matthias. He caught my eye and threw another goofy, boyish smile, and in that second I began to beam as well, my grin as wide and unabashed as his own. I reached out to pat his shoulder, noticing the firm, muscular curve of his arm. A dancing bear, inked in black, accentuated his bicep.

"Drink up," I said, knocking my empty glass against the bar. "The bunkhouse awaits!"

. . .

To our disappointment, four snoring cyclists accompanied by mountains of unwashed kit occupied the bunkhouse. So, we bedded down outside, unrolling our bivy sacks on the grassy pitch. Urban camping at its finest.

Sometime later, I awoke to a crinkling noise. The first thought in my sleep-addled brain was of Matthias—he was packing up to abandon me. My body reverberated in panic; an invisible cord cinched tight across my chest. I propped up onto my elbows, eyes blinking into focus. Luckily, my ride buddy remained dozing to my left, unkempt beard and slack mouth reminiscent of a caveman's post-hunt exhaustion. To my right, however, less than ten feet away, a cyclist unpacked his bivy sack.

Who is this guy? I wondered.

The man said nothing, and I questioned if this might be another nighttime apparition, like the time I thought I heard a freewheel spinning outside our hotel room in Dillon, Montana. I glanced back toward Matthias to confirm his presence. Once assured, I returned to my dreams without giving a second ounce of consideration as to why an absolute stranger was preparing to sleep next to me in a field.

Day Eighteen

JUNE 21, 2017

CHESTER, ILLINOIS TO MARION, KENTUCKY

DISTANCE: 148 MILES

RACE MILEAGE: 3,208 OF 4,264 MILES

Matthias actually did leave before I woke up, but it was part of our plan. The bottom bracket of his bicycle had succumbed to Missouri's rollers with a violent clanging, which had been growing worse by the day. Into the first glimmerings of an opalescent dawn, he set out for Carbondale, a college town with a bike shop forty miles down the road, six miles off-route. I shifted in my bivy to see him packing.

"Catch you later," I mumbled.

Matthias waved farewell, the stub of a half-munched granola bar in his raised hand. Best case scenario saw him arrive at the shop when it opened, have his bike promptly serviced, and meet me back on route later that day. There was no reason I had to join him at the shop—Epona, thankfully, had held up fine. After a tune-up and a new chain in Newton, she was just as swift and agile as when I brought her home from the bike shop, eight months prior. It was the rider—me—who was responsible for hindering our progress.

"You don't have to wait up," Matthias had said, yesterday evening. "My bike may be irreparable, or they might need to order parts. Who knows—it could be game over."

"Of course, I'll wait."

After everything we'd been through, how could I not?

I nodded back off to sleep after he rolled out. By the time I climbed from my bivy sack at the luxurious hour of 7:00 a.m., I'd forgotten entirely about the stranger cozied up beside me. The man lay in repose, eyes shaded from early morning sun with a forearm. A quick scan of his kit revealed he must be a Trans Am racer, though we hadn't met in Astoria. I packed up quietly so as not to wake him.

Unfortunately, I found myself lost at once. Technically, I remained on-course, but heading back toward the statue of Popeye guarding the bridge in the wrong direction. I reversed, pointing my wheels east, but pedalled only a mile before I was lured into a gas station for breakfast sandwiches and terrible coffee. Then I checked the Tracker. Matthias was making good speed—I didn't have time to dawdle. I also learned the name of the still-sleeping mystery rider outside the bunkhouse: Mitchell Potter. Since this was the first time I noticed his dot, I could only conclude he must have been pushing hard to catch us. After making my way through the first of the breakfast sandwiches, I stuffed the other two in my pockets for later, eager to get moving and establish a lead on Mitchell.

I had added motivation for that morning's ride: I wanted to get to the bike shop as well so that I could pick up a fresh pair of cycling shorts. My eyes had nearly popped out of their sockets that morning when I held mine under the bathroom's fluorescent glare and realized how threadbare they'd become. I knew excessive mileage and daily wear would take a toll, though I didn't predict they might disintegrate to the transparency of pantyhose after just a few weeks. For the first time, I was thankful race rules prohibited drafting, as someone riding close behind me could distinctly make out the pale moon of my bum.

Following Matthias to the shop—instead of meeting him on route somewhere—meant that I would also detour off-course to arrive in Carbondale. But with no other bike shops until we reached Charlottesville, Virginia, I couldn't afford to pass up this rare opportunity. I should have accompanied Matthias, but even if I'd known then about the sorry state of my shorts, I wouldn't have been able to forfeit the extra hours of sleep my body so deeply craved.

. . .

It took longer to reach Carbondale than I'd planned. I continued to make wrong turns, spacing out at directional cues, or interpreting turns backwards. What was wrong with me? Aside from my misadventures leaving the coast, I had been fine until that point. True, the arrow-straight roads of the plains required minimal navigation, and I could be guilty of drifting to autopilot from time to time when Matthias led. But there were also plenty of instances when we weren't riding together, and I'd managed well enough. What gives?

I maintained a good clip through the hilly countryside after leaving Chester, which afforded alternating views of deep woods and agricultural lands. Bushy trees slung with creeping vine edged the road in places, but then a cornfield bordering a red farmhouse would break the green monotony. Traffic picked up around Rockwood. Vehicles backed up behind me in places where the road thinned. Eric's passing prowled on the edges of my mind. He had died on impact, they said. I wished for more of a shoulder so vehicles could pass safely.

In addition to several inconsequential detours, I committed the more costly mistake of continuing off-course for several miles just before the turnoff to Carbondale. I raced to rejoin the route, annoyed with myself for wasting precious energy. I huffed the remaining six miles into Carbondale just in time to catch Matthias finishing up at the bike shop.

"Hey, did you see," Matthias said, pouring a handful of M&M's into my open palm as I caught my breath. "Nuno is catching up."

"Nuno?" I repeated, nearly choking on the candy. "Nuno Lopez—the Brazilian?"

Now it made sense: my sudden shoddy navigation skills and inability to map read.

"Nuno and I have a history," I explained. "I'm not sure if it's our Cannondale bikes or what, but whenever we're in proximity, there's trouble. I just can't stay on course if he's around."

Matthias lifted a quizzical eyebrow and finished chewing before he spoke. "So, you're telling me that someone riding the same model of bicycle inexplicably throws off your ability to navigate?"

"Yes!"

He didn't buy it.

We both agreed we wanted to maintain our lead on the Brazilian, however. Matthias's bottom bracket appeared cured of its noisy malady, and I hoped his presence would offer a degree of protection against the Curse of the Cannondale, as I called it.

But time was of the essence: if I still wanted to replace my bike shorts, I had to be quick. The shop only carried three pairs of women's shorts, each a different size and brand. I grabbed all three hangers and charged into a dressing room.

The size small didn't make it past my kneecap. Size medium made it only slightly farther, getting stuck mid-thigh. I whispered a Hail Mary as I reached for the last pair, a large. Luckily, these proved to be the Goldilocks fit: just right. I ripped the tags off to pay and threw my tattered old shorts into the trash on the way out.

. . .

With Carbondale behind us, Matthias and I pushed eastward into Shawnee National Forest. Just over a thousand miles lay between us and the finish line, a sum that actually felt surmountable. No longer did any doubt exist in my mind that I was doing this, wheels tracking east as each pedal stroke brought me closer to the Atlantic. And while my body continued to disintegrate before my eyes, the sinew holding everything together remained strong. I existed in a state of fatigued awe, dumbfounded by my very existence and the prospect of another 180-mile day in the saddle. Due to rider attrition, Matthias and I had miraculously been moving up the rankings: out of 131 starters, we found ourselves in the top thirty. The next milestone was Cave-In-Rock, where a brief ferry crossing would carry us over the Ohio River and into Kentucky.

Despite our renewed enthusiasm, it wasn't long before Nuno overtook us on a series of short, steep ups and downs.

"Hey, Meaghan!" he said, drawing out the "ey" sound for several beats. He paired his sunglasses with an enormous grin, the same green and gray jersey sporting the command RIDE! encrusted with salt and paling in the heat, considerably worse for wear than last time we met. "How many kilometres?"

"To where?" I asked. Next gas station? Next town? Until we reached Yorktown, Virginia?

Nuno had mounted his phone to his handlebars and the tinny speakers projected an upbeat, percussion-heavy beat.

"The ferry!" he said, bobbing his head to the tune.

"Seventy miles," Matthias responded.

Nuno nodded, and punched to the front of our little group, leading the way in an uphill charge. His legs were astonishingly muscular, with sculpted calves and quadriceps like bricks. I envied his tan—in sharp contrast to my own chronically peeling, lobster-red skin. Yet despite his friendly demeanour, I remained wary of riding with Nuno. I hissed to catch Matthias's attention and suggested we let our rival go ahead.

"He's going to burn out if he keeps up this pace," I said. "Then we'll pass him."

I didn't want to mess with the Curse of the Cannondale.

As Nuno pulled ahead, I noticed a pair of tiny punctures worn through the seams of his shorts, one in each butt cheek. I wondered which was worse: Lycra that was see-through, or shot full of holes. I thanked my lucky stars again that I'd been able to replace my shorts in Carbondale.

. . .

Matthias and I had all afternoon to make the cut-off for the last sailing at Cave-In-Rock. But exhaustion set in as the day wore on, and our pace became sluggish. This was a familiar and predictable pattern, yet it annoyed me to no end that I couldn't ride through one afternoon without falling victim to lethargy. The heat didn't help.

We pedalled through a parkland of rolling hills and leafy trees, leap-frogging Nuno every hour, our encounters foretold by the sound of his tunes. We also ran into the night stranger, Mitchell. He paused to check in on me and Matthias after we'd pulled over so I could mend a puncture, my first in weeks.

"Everything okay?" he asked, skidding to a stop next to my dismantled bike.

I assured him it was only a flat, and we made a round of introductions.

"Oh, the bunkhouse!" he said, after I mentioned we had already met. "I arrived in Chester late. Saw you two sleeping and figured it must be a good spot."

Mitchell was small-statured, lean, and seemingly hard-wired for suffering. From Arlington, Virginia, he went by Mitch and spoke with an accent that gave away his southern roots. His Trackleaders profile stated that he was fifty-nine, though he didn't look it. Our conversation was brief, with Mitch taking off in the same tornado of energy he had pulled up in, torso positioned low over the aerobars and legs cranking.

"ITT to the ferry!" he shouted over his shoulder, lips stretched in a grin as he set off at a blistering pace.

ITT stands for Individual Time Trial, a gruelling solo pursuit where one rides all-out over a set distance. No wonder he'd caught up to us: Matthias and I were having trouble remaining upright, let alone generate speed. Mitch was clearly made of tougher stuff.

. . .

We continued past forest and farms, a cluster of houses and a small white chapel every fifteen or twenty miles. While I was grateful to have escaped Missouri's hilly terrain, Illinois proved far from flat. Our biggest battle was not muscling up the inclines, however, but staying alert despite mounting fatigue. My eyelids crept lower as we inched toward Cave-In-Rock. Like moving through water, I felt bogged down and dreamy. I hoped talking would spark some animation, but like a pair of burnt-out stoners, Matthias and I couldn't conduct even the simplest of conversations. If only Nuno would come along with his rousing music. Perhaps that would pick me up—curse be damned.

Instead, Matthias and I amused ourselves by performing imitations of our Brazilian competitor's enthusiastic greeting. It became a game where one would sneak up on the other and holler into their ear.

"Heeeyyy, Matthias! How many kilometres?"

After the startled victim regained his or her senses, he or she would respond with a number—Matthias diligently checked his map to provide the correct distance to the ferry, while I just shouted something at random—and began plotting retribution. We repeated this silly charade at least a dozen times over the course of the afternoon. Immature, yes. But we were committed to whatever it took to maintain forward progress.

. . .

Finally, Matthias and I arrived in Elizabethtown, a charming village of manicured front lawns, tidy homes decorated with American flags, and red-brick storefronts of restaurants we didn't have time to visit. We sped the final few miles along the Ohio River toward the ferry dock at Cave-In-Rock in the swift descent of night. In an instance of perfect timing, we rolled onto the boat without so much as a pause, and by the time we'd parked our bikes we were sailing.

"Can you take my picture?" I said to Matthias. A cloud-combed sky deepened from lilac to fiery amber as the sun set in the distance. I threw both hands up, one straight toward the heavens and the other horizontally.

"I love ferry rides," I gushed.

"This hardly counts as a ferry," he teased. "You could swim to the other shore."

"Doesn't matter," I grinned. "Want me to take your photo?"

After I snapped his picture, we leaned our forearms against the railing, letting the cool river breeze sweep across our faces as we admired the glimmering waterway.

"I used to take the ferry to Vancouver Island every summer to go camping with my father and sister," I said.

Matthias remembered that ferry—the same one he boarded to get to Tofino, where he started his Trans-Canada bicycle journey in 2014.

I explained how I loved those voyages across the Georgia Strait, my sister Alisha and I racing around the upper deck, arms braced into the salty wind—on the lookout for eagles, or hinged over the guardrail, wondering what creatures lurked unseen in the blue abyss. When we disembarked on Vancouver Island, I felt as though I'd stepped into the skin of a character from Narnia, about to set forth on an adventure of my own. A world away from home.

The ferry from Cave-In-Rock shuddered, its course across the river slowing. The sun had drifted beneath the horizon, yet the sky still burned with streaks of fuchsia and gold. We returned to the bikes, checking tires for air and adjusting the angle of our lights. A metal clang reverberated through the boat to signify our arrival on the opposite shore.

"Welcome to Kentucky," announced Matthias.

"Bring on the fried chicken!" I replied, reaching to meet his palm for a high five. My sense of elation in reaching our second-to-last state was so great, the fact that Evan Deutsch had just crossed the finish line to claim first place did not impinge on my joy. A three-time Trans Am veteran living in Portland, Evan had honed his skills in each of those previous attempts to not only win the 2017 event, but beat Mike Hall's course record in a time of seventeen days, eight hours, and fifty-eight minutes. While I wondered how many more would cross the finish line before Matthias and I arrived in Yorktown, I wasn't bothered that we weren't among the race leaders. By Kentucky, I'd come to accept that I could only do my best; the brief fantasy I'd had about competing at the pointy end had long flown out the window. Instead, I was content to jockey for position with the other mid-pack riders as I pushed my own limits on the road.

. . .

Darkness galloped in. We pedalled away from Illinois along a rural road, everything obscured and undecipherable. Insects stormed the still air, the night even muggier than the day. Nothing except mailboxes hinted at human habitation until we reached Marion, ten miles from the river crossing. We satiated our hunger with burgers and milkshakes at McDonald's, the only place open. The staff appeared thrilled to see us.

"Where are you from?" asked the cashier, a woman in her mid-twenties with an accent that matched Mitch's friendly inflection.

"Vancouver, British Columbia," I said. Whenever I told people I was from Saskatoon, Saskatchewan, they just laughed—as if I were playing a strange joke, pretending to hail from a made-up locale. I used the name of my previous home city instead: Vancouver. Famous for its stunning mountain backdrop and host city of the 2010 Winter Olympic Games.

The cashier's eyes became large, then she turned to Matthias.

"I'm from Germany," he said.

"Really?" she squealed, then called over her shoulder to the kitchen. "Candice, come over here! Guess where these two are from?"

Candice, accompanied by another cashier who had been taking drive-thru orders, hustled over to meet us. We answered the trio's questions about the race, our hometowns, how we were enjoying our time in Marion. For a few moments, Matthias and I were superstars. That we weren't the first—

Nuno and Mitch had already passed through, as well as a whole host of foreign riders—didn't diminish our celebrity status. I tried to imagine how different life would be if I'd grown up in a place like Marion, where no one owned a passport and options for work, housing, and dating were limited. The stir we caused in McDonald's made me wonder if the annual arrival of Trans Am racers could be the most exciting thing to happen all year.

We stopped for the night there. It wasn't late, but I didn't want to risk being caught in the middle of nowhere at midnight, the hour in which my transformation into a sleepy pumpkin became inescapable.

"It makes more sense to stay in Marion and make an early start tomorrow," I reasoned, sucking down the last of my chocolate milkshake.

"What about the weather?" asked Matthias. "It's supposed to get lousy."

Last night, a beer-breathing farmer at the Fraternal Order of Eagles had muttered grim proclamations about an impending storm before stumbling back to his table, using the line of empty bar stools as a crutch to support his teetering weight. I didn't take him too seriously.

"We'll get up early," I repeated. "Better to put on solid miles in the morning when we're refreshed, than ride like zombies tonight."

We checked into the only motel in town. Our room smelled like the inside of a gym bag, everything slightly damp, as if the sheets and towels had been left outside overnight in the dew. Part of me wished we had continued on to find a more comfortable place to spend the night, while another part couldn't care less. The overhead light didn't work; neither did the hot water. I took a cold shower and fell asleep prostrate, face down into a pillow. Breathing so operatically loud, apparently, that I kept Matthias up.

"Heeeyyy, Meaghan!" he said, reaching over to startle me awake. "You're snoring."

When my alarm rang at 4:00 a.m. it felt far too soon.

Day Nineteen

JUNE 21, 2017

MARION TO SONORA, KENTUCKY

DISTANCE: 166 MILES

RACE MILEAGE: 3,374 OF 4,264 MILES

Kentucky remained an enigma. I struggled, in my pre-caffeinated state, to recall if we were riding into morning or night, the road shrouded in darkness. Then, the sun exploded to the east and an eerie, crimson glow revealed bushy trees and sprawling properties guarded by at least one unleashed canine. Widening beams of light battered the underbellies of clouds into shades of flower-box violet and bruised plum as the sun lifted into a window of sky. After a few minutes of stunning radiance, the slanting light vanished behind a ceiling of cloud that settled into a grey pallor. A breeze swept through, stirring leaves and bristling the hair on my arms—a forewarning of the merciless wind that would continue to ramp up over the following hours.

While the storm's arrival appeared imminent, showers held off until we reached Utica, sixty-five hilly miles from our dank motel room in Marion. The first drops came not long after our morning coffee stop. We were greeted with curiosity by the locals, fielding the usual questions about what compelled us to race our bicycles across America, in addition to a slew of solemn-faced warnings about incoming Tropical Storm Cindy. As ominous clouds blackened overhead and Matthias and I geared up for the inevitable downpour under an out-of-service gas station awning a mile further down the road, I silently congratulated the two of us for following through on our plan to crush the morning's mileage. We had been slipping, more often than not stopping short of our targets. I worried we might not reach Yorktown until mid-July if the trend continued.

I waterproofed myself from the toes up, first pulling on boot covers, then fastening the absurd neon rain chaps around my thighs and waist. I knew from the descent down Togwotee Pass that the chaps would fail to keep moisture out, yet hoped the garish colour might increase my visibility to other road users under poor conditions. I opted not to wear the blue Latex gloves I'd swiped from the clinic where I worked, since temperatures were forecast to remain warm. My hands would only become sweaty if they couldn't breathe. Finally, I stuffed my arms into the sleeves of my rain jacket and reached for the zipper. Unfortunately, my fingers came up short on dexterity. The condition of my hands had continued to deteriorate since I'd first discovered the nerve damage in Idaho. By Colorado, it seemed to have plateaued, yet unfortunately, by that point I'd lost much of my hand strength, and struggled to grasp anything smaller than my handlebars. Unable to straighten the fingers on my left hand, my palm remained in a perpetually cupped position, a disfigurement I nicknamed "Claw Hand," and Matthias endearingly referred to as "Clawey."

Why was I doing this? I wondered, fighting to pinch the zipper between uncooperative fingertips.

It was the same question we'd been bombarded with at our coffee stop earlier, the same I'd heard countless times when I first shared my intention of competing in the Trans Am. Now, here I was in this dilapidated Kentucky gas station, struggling to dress myself and about to set off into a rainstorm—what on earth compelled me to continue?

I was racing across America to discover if I could. That's what I told my friends, parents, and people I didn't know. I wanted to find my limits and test them.

But by the time I arrived in Kentucky, I was starting to second-guess myself. If I only wanted to find my limits, there must be an easier way—sign up for a road race or challenge myself on a twenty-five-mile individual time trial. Was it necessary to go through such extremes—crippling fatigue, a litany of aches and pains, terrible weather—to find out what I was made of?

Rain pummelled the awning's tin roof with intimidating ferocity. My mind went numb, a low-grade static hum filling the space between my ears. I had no answer but to keep riding.

. . .

The sky emptied itself on us, dispensing all of its pent-up precipitation in a lashing fury. Why had we bothered to don rain gear at all? Water came down in sheets, blurring my vision until the murky landscape resembled the scummy green algae of a long-neglected fish tank.

Why was I doing this?

To find out if I could, I reminded myself. But what type of person cycles through a torrential downpour just to discover if they can? An idiot like me, that's who.

I heaved my weight behind the pedals and shifted into easy gears for another long climb. The mystery cyclist from Chester, Mitch, emerged from the curtains of rain and we slogged it out together, passing Matthias's seemingly infinite supply of M&M's between us. Mitch appeared in good spirits, despite the curveball Tropical Storm Cindy had thrown into our itineraries.

"I left Astoria on antibiotics," he said. "Sick as a dog. Unsure if I'd arrive at the start line. But after months of planning, I couldn't stay home."

Mitch had experienced some sort of gastrointestinal crisis just before the race, from what I understood. His health had taken such a hit, he barely made it off the coast that first day. Week one became a study of suffering as the antibiotics took their time. In contrast to the rest of us—giving it every-thing we had with fresh legs and still-plentiful sleep reserves—Mitch fought for every mile.

By the time he reached the halfway point in Newton, however, the course of antibiotics had taken effect. By Illinois, Mitch was riding stronger than ever. Compared to debilitating pain and nausea, I suppose a little inclement weather didn't rank as such a terrible thing.

The three of us stayed our course eastward, tacking up steep climbs and sailing down quick descents, rear wheels throwing rooster tails of spray in our wakes. Mitch took every downhill pitch at breakneck speed, banking into corners with the finesse of an accomplished racer despite the wet road surface. I, on the other hand, white-knuckled the brakes, terrified that Epo-na might slide out from underneath me at any given moment. Under the guid-ance and mentorship of Matthias, my descents had improved over the past weeks, though my inexperience in rainy conditions revealed a still-amateur skill set. Instead of hovering low over my drop bars as I descended—where my centre of gravity would remain stable—I sat erect, like an exclamation point in the saddle. Anytime I inched toward the drop bars, the sight of wet asphalt zipping beneath my wheels scared me upright. I consistently arrived at the bottom behind Matthias and Mitch, every fibre tensed in prayer as my tires slashed through ponds that had accumulated in the terrain's low point. Please, just let me skim across this tiny lake unscathed.

Every couple of hours, we were blessed with a recess from the rain. As the clouds held their breath, we winked beads of moisture from our eyelashes to witness the million shades of Kentucky green. From celery to mint, emerald to lime, mantis to pistachio to bright budding green. Sometimes, crop fields or a simple one-storey home with a rambling front porch replaced the leafy deciduous trees that hemmed in the road like a narrow, winding hallway. Yet when I reflect back on those waterlogged days in the South, everything is eclipsed by wet, wet green. The plus side to all that water, however, was that it kept the dogs away.

My anxiety over furry four-legged creatures stemmed from narrowly escaping the gnashing jaws of a farm dog during a training ride in the Prairies that spring. Trepidation grew as posts circulated about Kentucky's rampant dog population on the Trans Am Facebook Page. Then, when I learned the top three riders—Evan, Jon, and Janie—had been inflicted with dog bites in Kentucky, my fear exploded into full-blown terror.

"Watch out for the pit bull guarding Pippa Passes," Janie posted to Facebook.

That the same dog had bitten all three of them, on different occasions, did nothing to assuage my anxiety about dogs in general. Janie relayed the incidents to Animal Control while she waited in a hospital emergency room for a rabies shot, and they reportedly contacted the owner to request the dog remain indoors, or at least leashed, for the remainder of the race. I found this only somewhat reassuring. Thankfully, as long as the rain continued, roaming dogs with a taste for cyclists were one less thing to worry about.

. . .

After gorging ourselves on sandwiches at a café with Formica furniture and a checkerboard floor, Matthias and I disconsolately watched Mitch dissolve into a dreary hillside, unable to summon a further watt of increased power from our legs. If Mitch kept upping the pace as he'd done over the past week— on a rigid mountain bike outfitted with slick tires, no less—we wouldn't see him until Yorktown, and only then if he stuck around to shake our hands. He was as hard as they come, and I? I still couldn't figure out what I was doing here. I returned to following the thin line of my GPS unit, thinking no farther ahead than the next twist or turn in the road.

Later, we caught up with Nuno and Brian at a gas station. Among racks of pre-packaged carbohydrates, we acknowledged our competitors with weary nods, failing to muster sufficient energy for a verbal greeting. I was sick to death of the rain, but to make matters worse my body appeared hellbent on its train of self-destruction. Both of my knees and my right

Achilles ached, and my hands had exhausted themselves from the day's frequent shifting of gears on hilly terrain. Claw Hand had regressed to where the only way I could use my left gear lever was if I reached over with my right hand—my so-called "good hand"—and wrenched the lever using the force of both hands, a precarious manoeuvre I avoided unless absolutely necessary. When I considered the circumstances, my heart rate quickened: what would happen if I lost ability to shift with my right hand, or if I got a flat? I knew Matthias wouldn't be able to save me.

Moisture pricked my eyes as I stood in line to buy a roll of mini-donuts. When I pulled out my change to pay, I dropped coins all over the floor. The metal rang with a premonition that recalled the first raindrops colliding against the tin awning as we geared up that morning outside Utica. Instead of stooping to collect the coins—which would only result in more fumbling—I tugged a bill from my wallet and abandoned the change, cringing as I sensed the watchful eyes of customers lined up behind me. The rain had pared away my defenses. Stripped me of emotional armour. In that moment, I only wanted to be alone, curled up with my sleeping bag until the world dried out.

Instead, I walked through the sliding glass doors and stood by Epona, my back facing the ads for cigarettes mounted beside store windows. I tore open the plastic packaging of the mini-donuts with my teeth, devouring them conveyor-belt style, one after another in a series of gnashing, messy chomps that left my shoulders dusted with icing sugar. Taste buds satiated, I glanced inside and remembered the spilled change, pulse quickening as I relived my embarrassment. The undertow of my thoughts pulled me down, threatening to drown me in self-pity like the deluge flooding the parking lot.

Get it together, Meaghan. Get. It. Together.

I exhaled, trying to re-establish control. Roof runoff sprayed my ankles before it pooled just an inch or two from my cleats, marooning me and my bicycle on high ground by the window. Yet I couldn't make myself return indoors to face Nuno, Brian, and the air conditioning that made me shiver. Besides, I couldn't get any wetter. Matthias joined me on the concrete island a minute later.

"Can I have a hug?" I asked, trembling jaw a harbinger of tears.

Matthias opened his arms, and I fell into him. Seconds passed. My heart slowed. It was as if I'd been granted a vertical micro-nap, the reassuring weight of Matthias's body a winter comforter I could snuggle underneath, if only for a moment.

"Thanks," I said, peeling my face from his rain jacket. Already, I felt calmer. "I might ask for another later."

"Anytime," he said. "You can have a hug anytime, Hackinen."

. . .

Clouds parted as we rode toward Sonora, revealing blue sky and promise of a clear night. I inhaled deeply as I dug into a climb, fragrances of grass and wet earth thick after rainfall. Sonora was just a name on the map at a crossroads, significant to us only because it marked where we'd reserved a room at a bed and breakfast. Everything in my seat-post pack was soaked, but the prospect of a good sleep in dry bedding put me in a better mood. I pulled over on the hilltop to shed my rain jacket, fighting once again with the zipper. A sound I mistook for thunder reverberated across glistening clover fields, and I squinted past a rickety fence to see distant horses galloping in play.

A perfect moment. I paused for Matthias to catch up so I could point out the horses, though surely he would notice. While I waited, my mind spun back to that lingering question: Why was I doing this?

Suddenly, it seemed so simple. All this time, I had been overthinking it, when the answer existed in the most universal tenet of travel: why does anyone voluntarily go anywhere? To find out what is out there. I could locate my "Why" not just in the overarching goal of reaching Yorktown, but in any singular moment of the travel itself. I trained my eyes into the fields to follow chestnut and white horses as they cantered past a backdrop of achingly blue sky, my cheeks pulled tight into a grin. All the while I'd been searching for a profound explanation, but the explanation stood in front of me. This, here. This is it.

Just like the million shades of green in Kentucky's countryside, there was not one, but infinite explanations for my journey. Unpredictable and circumstantial, they revealed themselves as I encountered them, at times surprising, disappointing, and overwhelming: to know the sound of horses romping in wet pasture; to learn to manoeuvre one's fingers without sensation or feeling; to soak in the day's final rays after a storm.

While far from cultivating a Zen-like acceptance of each passing moment, from that point on I became more at ease. I didn't owe myself, or anyone else, an explanation other than my sincere desire to experience the world outside my doorstep.

Day Twenty

JUNE 22, 2017

SONORA TO HARRODSBURG, KENTUCKY

DISTANCE: 98 MILES

RACE MILEAGE: 3,472 OF 4,264 MILES

We rode nearly a hundred miles before Tropical Storm Cindy reared her ugly head again. The morning sky appeared crisp and blue, scrubbed clean from the day before. In a bout of wishful thinking, I hoped the storm had burnt itself out, and we would be blessed with clear sailing and tailwinds until the finish. Not so, I would soon discover.

Matthias and I joined Brian, who had stayed at the same Sonora B&B as us the night before. The room Matthias and I shared could have been pulled straight from a colonial doll house: cream and pink accents, antique lamps, everything fringed in lace. We attempted to ditch Brian as we left Sonora, but unfortunately, we took a wrong turn leaving town. I couldn't even blame Nuno, since he was still asleep at the B&B, his bike stabled on the porch out back. By the time Matthias and I returned to the route and caught up with Brian, we had drained our tanks. We could barely ride alongside, let alone sweep ahead for the pass, both of us panting like the potentially rabid dogs that chased us down the switch-backed rural roads.

Brian didn't notice (or ignored) our failed drop tactics and chatted merrily as though we were old friends, telling us about the stunning beauty of the Swiss hills he trained among, having relocated from the United Kingdom to live near Lake Geneva with his globetrotting South African wife, Stacey.

"Why did you decide to do the Trans Am?" I asked. While Brian made his living as an endurance coach, a coast-to-coast bike race still sounded a tad excessive, even for someone immersed in the particularities of suffering.

"In 2014, I attempted solo RAAM—Race Across America—but everything went wrong." He chuckled. "To be honest, love, I was hopeless."

At 3,000 miles, the Race Across America has a reputation for being the toughest ultra-distance event in the world. I was surprised to hear that Brian—white haired and almost sixty—had signed up. Aside from the start and end point, Oceanside, California, and Annapolis, Maryland, respectively, and the fact that riders are followed by a support crew (complete with massage therapist, medical expert, and dietician), I knew little about this event. Brian described some of the gorier details, such as how competitors regularly scratched due to Shermer's Neck, or because of elevation-induced pulmonary embolisms in the Rocky Mountains, as well has his own particular failings.

"We had just moved houses from Germany to Switzerland. My lovely wife, also my crew chief, had organized all this. By the time we got to the start line in California we were both tired. Exhausted. I was a rubbish rider, and Stacey couldn't hold the inexperienced crew together. After 2,000 miles, I went home."

The Trans Am was his redemption ride. After failing to finish RAAM, Brian had taken time to regroup, settle into his new home, and get his head back into the game.

"I trained hard, love, but I trained my mind harder," Brian reflected. "So that in the tough times—like that bloody, pissing rain we had yesterday—I can just get on with it, you know?"

Brian had a habit of ending his sentences with a question and fixing his eyes on you in such a way that not only acknowledged your presence, but made you an integral part of the story. I realized then there was absolutely no chance I could dislike this man who referred to me as love, and welcomed me into his world as if I'd been there all along.

Mitch joined us an hour later when he spotted our trio from the parking lot of a motel he had overnighted in. Cauliflower clouds sprouted on the horizon, occluding the faint blue sky. Yet my body still revolted in Kentucky's muggy heat. Sweat percolated from every pore, covering my arms and face with an oily film I wiped with the filthy backhand of a glove. I shifted in the saddle, painfully aware of the angry red saddle sores that had blossomed after yesterday's bout of wet weather. I was all out of chamois cream to ease the chaffing, and cringed when I imagined the bumps, now fermenting in the heat.

. . .

The four of us rode the next few hours together, eventually stopping to resupply at a gas station on the outskirts of Harrodsburg.

"You're biking in this weather?" the attendant asked. He wore mechanic's overalls and a trucker hat, his rosy complexion disguised beneath a whiskery moustache. The shop smelled of burnt coffee and motor oil.

"It's fine weather for cycling," I replied indignantly. "Any more sun and we'd be melting."

"Not for long," he said, jabbing a finger toward a TV behind the counter.

The four of us edged close for a better view of the broadcast, which depicted a map of the southeast with the headline "Storm Warning" stamped in bold letters. A montage of broken telephone poles, toppled trees, and reckless overflow from streams and ditches followed, accompanied by dramatic music. Matthias, Brian, Mitch, and I watched in horror as the twenty-four-hour radar forecast projected a spiralling rainbow of precipitation over eastern Kentucky.

"You'd better hole up in Harrodsburg," advised the attendant. "Tropical Storm Cindy ain't nothing to mess with."

"We biked all day yesterday," I said, still defiant. "It wasn't so bad."

"It's going get a whole lot worse."

The attendant pointed out another map on screen, this one showing high winds. Nuno walked in just then, face lit up in delight to have caught us lounging around a gas station. It was both humorous and heart-wrenching to watch his expression fall when he learned that we were about to call it quits for the day.

"Now?" he said. "You're kidding, right?"

Brian pointed to the onscreen weather forecast and its mesmerizing swirl of colours. I turned to Matthias to get his thoughts, but before I could speak another gust of wind rattled the door chime, its unaccompanied ring somehow sinister, hinting toward elements beyond our control.

"You'd better hurry into town," interrupted the attendant. "Looks like Cindy will be here any second."

Fifteen minutes later all five of us stood in the reception of a budget motel in Harrodsburg, as dripping and dishevelled as shipwreck survivors after hauling themselves onto shore. We convened in Mitch's room before separating ways for the evening, plotting our next move *Ocean's 11*-style as wind whisked the rain into a frenzy, hurling discarded aluminum cans against the building in rickety song.

"It's two o'clock now," I said. "When do you guys expect this to clear?"

It felt too early to be calling it quits, but if Cindy lived up to her reputation, the road would be underwater for the next few hours anyway. No point in wading across Kentucky. Better to wait it out and hit the road once conditions improved.

"The storm should pass through by midnight," said Matthias decisively, brow crinkling as he studied the forecast on his iPhone. "Meet in the parking lot at quarter to twelve?"

"Sounds good to me," Brian replied.

Mitch, Nuno and I nodded agreement before shuffling off to wash our kit and purchase takeout bags of fried chicken and home fries from the gas station across the street, venturing from the safety of our rooms into a world of chaos: sidewalk submerged in two inches of water, traffic in gridlock as vehicles crept through intersections without power. I dried my clothes with the blow-dryer once I returned to the room I shared with Matthias, thankful for heeding the gas station attendant's advice to hunker down. Mother Nature seemed intent on doling out her worst with Tropical Storm Cindy. I doubted we'd be able to maintain a decent pace had we continued, and the risk-reward ratio of chasing miles in horrendous weather just didn't seem worth it.

In the shadow of Eric's death, I could no longer ignore the precariousness of my own existence, or the reality that a degree of danger would always be present in cycling. It remained the rider's responsibility, however, to mitigate risk. Staying put would set us back, yet I knew it was the right decision, as far as safety was concerned. Eric's passing likely weighed on Matthias as well: after the race, in New York City, he would get a tattoo of the Grim Reaper inked on his right calf—a permanent reminder that, regardless of our cushy jobs and safe, warm beds, we are all just one unlucky shoulder tap away from death's merciless scythe.

I yanked the motel blinds shut to block out the daylight and tucked into bed. Butterflies batted my insides as I imagined the turbulence outdoors, wondering if the weather would blow over when midnight rolled around.

Day Twenty-One

JUNE 23, 2017

HARRODSBURG TO LOOKOUT, KENTUCKY

DISTANCE: 212 MILES

RACE MILEAGE: 3,684 OF 4,264 MILES

Traffic slowed on Kentucky's backroads after dark. Tree branches poked skeletal fingers from the fog, and I wondered why we didn't wait until daybreak, when we could actually see, before recalling in a hidden-away part of my brain that I still hoped to reach Yorktown in under twenty-five days. Our cobbled-together fellowship—Brian, Mitch, Nuno, Matthias, and I—rolled through puddled streets, slinging stories between ourselves as we dodged downed branches and storm debris on dicey descents. We were closing in on the Appalachian Mountains, but our crisp white bike lights illuminated only snapshots, a handful of jigsaw puzzle pieces that, when assembled, depicted an incomplete hilly countryside.

"Where's Matthias?" someone asked.

I looked around to see only four sets of lights. "I'll text him," I volunteered.

Took a wrong turn, Matthias messaged back. *Don't worry, I'll catch up later.*

But everyone agreed we should wait. Shadowed trees arched overhead; the sharp, citrusy scent of wet bark infused the air. Behind an unseen fence, a dog barked. Brian told it to bugger off. We laughed but moved a few hundred feet down the road in case the animal broke loose, or the owner charged out with a shotgun. I heard Southerners packed guns like Californians toted Starbucks soy lattes and over the past few days, I'd seen enough open carry firearms to be convinced. In a Dairy Queen that featured the Ten Commandments on its wall, the back of my neck prickled as I realized everyone (excluding staff) holstered a gun on their hip. Long after we'd continued on our way, I remained baffled by the juxtaposition of friends catching up over Dilly Bars, and the deadly weapons at their sides.

The dog went quiet once we relocated to wait for Matthias. A surging wind tossed droplets from overhead leaves, the resulting patter against our rain jackets soft and small, like babies' hands. A soothing contrast to the frenzied storm responsible for wreaking havoc on the countryside mere hours ago.

Matthias turned up ten minutes later.

"Thanks for waiting," he said, gasping from his effort to meet us.

"No worries," said Brian. "I'd want you guys to wait for me if I got lost."

As we set out into darkness again, I continued to mull over Brian's words. I looked from Matthias to Brian and the others, heart warming with gratitude and camaraderie. Buoyed by the assurance that if I found myself separated and alone on a soulless night in the dog-bite capital of America, these competitors-turned-friends would not abandon me.

. . .

Night transitioned to dawn, and dawn to day. Our perseverance had been rewarded, yet I emerged into the shimmering light of morning dazed, as if I didn't quite know how I got there: the five of us still rolling eastward.

Stick close to the others, I counselled myself. *Just follow their lead.*

I trailed Brian around a convenience store, mentally flayed. Replicating his actions down to the T: large coffee, four granola bars, bottle of Gatorade, bag of sweets. The bitterness of the coffee overpowered all other flavours, its acidic lash persisting in raw skin at the back of my throat long after I'd tossed out the Styrofoam cup.

We continued east as a loosely assembled group, stretching like an accordion on ascents and clumping together on the flats in between. I lost all sense of time and place as we climbed into the heartland of the Appalachians. Rock walls rose into pillowed clouds, gauzy hills just out of reach behind the veil of morning mist. Scenery reeled by like a video game dream land—but what was I doing there? I was no hero.

Eventually, drowsiness crept in. I slipped into a road-sick delirium, untethered, as if my head had been filled with helium and affixed to my shoulders by only a thread. The rational, thinking part of me had checked out, and yet a small but relentless stronghold remained. One arm tugged the balloon back to earth to bear witness to the slow devastation of my body. I achieved forward motion by absorbing energy from the group, never letting myself fall too far off the last rider's rear wheel.

For some reason, I remained dead-set on maintaining the visage of competency; the last thing I wanted was to telegraph my exhaustion for all to see. Perhaps if I acted the role of the unshakable, indefatigable bike racer, there was a chance I could become it. I drifted between the others, conversing as long as road space or topic permitted, savouring the company of each person in turn. Mitch's bikepacking anecdotes about tackling long rides in New Zealand and the States proved him to be as resilient as I'd guessed; Nuno remained upbeat and grinning, although the holes in the butt cheeks of his shorts had doubled in size and his jersey was now fastened with zip ties. Brian turned out to be more complex than the "Tough Ol' Bastard" nickname let on—his willingness to endure matched by a wry sense of humour and a thoughtful consideration for others I would not fully comprehend until a year later. Matthias continued to be as practical and steadfast as ever, always calculating how many miles separated us from resupply, available for a hug whenever I needed one.

. . .

The Appalachians devolved into a timeline of climbs, pit stops, and more climbs. We cycled on meandering rural roads that wound like an unravelling skein of yarn. Everything was off-kilter. Hand-painted American flags graced the sides of barns, and Trump supporter signs adorned front lawns. Next to patriotism existed squalor: beer cans littered ditches; machinery rusted outside dilapidated sheds; entire towns were entrenched in poverty and disrepair. Layoffs in the coal-mining industry had hit Kentucky hard, and now people were struggling to make ends meet. Breezing through on our expensive bicycles, it was no wonder folks more often than not acknowledged us with stone-faced stares of suspicion. The gulf between us appeared deeper than I'd imagined, my month-long vacation a privilege most folks here would only experience under the more sinister guise of unemployment.

In an isolated mountain town, a woman we asked for directions to a restaurant acted as if we were Lycra-clad invaders from another planet, hardly speaking the same language. For some reason, I yearned for a photo of the five of us and handed over my iPhone. She clutched the screen at face level, repeating, "I can see ya'll, I can see ya'll through the lil' window!"

"Love, she's never held a smartphone before," whispered Brian.

I took back my iPhone. A selfie would have to suffice.

. . .

We reached the infamous Pippa Passes—renamed Pit Bull Pass—just before daylight ran out. From what we'd gleaned online, the dog that had taken bites out of Evan, Jon, and Janie lived somewhere in the valley, just before the climb over the pass. As we approached, the others picked up tremendous speed on the descent into the lowlands. A jolt of fear shot through me when I noticed that I'd fallen behind. No matter how hard I pedalled, I couldn't catch up. The scenario of my demise played out in my head: the other four would shoot past one by one, rousing the pit bull of Pippa Pass from slumber and whetting its appetite with the smell of human flesh. By the time the dog saw me coming, it would be whipped into a slobbering frenzy and break free, trampling the flimsy screen door or catapulting over a low wire fence to sink its two-inch canines into my juicy calf meat.

"Assholes," I said aloud. They thought nothing of waiting for Matthias last night, yet they didn't hesitate a second before ditching me.

I made it through the valley without incident, but my blood pressure remained sky high, even after we regrouped.

"Thanks for abandoning me back there," I said. The ferocity sprang from my lips. I had no right to be angry, but was, regardless.

The others glanced around sheepishly.

"I could have been dog food!" I shouted. Secretly, I was now enjoying my moment of self-absorbed guilt-mongering. "How would you like that on your conscience?"

"Poor Meg," said Brian, shaking his head in what I hoped was remorse. "We just buggered off on you."

"After all we've been through together," I continued, "I expected more."

. . .

Perhaps it was the need to prove myself after Pit Bull Pass that led me into a hill climb challenge with Nuno later that night. Under darkness, the world had shifted to grey-scale: no colour other than the flashing red of our rear lights. The sawtooth pitches were steep and relentless, sharp as the gnashing canine teeth of the dogs that burst from the pitch-black driveways on our descents. My throat became hoarse from hollering ugly strings of obscenities. When had I ever talked like this? I thought about the dogs we had growing up and felt ashamed. Our family pets wanted nothing but to be our companions, and here I was hurling curses and threats at their distant American relatives.

"I've turned into a monster," I confessed to Matthias.

He flicked his headlamp toward me in grave appraisal. "You look fine to me, all things considered."

Despite losing grip of my cognitive capacity as the clock approached midnight, my legs remained strong. When Nuno began to ratchet up the pace on a punchy climb with no end in sight, I shot up next to him, grinning as his inhalations became laboured. Our front wheels were neck and neck. I torqued on the pedals, rocking my weight from side to side until the burn in my thighs became unmanageable, adrenaline insufficient to mask the pain. Nuno edged ahead just before we crested the apex and waited for me at a pullout, crumpled over his bike frame and breathing hard.

"Nice work," I said. My legs were shaking so severely after I unclipped that I would have collapsed, had not the bike been there to support my weight. Yet muscle fatigue aside, I was soaring—as if I'd finally arrived in the moment after floating outside of it all day.

"You too," wheezed Nuno.

We repeated this charade half a dozen more times before rolling up to a Baptist church in the tiny settlement of Lookout where we would spend the night. The deacon gamely answered his door after midnight to let us in, commending us on our efforts of pedalling non-stop for twenty-four hours. The church was equipped with showers and a kitchen stocked with no-name coffee and cookies for breakfast, an improvement over the leftover slices of Hawaiian pizza I'd been carrying around in my jersey pockets since supper.

"We're open to all who need us," proclaimed the deacon.

I was certain this was some sneaky conversion tactic—a cue for him to launch into a religious pitch—but to my surprise he pointed us in the direction of the sleeping area, and requested we sign the guest book on our way out. Perhaps he could see how worn down we were, wavering toward sleep's surrender in the church's entrance. Or maybe he meant it. Either way, as we laid out our sleeping bags on sofas and thin mattresses in a room upstairs, I realized how grateful I was to cap off a surreal day with genuine southern hospitality.

Day Twenty-Two

JUNE 24, 2017

LOOKOUT, KENTUCKY TO MAX MEADOWS, VIRGINIA

DISTANCE: 164 MILES

RACE MILEAGE: 3,848 OF 4,264 MILES

I woke in the Baptist Church with a sense of dread accompanied by lethargy so deep, it took formidable willpower to heave both legs over the edge of the bed. Shivers seized my body before my feet touched the floor.

Brian, Mitch, and Matthias were already up. Nuno snoozed on a cot across the room, one arm shielding his eyes from piercing hallway light. I wondered if he planned to sleep late and join us down the road, as he'd done the other day. Perhaps I might rest a little longer and accompany him. Then I remembered that I couldn't pedal quick enough. Despite my solid effort on the hill sprints yesterday, the rivalry remained a facade—Nuno was the stronger cyclist. I represented the proverbial tortoise, while he was the hare. I'd never catch up if I gave the others a lead. My muscles ached to the bone, but I hoisted myself from bed and rummaged through my things for Ibuprofen pills.

It took longer than it should have to dress, wash up, and use the toilet. Every movement initiated a chain reaction: a domino-effect of low-grade pain coursing up one arm and down the other, neck and shoulders to quadriceps to toes. I maneuvered with caution, wary of speed. Infected with a deadly torpor. I didn't arrive in the kitchen until everyone—even Nuno—was ready to leave the church. A crumb trail led to a half-eaten box of black and white cookies on the table. Panic sheared the fog of my still-sleeping brain. I was about to be left behind—Pit Bull Pass repeating itself all over again. As I stuffed my jersey pockets with a bounty of cookies, I noticed the familiar clip-clop of cycling cleats against linoleum floor. Matthias appeared next to me, a groggy half-smile on his face as he presented a red mug.

"Figured you'd need coffee," he said.

I accepted the mug with both hands and brought the rim to my lips. The coffee tasted hot and strong, suffused with instant creamer and plenty of sugar.

"This is the kindest thing anyone has ever done for me," I whispered, clasping the mug under my chin to inhale the warm, wafting steam.

Matthias made a face. "Really? It's not a big deal. I was making a cup for myself, anyway."

"No," I insisted. "This is amazing. Thank you."

In an instant, I had pivoted from a state of disoriented panic to rational calm. This journey had taken more from me than I thought I had to give, and yet each day, I found the strength to give some more. I dunked a chocolate cookie into the mug and as I chewed, my brain kicked into gear to generate a to-do list of everything I needed to accomplish to depart alongside the others.

But first, I'd finish the coffee.

．．．

Kentucky Route 80 turned into Virginia Route 80, and all five of us crossed the state line at Breaks Interstate Park by 8:00 a.m.—nine states down, one more to go. We snapped photos in mock-triumphant poses in front of the heart-emblazoned "Virginia is for Lovers" billboard before zipping into Breaks for a greasy diner breakfast at a gas station. The difference between

Kentucky and Virginia occurred instantaneously, ramshackle porches replaced by tidy homes with flower box planters and healthy green lawns. As we converged around a tiny table the mayor of Breaks welcomed us, enthusing with conviction and delight about Virginia's charm.

"We have the coast, the Blue Ridge Mountains—you're in for a treat, folks. And there ain't no better way to experience the state than on a bicycle."

Though a small gesture, the mayor's well-wishes buoyed my spirits. The last person we spoke with in Kentucky was a solitary young girl lurking in dim morning light.

"Watch out," she said. Her vacant expression matched the washed-out pastels of her summer dress.

"Why?" asked Matthias.

"Dog's gonna get'cha, Mister," she muttered, before turning on her heels to chuck a stick into the woods.

I wondered if her warning regarded one dog in particular, or dogs in general—and what on earth was she doing up at 5:00 a.m.? Though we arrived at the state line without incident, the encounter with the girl left me spooked. Despite the hospitality of the Baptist Church, I was ready to say goodbye to Kentucky.

After a brief stop in Breaks, I hit the road buzzing, fuelled by caffeine and more carbohydrates than the average person should consume in an entire day. Threats of unleashed canines and Tropical Storm Cindy were a thing of the past. Our arrival in Virginia—the last state of the TransAmerica Trail—signified the home stretch. Over breakfast, we had even discussed continuing on to Yorktown as a group, five sets of wheels crossing the finish line together.

. . .

Sunlight radiated between leafy boughs of slender trees that pinched the road as it traced the valley's basin southeast. I marvelled at cottages tucked into the hillside and thick, enchanted vines blanketing everything from telephone poles to barn doors. But while I was experiencing a euphoric high, the others fought a futile battle against fatigue. Despite our best efforts, our merry band had strung out, losing sight of one another and regrouping upon arrival in each later town. I became concerned about the inefficiency of attempting to synchronize five individuals' rhythms—how had we managed so well over the previous thirty-six hours? Matthias zipped ahead on an ascent and didn't wait up. When the rest of us reconvened, someone called for a break. I decided my turn to split had come. Matthias's location on the Tracker showed he wasn't stopping, and so I dug in and picked up my pace. Fifteen miles along, I caught him at the summit of a leg-crushing climb after Council. He had pulled alongside the guardrail to admire a panoramic view of undulating emerald hills that rolled out like the scaly, serpentine backs of dragons.

"Heeeyyy, Matthias!" I exclaimed, sporting an exaggerated grin. "How long have you been waiting?"

"Heeeyyy! Just a minute or two. I was watching your dot."

I nodded, pleased he had also monitored my whereabouts.

"You good to go?" he asked.

"Sure."

Noon-day heat surged to suffocating levels, but the fast descent delivered a cooling breeze. I eased low into the drop bars, relishing the free speed and freedom from pedalling. As we pulled farther ahead from the others, I felt like an entirely different person than the one who could hardly haul herself from bed that morning. So long as I kept myself caffeinated and dosed with Ibuprofen, nothing could stop me.

. . .

Matthias and I picked up the groove we'd established before conglomerating into the five-rider mega-group with Brian, Nuno, and Mitch. While I found strength and security—and more than a few laughs—in cycling with the others, travelling with Matthias undoubtedly proved easier. Our daily rhythms followed a similar pattern; we didn't need to discuss pace, or how long we planned to stop. We simply fell into sync. I had come to view Matthias like a mid-ocean wave: calm and steady, forever rolling toward the shores of Chesapeake Bay, while I trundled along after him like flotsam picked up in the current, prone to erratic fits and starts in my sleep-deprived, worn-down state. To this day, how I managed to keep pace remains a mystery.

A quiet rural road transitioned into an even less trafficked single lane climb through a shaded, fairy-tale woods where I imagined Disney chipmunks with cartoonish-wide eyes batting eyelashes at robins sporting suave bow ties. Though my legs quaked with fatigue during steeper pitches, I welcomed the cooler air, and an opportunity to avoid the sun's glare during the hottest part of the day.

"Guess what?" said Matthias. "My brother's wife is supposed to give birth any day now."

Like me, Matthias had one sibling, and our younger siblings had achieved a respectable stability in their lives. My sister, Alisha, had a career in office management, with money set aside in her saving account and RRSPs; Matthias's brother, Sebastian, moved into a cottage in the woods to put down roots and start a family. I, on the other hand, was cursed with a restlessness that led me from one city to the next, choosing jobs more often seasonal than career building, and saving for upcoming travel instead of any distant future. This caused a degree of inner conflict: I wanted to be reliable, and I enjoyed stability. Yet I yearned for new experiences and changing scenery. I voiced these concerns to Matthias.

"I wouldn't agonize over it," he assured me. "No sense in letting other people dictate your life."

"I just worry about falling behind, you know? My friends are making mortgage payments and having babies, and meanwhile I'm bicycling across America."

"So long as you are happy, you're doing the right thing," he replied.

Although Matthias ran a successful business and had a long-term partner, I sensed that he was still searching for something; however, he had definitely got his shit together more than I did at that point.

After taking a slug from my water bottle, I switched topics.

"Only five hundred miles to go," I said, eliciting an eye roll from Matthias. By that point, I knew better than to describe any distance as only x miles—I just did it to annoy him.

"Look at the race winners," said Matthias, turning serious. "They weren't lounging around gas stations with bottomless fountain drinks and ice cream. They got in, got out; stayed focused. That's how we need to be."

"Smart and efficient," I concurred.

But it would only become harder from here on in, our fatigue mounting as we approached Yorktown.

"Let's motivate each other," he suggested. "Keep the breaks short and avoid wasting time."

We both hoped to finish with a bang, not a whimper.

"Agreed," I said. "And if I look drowsy, give me a pinch or a punch."

"A pinch or a punch?"

"Your choice."

The words had barely escaped my lips before I was blindsided by a biting pain in the soft tissue of my underarm. I shrieked and spun in my saddle to see Matthias chuckling as he returned the offending fingers to his handlebars.

"You looked tired," he said. "But I'm sorry. That was mean."

"I'll get you back," I promised.

. . .

We stopped for lunch in a colossal travel centre at a crossroads with the Interstate. Rural Virginia's lovely secret garden had morphed into a dull, cement conglomeration of restaurants, gas pumps, and parking spaces. The break coincided with a sudden nose-dive in my energy levels, my temperament penduluming from bright optimism to solemn lethargy. While Matthias took off to find a restroom, I lurched around the food court like the walking dead, unable to choose which fast food to feast on. After an overload of sausages and grits at breakfast, I couldn't stomach the thought of a second greasy meal. My appetite that day seemed only for suffering. Everything reeked of frier fat and seasoning salt—the only healthy option appeared to be Subway, which featured a lineup that snaked through the food court.

"Smart and efficient," I reminded myself. "Pick something, dammit."

I put an end to my decision paralysis and queued up at the Subway. Matthias joined me a few minutes later, and we waited wordlessly, the surrounding commotion washing over us like ocean surge. I felt myself fading, sinking deeper into an imagined sandy bottom, my body inching toward slumber even as I stood in line. Sandwich artists moved with a sluggish indifference that matched my own. By the time we paid for our subs, I realized only a serious intervention would enable me to remain lucid. Instead of sitting with Matthias, I took my sub to go and beelined across the parking lot in search of a caffeine fix. I grabbed two 5-Hour Energy drinks from a gas station convenience store and placed them on the counter.

The attendant shook his head, glancing from me to the three-ounce bottles and their laundry list of questionable ingredients. "I can't believe a healthy young athlete like yourself would put this crap into her body."

"Don't you dare judge me," I replied, my face burning as anger roiled beneath the grip of stupor. "You have no clue what I've been through."

We held eye contact for a moment, and he rang up my drinks without another word. I threw down the cash—or, more accurately, coaxed my nerve-damaged hands into dumping small bills and change from my wallet—and let him sort through it. Then I uncorked a bottle of high-octane rocket fuel and gulped its contents in front of him. But my pseudo-rebellious act may not have had the intended impact, since the attendant had moved on to the next customer by then.

Back on the bike and heading toward Damascus, I cracked up, the distance between myself and the outburst rendering it ridiculous.

"You said that, Hackinen?" replied Matthias. "Are you sure? Doesn't sound very polite for a Canadian."

"Yes! And then I stormed out."

While short of being apologetic—it was none of that attendant's business what I purchased—losing my cool over such a minor thing seemed symptomatic of a bigger issue. The race was taking its toll on my body and mind, and in the midst of it, I wasn't willing or able to face the full effects. Caffeine and Ibuprofen masked exhaustion, but only to a point.

Daily, I pushed boundaries of self. My changing appearance documented this transformation. After three weeks on the road, I'd become a Ripley's Believe It or Not exhibit of bodily catastrophe: swollen knees, sunscreen-clogged pores, taped Achilles, nerve-damaged hands, saddle sores, and blistered, scabby earlobes from prolonged exposure to sun and wind. The slow accretion of mental and physical damage had undeniably left its mark.

I also knew that sleep deprivation coupled with a nutrient-deficient, sugar-heavy diet only exacerbated my mood swings, yet saw no alternative. Four or five hours appeared to be the maximum window for rest; healthy options proved few and far between. Besides, my body craved sweets and crunchy carbohydrates—that Subway sandwich was the healthiest thing I'd eaten since Newton Bike Shop. Had I come across a salad bar, I probably would have walked right past.

. . .

From Damascus, we climbed. Bathed in dappled afternoon sunshine, Matthias and I kicked into the slope, grinding through Jefferson National Forest as slanted light transitioned from copper to gold. Past Hurricane and Grave Mountain, Mount Rogers, and High Knob. Up through the tiny settlements of Konnarock and Troutdale before we chased the last lingering rays down into Sugar Grove and Cedar Springs.

Mitch joined us along the way. No longer struggling as he had been that morning, he provided animated company, and I remained amazed by his even-keeled temper and unyielding determination. I endeavored to entertain him and Matthias with Schwarzenegger impersonations, shouting famous one-liners in machine-gun rapid-fire:

"Get to the chopper!"

"It's not a tumour!"

"I did nothing—the pavement was his enemy!"

Their laughter only encouraged me, and I continued, more boisterous and nonsensical every minute, hollering *Terminator* catchphrases alongside my own Austrian-accented descriptions of the hillside.

"Schwarzenegger once walked around Munich in his posing briefs to promote a gym in the middle of winter," I boasted, keen to merge insight of my favourite action hero with Matthias's home country.

"Really?" asked Matthias.

"Just before he came to America."

Unlike me, Schwarzenegger seemed to have no trouble embracing his assets in the face of adversity: to parade down a busy street in next to nothing is something I would never have the confidence to pull off. But then again, isn't that exactly what I did in roller derby—race around a flat track in torn fishnets and booty shorts for an audience of screaming fans? Why, then, has it been such a struggle for me to pin down the same level of self-assurance in cycling; what differentiated Schwarzemegger—my roller derby persona— from Meaghan the self-doubting endurance cyclist?

Perhaps it had something to do with the fact that despite my years of experience on the bike, I was still very much finding my footing in the realm of competitive cycling. But I had to admit, both confidence and competence were improving. I no longer felt as anxious as I did in those early race days, when I wrestled with everything from attaching my Spot, to interpreting the elevation profile. After weeks on the road, I was beginning to feel at home in the unknown. Comfortable in the in-between. I had proven, just by hanging in there, that I was capable. Something had clicked. Though my temperament was now marred by mood swings, each day I felt more convinced in my newfound abilities, assured I was on the right track.

. . .

As the sun dipped behind the treeline, we rode into an isolated mountain community to discover a cluster of townsfolk surrounding a police cruiser.

"Someone drove into my fence," exclaimed a distraught man in overalls. A thick-knuckled hand waved toward the half-demolished white fence on the right-hand side of the road.

A witness described the suspect's vehicle as the officer took notes. The man in overalls continued speaking, repeating himself like a sleepy late-night broadcaster re-reading blocks of script from the tele-prompter.

"He just drove right through it. Drove right through my fence," he said. "Officer, I just put up that fence. Just put it up. You've got to arrest whoever done this."

"He just put the fence up," echoed an equally distressed woman who may have been his wife.

Mitch, Matthias, and I stared at the fence. You could almost smell the fresh white paint. The bulldozed section appeared unsalvageable, wood beams cracked in several places.

"Someone needs to pay," demanded the man in overalls. "Officer, I'm telling you, someone must pay for my fence."

The police cruiser took off, lights blazing. The three of us moved along as well, stepping away from this slice of Americana as abruptly as we had entered. Life continued, but we existed outside of it. Somewhere in my cross-continental journey, I had passed through a multi-dimensional doorway. Now, I inhabited the Trans Am Bubble, a parallel universe that functioned according to a very different set of principles—ride, eat, sleep, repeat—than the existence I had left behind. With each day, the cognitive dissonance increased: the man and his fence served as a reminder of the departed world, though these real-world intrusions infiltrated my headspace less and less frequently as I pushed farther east.

. . .

At Rural Retreat, our group of three hooked a right, following West Lee Highway until the spellbinding lights of a gas station brought our wheels to a halt. I skipped into the convenience store after checking the Tracker to discover Nuno and Brian carving a star-lit path through the mountains, the distance between us stretching. Mitch wanted to continue together, a prospect I remained leery of, fearful of jeopardizing the easy harmony established between Matthias and myself. Though Mitch was an undeniably strong rider, our patterns didn't mesh. This became apparent once Matthias and I had purchased our to-go items, only to lose sight of Mitch. We found him examining a menu at the attached diner. The hour was closing in on 10:00 p.m. and I was eager to roll.

"I'll grab something quick," promised Mitch.

Matthias seated himself across the table from Mitch while I returned to the bikes. After stockpiling snacks in my frame bag, I settled onto the pavement with a Rice Krispies Square, legs spilled out in front of me. Two bites in, my mother called.

"What are you doing?" she asked. Her accusatory tone caught me off-guard.

"I'm taking a break," I said. Then added: "Waiting for Mitch and Matthias."

I hadn't spoken to my mother since Eric's death, but it took only a minute to realize how much I'd missed our conversations. She still didn't grasp why I insisted on doing this race, yet supported me regardless—the ultimate cheerleader. Our chats always left me pumped, confident I could undertake whatever unknown challenges lay ahead. Outside the gas station in Rural Retreat, I rambled about the past few days, filling her in on Tropical Storm Cindy, but omitting how destroyed my hands and undercarriage had become—she didn't need to know all the details.

Then she cut in to ask again what I was doing.

"I told you," I said. "Waiting for the guys. They're eating dinner or something."

"Meaghan," she paused, considering her words. "This is a race, right?

And you've been wasting time at this gas station for nearly an hour."

"I need to get moving." The realization knocked me in the chest like a fist.

"Yes."

"What about Mitch and Matthias?"

"That's up to you. But remember, it's a race."

I ended the call and hauled myself back inside to find the others. She was right: regardless of what I was up to, the race clock was ticking away. It felt strange to be taking advice from my mother, a vegan yogi who didn't have a competitive bone in her body. But I'd never been great at tactical decision-making, and perhaps in my weary, discombobulated state, I needed someone else's hand to pull the strings of the Meaghan marionette and realign me with my purpose. I bumped into Matthias first.

"Where's Mitch?" I demanded. "I'm ready to go."

Matthias was antsy to hit the road as well. He told me that Mitch had disappeared into the restroom. "I think his stomach is bugging him again," he added.

I waited at the table beside Mitch's things, secretly relieved that Matthias was at least prepared to leave. As much as I wanted to follow my mother's urging and take off as quickly as possible, a pact existed between Matthias and me. He'd stuck it out and waited for me to get it together on several occasions; I was sure there'd be Karmatic hell to pay if I ditched him at a gas station during the final leg of the journey. Luckily, it wouldn't come down to that.

Mitch looked unwell when he finally returned, his skin sallow and moist. I didn't want to guess what ghastly events had taken place in the men's room. He asked if I could wait a few more minutes. I reluctantly agreed. In the end, we wasted well over an hour at that stupid gas station, engaging in exactly the time-frivolous behaviour that Matthias and I, with our recently coined maxim of "Smart and Efficient," hoped to avoid.

. . .

An hour later, we parted ways with Mitch at a baseball diamond in the sleepy town of Max Meadows. While the break at the service station had sapped my energy, it left Mitch rejuvenated. When Matthias and I decided to bivy in the dugout, he continued alone. I'm convinced Mitch pedalled the remaining 416 miles to Yorktown without stopping more than an hour to sleep, eat, or use the toilet.

"ITT to the finish!" I imagined him saying, echoing the words he had used en route to Cave-In-Rock Ferry in Illinois.

Where he pulled the energy from remains a mystery, though I eventually forgave him for delaying our progress that night in Virginia.

Day Twenty-Three

JUNE 25, 2017

MAX MEADOWS TO LOVE, VIRGINIA

DISTANCE: 172 MILES

RACE MILEAGE: 4,022 OF 4,264 MILES

I awoke under a cobalt ceiling of sky. Dew twinkled on grass in the outfield like tiny stars, each blade reflecting a shard of moonlight. It took a moment to realize where I was and place a name to the body sleeping next to me. But frigid air quickly roused the senses, and within minutes, Matthias and I were on our way, pedalling toward the rose glimmer of dawn.

Two miles along, we pulled into a gas station at the junction of Interstate 81. While neither of us wanted to take a break so early in the day, we were both freezing. Not only was I out of Latex gloves, but I seemed to have lost one of my long-fingered cycling gloves as well. My hands were useless in the cold, and until I could subdue the shivering, my legs couldn't produce power. We huddled next to the coffee machine inside, warming hands against paper cups as Matthias detailed the upcoming terrain, and I racked my brain for where that glove could be.

"Hills," he said. "Short, steep ups and downs. Then we hit Lexington, which might be a smart place to stop for dinner before we tackle Vesuvius."

"Vesuvius," I repeated.

Though Mount Vesuvius was an ocean away, my mind could no longer separate the infamous volcano—responsible for burying ancient Pompeii under ash and stone in its 79 AD eruption—from Virginia's more benign counterpart. At 3,300 feet, Vesuvius marked our high point in the Appalachian Mountains, yet in comparison it proved lower than both Italy's Vesuvius and the high passes in the Western Rockies that we had already scaled.

"But we shouldn't underestimate it," warned Matthias. "From Lexington, we'll gain over two thousand feet of elevation on grades up to twenty-four percent."

I groaned. "My legs hurt just thinking about it."

"They will hurt even more once we start climbing."

. . .

The first few hours went well. Distant hills backlit by heavenly light were laced with soft morning fog; crisp white church steeples pierced a brilliant blue sky. Green vegetation appeared as much a hallmark of Virginia as Kentucky, with old-fashioned mailboxes and brick buildings interrupting the trees, shrubs, and fields. After our first stop, we kept the momentum going until early afternoon. I never did find my glove, but I took my revenge on Matthias for that awful pinch the other day, though he got me a few more times, sneaking up just as my eyelids began to droop.

We charted our course along scenic rural roads that paralleled Interstate 81. Every time the gasp of traffic on the busy freeway reached my ears, it reminded me of how fortunate we were to follow quiet byways instead.

The TransAmerica Trail, which the Trans Am Bike Race follows, originated in 1976 when convoys of explorers set out across the country on two-wheeled transportation to celebrate America's bicentennial. The route was drafted through a collaboration between local cyclists familiar with the best regional routes, and a non-profit organization called Bikecentennial (which later became the American Cycling Association). Over the years, the TransAmerica Trail has become one of the most popular long-distance routes in the United States. Though bicycle travel has since modernized—with digital maps supplementing or even replacing paper ones, and brighter, USB-chargeable lights favoured over bulky, battery-operated devices—at times when I found my morale lacking, I thought of those first intrepid souls who braved the Trans Am in the summer of 1976.

. . .

Matthias proved correct in his prediction: the journey was challenging. By noon, my quadriceps rebelled against the recurrent calls to action. I worried how they would fare under the strain of prolonged climbing, but banished the thought of Vesuvius for the time being.

In the typical pattern of the day, I lagged after our meal. Matthias and I split up, parting with a plan to meet in Lexington for dinner. Alone, I slipped even further in pace—a riptide of fatigue dragging me. I collapsed in front of the town hall once I reached Troutville, splayed like a gutted fish on the spongy grass. Sleep snatched me away the second my cheek touched down. I awoke to the buzz of my iPhone with an incoming text from Matthias.

Hurry! Nuno is catching up.

I had dozed an entire hour.

My first impulse was to check the Tracker, but with poor service since Kentucky, I knew the webpage would take minutes to load. Instead, I hoisted myself from the grass, wiped the pooling sweat from my face with my neck warmer, and filled my bottles with tepid water from a nearby tap.

Awake now, I texted. *See you soon.*

. . .

Sky-rocketing humidity and sweltering temperatures made every pedal stroke a chore. Despite an hour-long nap, I felt far from fresh: my quadriceps lifeless and limp; my back and shoulders ached as if I'd been carrying a backpack of encyclopedias. But I had learned to differentiate the minor bodily nuisances that could be pushed through from the more serious concerns that required treatment. I knew most of those annoying pains would dull if I could simply detach from what ailed me, and shift my focus elsewhere.

Upbeat dance music in my earbuds helped me through the following hours. I caught up with Matthias a few miles before Lexington on a narrow winding road that swept like a giant serpent through the hills. Adrenaline surged as I whipped around corners, taking in scenery with the quick capture speed of a camera flash. Despite the ache in my limbs, I enjoyed myself; Matthias proved to be in similar spirits. We kept each other motivated on the climbs with senseless humour, like repeating the name of the state until it transformed into the word for an intimate part of the female anatomy: "Virginia. Virginia. Virgina. Veer-gina. Vagina!"

I was gasping for air by the time I reached the final iteration, my abdomen clenched tight with laughter. Matthias snickered, his typically austere face replaced by a loopy grin as we inched uphill, our surroundings gorgeous and green, with mottled sunlight peeking through a leafy ceiling. It was as if the road had been constructed with cyclists specifically in mind. At a bend, Matthias and I spotted a mossy wooden pedestrian bridge arching over a creek that paralleled the route. Instinctively, we slowed.

"Stop for five?" I said.

"Why not?"

We dismounted and continued on foot along an earthen path. At the bridge, we removed our shoes and seated ourselves near the edge. The water ran shallow and clear, revealing streamers of algae on smooth river stones below.

"Listen," said Matthias.

The creek's babble intermingled with the rustle of leaves overhead. From an unseen perch, a songbird trilled. Matthias dangled his legs, toes like pale fish in the stream.

"Delightful, isn't it?" he said.

I nodded and hooked my knees over the bridge's edge. Cool relief ebbed over my tender, swollen feet. Waves of calm emanated up my legs. I rolled back my shoulders, noticing how my movements were stiff with accumulated tension, as if someone had jammed stones between my rhomboids and scapulae. Minutes passed.

"We should get going," Matthias said.

Dread seized my chest. I remained anchored to the bridge, lower limbs heavy with accumulated lactic acid. Unwilling to move. I looked toward my bicycle, lying next to the road, and tried to imagine myself pedalling into the night. Then my mother's words from yesterday's phone conversation came back to me.

"Remember, it's a race," she'd said.

It was late afternoon, and I guessed she would be at home, unfurling her yoga mat or preparing a salad to accompany supper, her iPad nearby so she could check in on my progress. I imagined Marj, Bob, and the other Prairie Randonneurs keeping tabs as well, all of them watching and waiting to see when my dot would move. Like fans watching a basketball player on the free-throw line, all eyes were on me. I didn't want to disappoint.

"Right," I said. "Let's ride."

. . .

After dinner in Lexington, we began our gradual ascent along the South River into the foothills of the Blue Ridge Mountains—John Denver country—the air scented with wildflowers whose sweet perfume lingered long after their buds had shuttered tight. Under towering trees, fireflies signalled dusk's metamorphosis to night. Matthias taught me the German word for firefly: *Glühwürmchen*.

"Glow-worm-song," I sang. "Gloo-wop-sing."

He repeated it, dragging out the syllables: "Gluuuuh-würrmmm-chen."

But I continued to stutter over the first part.

"Glu," he repeated, feigning annoyance. "Just like 'glue,' the sticky stuff!"

"Glow," I said, slipping into hysterics.

Matthias took his responsibility as ambassador of the German tongue seriously. He repeated the word once again, but my concentration had evaporated. I collapsed over the handlebars in laughter. My botched attempts at speaking what Matthias playfully referred to as "the most beautiful European tongue," would have to wait.

Meanwhile, the fireflies blinked on and off in magical bursts. Yorktown was just around the corner, or more accurately, less than three hundred miles away. Our plan to attack Vesuvius under nightfall was right on schedule, though that meant we would roll through the Blue Ridge Mountains in darkness and miss our chance to view the rugged Appalachian highlands by daylight. But from the Blue Ridge Parkway, it actually was downhill to the coast. A post office in Afton, a tiny settlement in the eastern foothills, marked our proposed evening finishing point. We planned to snag a nap in the foyer before the last big push to Yorktown.

. . .

Our lighthearted conversation dissolved by the time we reached the fabled Vesuvius. A town bearing the same name preceded the climb, but we halted only a minute to catch our breaths before plunging into woods, the maw of night swallowing us whole. By the third switchback, my leg muscles had turned to mush. By the fifth, I wondered if it would be quicker to walk my bicycle. The yips of dogs, or coyotes, sounded from the deep bush. I stood to pedal, every stroke stoking the fire in my quadriceps. I could no longer summon the strength to ride seated, yet my pride prohibited me from walking. So, I stood. Heaving weight from side to side until my breath grew ragged, and the burn engulfing my legs forced me to set a foot down.

Every switchback or two I paused, my lights flashing lonely beams into the void. Matthias and I communicated in grunts and groans, the skitter of gravel from beneath our tires a game of Marco Polo between us, ensuring neither strayed far. I continually brought the focus back to my breath; the attention to the parts of my body that remained strong. My legs wanted to buckle. I lost track of the hour as the road threatened to pitch me time and time again into the woods. I told myself that I was dying a slow death on this hill, yet knew as I said it that I was being overdramatic. Of course, I would survive just fine: wobbly legs were an inconvenience, not a death sentence. I reminded myself that I'd felt worse walking home from the bar after drinks with Tyler and his pals.

Though I stopped more frequently than I'd like to admit, I took comfort in the knowledge that with each revolution of the wheels, I inched closer to the summit. And while looking to Schwarzenegger's macho action hero persona for guidance may have served me well when I started this journey, it was all on me now. It would be me—not *Kindergarten Cop*'s Detective John Kimble or *Total Recall*'s Douglas Quaid—that hauled myself up Vesuvius. Me that would drag my thrashed body across the finish line in Yorktown. I recalled an expression from my roller derby days: "Be your own hero." Cheesy, sure. Yet now more than ever, the motto rang true. I would have to push against the limits of my endurance just a little bit longer tonight, but after weeks of digging deep, I knew that I possessed the grit—the mental fortitude—to get there. With or without an imagined Austrian body-builder-turned-actor-turned-politician muttering catchphrases in my ear.

. . .

By the time we escaped from the cover of foliage at the summit, our Herculean feat felt closer to summitting sacred Mount Olympus than America's Vesuvius. I rejoiced to be back in the open air.

But Vesuvius had left Matthias shattered.

"Just leave me," he moaned.

"C'mon," I urged, surprised to be coaxing him for a change. "Only a little farther to Afton."

We eased off the pedals to coast along the Blue Ridge Parkway, seeing nothing but the nearby silhouettes of trees and house lights interspersed among the distant highlands. It didn't take long before I started to tunnel as well, senses dimming as the spotlight of my front bike light entranced me like a hypnotist's charm.

Snap out of it, I told myself. *Get a move on!*

But it was well past midnight, and my last 5-Hour Energy drink had expired over an hour ago. We veered off at the next pullout for a pit stop. I hinged one leg over the frame to dismount. Everything below my waist felt flimsy, as if toothpicks supported my torso. A breeze hissed overhead. Bone-deep fatigue necessitated slow, deliberate movements as we flattened ourselves onto the still-warm pavement, spreading limbs like a pair of misplaced snow angels. The road remained quiet, disrupted only by the scrape of wind in the trees and our own mortal beating hearts. I looked up and noticed, for the first time, the night aglow with starlight.

"How's this for romance and adventure?" said Matthias, his voice sliding over asphalt into my ear.

I grinned. Dazed, deeply tired, but also in complete awe of the mountaintop sky. Bewitched by the fragile disc of battered moon set among a flickering expanse of stars.

"Surrounded by stars on a desolate peak—I suppose this passes the test," I conceded.

"Told you not to give up hope."

In a few minutes, our sweat would chill. We would not make it over the Blue Ridge Mountains that night. But the opportunity to witness the picturesque landscape by daybreak tempered the blow of failing to complete our mission to reach the post office in Afton. For a moment, I laid still. Resting on asphalt, I gazed toward stars that blinked like distant fireflies—*Glühwürmchen*.

As much as I was ready for this whole mad race to be over, I could not resist the urge to linger.

Day Twenty-Four

JUNE 26, 2017

LOVE TO ASHLAND, VIRGINIA

DISTANCE: 142 MILES

RACE MILEAGE: 4,164 OF 4,264 MILES

Matthias and I overslept. It was after 7:00 a.m. by the time the sun burned through our eyelids, snapping us back into the land of the living. In our case, that meant waking to the acute stiffness that comes from sleeping on wooden picnic tables. But instead of chastising ourselves for a late start, we duly accepted our fate. Perhaps failing to reach Afton yesterday had inarguably demonstrated our total depletion of energy, and the necessity of re-establishing a sleep base to see us through to the finish. Neither of us had much in the way of provisions—though my missing glove had miraculously turned up in the foot of my sleeping bag. It was a godsend when a pair of dotwatchers with granola bars and bottled water greeted us on the Blue Ridge Parkway.

"Where did you stay last night?" asked Gretchen, an athletic-looking woman in her mid-forties with the wavy blonde hair of a goddess.

"On picnic tables," said Matthias.

"In Love?" said Tim, a big, friendly guy with a booming laugh.

We nodded. Love was the name of the tiny valley settlement where we had overnighted.

The thought made me blush: we woke up in Love. What a place to find ourselves. My inner narrator couldn't help but highlight the potential symbolism, though I mentioned nothing to Matthias. Hopefully, he didn't notice my reddening face as we chatted with Gretchen and Tim.

"You both are absolutely killing it," said Tim. "By this time tomorrow, you'll be in Yorktown."

"It's not far now," agreed Gretchen. "More downhill than up!"

Gretchen and Tim's encouragement proved exactly what I needed to get back on track after cutting it short yesterday. We could do this; we were doing this. And now that we were rested, it might even be easy.

I knew that last part to be wishful thinking—a pipe dream. In this race, nothing was ever easy. Yet as we bade Gretchen and Tim farewell, I remained determined to harness their positive, hopeful energy and hold onto it as long as possible. Around us, the Blue Ridge Mountains rose from deep green valleys, their distant sapphire crowns draped with sweeping banners of clouds on the horizon.

Enjoy it, I told myself. *You are lucky enough to be here, so damn well enjoy it.*

. . .

We ripped down the slope so fast, we almost flew past the turnoff to Afton. In the span of minutes, the mountains fell away, replaced by a rolling descent I imagined would carry us to the finish line in Yorktown.

"Finally," I said. "All downhill from here!"

But alas, it wasn't.

In fact, from Afton we found ourselves ascending, ambushed by erratic sawtooth climbs reminiscent of Missouri's virulent rollers.

"What the hell is this?" I exclaimed, brow furrowing as the sad click of my derailleur indicated I had run out of gears. "Are we on route?"

Matthias nodded, struggling himself.

"Gretchen lied!"

"Technically, she said 'more downhill,'" he corrected me.

"She lied."

We stopped to replenish our supplies at a market in Owensville. The combination of hot breakfast sandwiches and the store's delightfully kitschy décor improved my mood. As we chomped into our meal on a bench outside, Matthias talked me through the day's elevation profile—the last remaining cue card in his stack. Relief came when I saw we were indeed trending downhill. I'd been complaining about molehills compared to the backbreaking mountain ranges we had conquered already.

"But why is everything so hard?" I whined, my voice gaining pitch as I slipped into desperation.

"You're just tired, Hackinen. After riding across a continent who wouldn't be?"

Matthias could be frustratingly pragmatic, I thought to myself, tossing grease-splotched sandwich wrappers and empty drink bottles in the trash. But he was also the most steadfast cycling companion I could have asked for.

. . .

The day lurched along, punctuated by stops and starts, twenty-minute cat-naps and gas station pit stops for Gatorade with a side of fried chicken as we attempted to stick to our credo of "Smart and Efficient." Gretchen popped out from an office building to wish us well in Charlottesville, her repeat performance a pleasant surprise, even if that comment about the terrain had been painfully misleading.

"You've got this," she said, offering a firm handshake as we parted ways for the second time.

"She looked so bright-eyed and healthy," I observed. "I can't remember the last time I checked my reflection and the bags under my eyes weren't as big as potholes."

"Bet she drinks smoothies for breakfast," said Matthias.

"And eats kale," I added.

Just six weeks later, on August 11-12, 2017, a right-wing rally of neo-Nazi white nationalists strewed terror on Charlottesville's streets. I watched the news from Saskatoon in horror as Unite the Right marchers waved Confederate battle flags while chanting racist slogans, protesting the removal of Confederate monuments, including a statue of General Robert E. Lee. I had fond memories of Gretchen and Charlottesville; it seemed like a progressive city (many of the protesters, it turned out, arrived from out of town). But I was also forced to confront the fact that despite my recent time in the States, I did not have much of a grasp on the political climate. My focus had been self-centred and inward-looking. While I felt blessed by the support of dotwatchers, most of my interactions with residents were in passing, and I couldn't claim to have an understanding of the trouble brewing in Trump's America.

. . .

We managed to maintain our lead on Brian and Nuno, but by late afternoon, fatigue had undeniably caught up with me. I needed to flip the script. Transform my drowsiness into action. Yet all of my tricks—chewing gum, music, rigorous spinning of the legs—proved futile. In frustration, I pinched my left inner bicep with my "good hand" until the skin blossomed violet, but even pain failed to shake the lethargy. Matthias abruptly pulled over ahead of me near Anna Lake, where I nearly collided with him as I skidded to a halt.

"We should go swimming," he announced.

I glanced from the stream of evening rush hour traffic to the idyllic lake with its lone dock thrusting a rickety finger into placid waters. I could smell the waterline, the slightly swampy odour of wet reeds and long grasses. We had recently stopped to eat and hadn't planned to break again until Ashland, on the outskirts of Richmond.

"Are you sure we have time?" I asked.

"A refreshing dip will do you good."

No one was around to see us duck underneath the chain barring the path to the water. A crescent of pebbled beach opened up. After a solemn oath to avoid looking at one another's saddle sores, we stripped down to rush in, giggling as our feet struggled for purchase on the slippery stones. I dove in once the waterline slapped my belly, reaching for a few wide strokes before resurfacing. Cresting waves shimmered like a secret cache of scattered gems. I paddled past the dock, then trod water in rhythmic circles, letting the aquatic surrounding perform its soothing alchemy. Matthias appeared alongside me a minute later. We orbited each other, the refracting surface distorting pale outlines of flesh beneath.

"I bet that's a nuclear plant," he said, pointing toward an industrial-looking structure puffing toxic fumes across the lake. "Explains why no one is swimming."

I looked down expecting a three-headed fish, but glimpsed my own legs, frog-kicking to keep my body afloat.

"I'm not concerned. 'Worry less; pray more,' right?" I said, quoting a church signboard we'd seen in Kentucky. It was one of my favourites, up there with 'Honk If You Prayed Today,' and a convenience store advertising 'Water Colder Than Your Ex's Heart.'

We paddled around the dock, the lapping waves muffling evening commuters on the roadway nearby. I thought back to when we met in Idaho and dared each other to dunk in the Clearwater River. I didn't even know Matthias's name—and half-expected to be out of the race by day's end, anyway. But weeks later, here we were. Our friendship staked in the ever-changing reality of the road, an adaptation to sustained hardship. I had found comfort in his company, solace in our shared experiences.

I sighted our clothes on the beach. We should get back. A few feet away, Matthias's head emerged from the surface. He grinned boyishly, hair slick against his skull. Eyes as clear and blue as the late-afternoon sky. Again, I flashed to the river in Idaho. What I remembered most of that day was not the century-long low-grade climb to Lolo Pass, the monotony of trees, or relentless boredom. Instead, it was those few minutes of unapologetic silliness as we took a time out. I wondered what I'd recall of this journey twenty years down the road. Where would I find meaning? I knew that situations where I persevered—like the day I starved myself over three peaks in Central Oregon after my stomach turned, or the Three Musketeers' heroic triumph over headwinds as we fought to reach West Yellowstone under the cloak of darkness—would withstand the test of time. But I also hoped those simple, satisfying moments when I stepped outside of the race would stick as well.

. . .

Back on the road, I had no trouble staying alert. In part because of our revitalizing dip, but also because Matthias had given me some of his chamois cream. I had run out in Kentucky, and my tender parts were now in excruciating pain. So extreme was the discomfort that I could no longer maintain one position for more than a few minutes. I shifted my weight in the saddle, resting gingerly on the nose, or slouching back in the seat, but my efforts provided only momentary relief. I was embarrassed to borrow such a personal item from Matthias, but he met my request with relaxed nonchalance.

"This isn't my usual brand," he warned. "I picked it up in Newton after mine ran out."

I took the bottle and disappeared behind a hedge to slather my intimates.

Five minutes later, my lady bits tingled. It wasn't a burning or prickly sensation, but rather an uplifting, mentholated cool.

"Dude," I said, "is there something you forgot to mention about this cream?"

Matthias's eyes met mine, his lips revealing a cheeky grin. "It's rather fresh, isn't it?"

"I feel like I smeared myself with peppermint toothpaste and can't decide if I love or hate it."

"It is a little weird at first," he admitted. "But you get used to it."

"Do you think this stuff comes in other flavours?" I wondered. "Bubble gum, or wintergreen?"

"Or chili pepper?" he offered.

This sparked a brainstorming session of undesirable chamois creams that lasted until our meal stop in Ashland.

Final Hours

JUNE 27, 2017

ASHLAND TO YORKTOWN, VIRGINIA

DISTANCE: 100 MILES

RACE MILEAGE: 4,264 OF 4,264 MILES

I had imagined hammering out the final hundred miles in one fell swoop—a last ditch *tour de force* before triumphantly crossing the finish line.

The reality couldn't have been more different.

The final hours were slow. Mile by painstaking mile. No shortcuts; no tricks. Matthias and I departed the gas station in Ashland at 10:00 p.m. just as Brian and Nuno were pulling in, both of them looking as thrashed as we undoubtedly felt. With an assortment of chocolate bars and gummies in our pockets, the two of us chased backcountry roads that detoured north of Richmond, carving a wide arc around the city's halo before joining the Virginia Capital Trail. The Trail would take us as far as Williamsburg, and then we'd hop back on the road for the last cobblestoned miles of the Colonial Parkway to the finish line on Chesapeake Bay.

My memory of those hours exists in bursts. Brief flashes that don't quite take hold: a collection of houses, a thin slice of moon, a silent pause as we oriented ourselves at a dark crossroads. The sound of our names from the window of a silver minivan and a dotwatcher fist pumping the air in encouragement. But fear burgeoned in my gut as we rode deeper into the night, my thoughts percolated in panic: what if we didn't make it? What if the end never came?

By midnight, I felt queasy. Sick to my stomach. The stagnant, humid air clogged our throats, suffocating us slowly like a steam room. No escape. By the time we reached the Virginia Capital Trail at 2:00 a.m. I was close to maniacal. To my unfocussed eye, the surrounding forest appeared nightmarish in its all-encompassing darkness, every gnarled tree branch a skeletal limb reaching to snatch us into the underworld. I imagined the grotesque swamp monster from Missouri, dark-limbed and dripping sludge, its eyes pinpricks of jaundiced iridescence in the wooded gloom. But the swamp monster wasn't real—or was it? My heart palpitated with an urgency I worried would send me to the emergency room. How many Red Bulls and caffeine pills had I consumed over the past twelve hours? Was I having a heart attack? I'd heard of ravers and partiers dying from caffeine overconsumption. I regretted the absence of a will, not that I had much to distribute. To my sister, my bicycle; to my boyfriend, my outdated MacBook—that was it. I considered mentioning my wishes to Matthias, but he had his own demons to fight, and I didn't want to burden him with mine.

We kept each other alert with pinches and punches, delivered without warning or mercy. Unlike the night before on the Blue Ridge Parkway, our resolve held strong. We did not stop. The pesky, chattering voice of my inner critic remained as loud as ever, but unlike those times I'd waffled in the wind in Wyoming or Colorado—leaving it up to Matthias to haul me up from the self-pitying mess I'd become and cajole me back on the bike—I continued on. Nagging doubts overridden by firm, grounded self-assurance: I could do this. I *was* doing this. While I couldn't know what was going through Matthias's head, that the end had finally appeared within our grasp perhaps enabled us both to push past the barriers—both physiological and psychological—that grounded us in Love, Virginia.

But our persistence wasn't pretty: pedal strokes clunky and out-of-sync, legs sluggish to spin after weeks of being pushed close to breaking. The final test. As the route undulated through forested countryside, I lost all notion of speed, although Matthias provided intermittent updates: we hadn't managed over twelve miles an hour since encountering Nuno and Brian in Ashland. I wondered if they fared any better.

. . .

"Hey, can we pull over?" said Matthias around 4:30 a.m.

We had entered Charles City, a settlement about forty miles from Yorktown.

"Here?" I said, pointing toward a closed gas station lit by the blue and red glow of a Pepsi vending machine.

We rolled up and dismounted. Matthias began to text rapidly while I fed the machine with quarters.

"My brother's wife just had the baby," he said, his voice faraway, eyes focused on something I could not see. "It's a girl."

I'd lost him. Matthias had stepped outside the Trans Am Bubble, into the real world. His happiness appeared tangible, a vibrational aura resonating from sweat-soaked Lycra and grimy, bug-streaked limbs. Suddenly, I felt alone. My presence diminished as Matthias traded me and the race for a digital reunion with his brother on the other side of the globe.

"Here," I said, handing him a Pepsi. "When will you meet her?"

"After the race. I'll stop by on my way home to Freiburg."

He continued texting, and I unlocked my iPhone. I didn't want to be on my own just then. In addition to the usual message from Marj, to my surprise I'd also received a dozen messages of encouragement and support. A friend had even posted the link to Trackleaders on the local Saskatoon Cycling Facebook Page: *Looks like Meaghan is very close to finishing the Trans Am Bike Race...pretty amazing.*

As I held the cool can to my neck, a tightness of emotion worked its way up my throat. All those people; I'd forgotten some of them existed. The panic that had seized me earlier on the Trail dissolved as all those long-distance love bombs sunk in. Indisputable proof, along with Matthias's new niece, that we were connected to a world that continued turning, regardless of our absence.

For weeks, I'd been alternating between wanting this race to be over and savouring the delightful moments as they were handed to me. I thought back to Anna Lake, the sensation of weightlessness as I gave myself over to water. Then I imagined floating into a hotel bed with plush white sheets as I tucked myself into sleep without an alarm.

There was no space left on my arm for bruises. It was time to rejoin the outside world.

. . .

At 8:01 a.m., after twenty-four days, twenty-two hours, and one minute, we arrived in Yorktown, Virginia. Matthias and I rolled over the finish line side by side as twenty-third and twenty-fourth place finishers, making a victory lap to the applause of bystanders before coming to a halt at the steps of the hundred-foot-tall Yorktown Victory Monument, a marble statue commemorating victory in the American Revolutionary War. We leaned our bikes against the stairs and embraced. Like the moment before liftoff, our bodies quaked. Between us, three weeks of living on the road. A roller coaster of ups and downs, headaches and heartaches, calories consumed and expended. My face melted into his chest, the hairs on his neckline brushing my cheek.

"We made it," he said. Creases around his eyes softened into a tired, weather-worn grin.

My arms fell away as I met his gaze. "We did."

Then we pulled apart. Our journey—at least this segment—had reached its natural conclusion.

Rolf was there to hand us a beer, as well as Mitch, who had arrived the night before and dragged himself from well-deserved slumber to greet us. Brian's wife, Stacey—a triathlete with mean-looking calves and tan lines as impressive as our own—and a few local dotwatchers rounded off our unexpected finisher's party. We mingled in the monument's shadow with our early morning beers as the reality of our accomplishment sank in. Brian and Nuno arrived an hour later, complaining bitterly about the terrible condition of the last twenty miles of cobbled river rock on the Colonial Parkway which shook our bikes with bone-jarring, jackhammer ferocity.

"Cheers!" shouted Stacey, exploding a bottle of champagne.

We ducked the spray, then passed the remainder around. The champagne's tiny bubbles tickled my tonsils. Even after handing the bottle off, I couldn't smack the smile from my face. I felt like a champion. The ride was finally over. Already, I realized that I was not the same person as when I set out from Astoria on June 3rd. Over the course of 4,300 miles, I pushed past preconceived limits time after time, putting my body through trials far beyond what it had previously endured to emerge more confident, less afraid of the unknown, and with hard-won trust in my legs and navigational abilities—so long as Nuno wasn't around to throw me off. While there were days I stopped short, that I'd been able to continue at all remained somewhat of a miracle. Grit, determination—these are not adjectives I would have applied to myself before. Yet over the preceding weeks, I'd build reserves of both.

Near a hedge, a small tribute to Eric had been erected. Just a photograph of him at the start line in Astoria—gazing past the photographer's lens in his highlighter yellow rain jacket and helmet—accompanied by the white plastic flowers left by previous finishers. I watched as Matthias crouched with his flower, but then turned away, not wanting to intrude on his private grief.

Over the past days, I had replayed my memories of Eric. But at the finish, I settled on a single incident. As Matthias stood to return to our celebration, I cut the plastic flower from my handlebars and paced over to the tribute, aware of each footfall, the gravel etching tiny craters in my knees as I knelt in front of Eric's photograph. During the months to follow, I would continue to process Eric's death: frustration, anger, and sadness boiling over to leave me flat and empty. At the finish line in Yorktown, however, I wished to honour his life. Memorialize our short time together.

I shut my eyes. The sound of the finishers' party fell away. Residual tension in my forehead dissolved like a line going slack. In my mind, I drift back to Central Oregon. Eric rides ahead, jersey rippling in the wind. We've just left Sisters. Scorched red rock surrounds us and the hot air tastes like bitter pine.

"Yorktown, we're coming for you!" he yells.

Pure, uninhibited joy.

· · ·

I returned from Eric's tribute to the steps of the monument to find myself surrounded by competitors I now counted as friends: Brian, Rolf, Nuno, Mitch, and of course Matthias. Rolf cracked another beer for me, and I settled onto a step, basking in 10:00 a.m. sunshine and the pride of finishing.

"Do you remember the last words I said to you?" Rolf asked.

"No, what were they?"

"I said I'd never drop you," he replied, chuckling.

"Then you sped off!" I swatted his arm, memories of that frighteningly windy day in Colorado flooding back.

"I'm sorry," he said. "I really hoped you guys would catch up."

"You could have waited in Newton," Matthias said. "Instead of taking off twenty minutes before we arrived."

Rolf rooted in his pack for another beverage and handed it to Matthias. "Please accept this beer as my apology."

I expected my journey across America to be a lonely affair, full of hardship, strife, and spellbinding sunrises. I was correct about everything except for the loneliness: the experience was far from solitary. So much of my own story remains wrapped up in collective experiences of glory and sadness, self-inflicted suffering and small triumphs. Flights had to be booked, transportation to airports sorted out, but that could wait. This moment was ours to celebrate, and I could think of no better company than the unexpected cast of characters with whom I shared the adventure.

Epilogue

I rode into Prince Albert, Saskatchewan, just after midnight. The staff at the Tim Hortons next to the casino were unexpectedly sympathetic to the plight of a solo late-night cyclist, stuffing a paper bag with an assortment of complementary muffins as I rolled through the drive-thru for a large double-double. I devoured a bran muffin on the curb, my phone plugged into a nearby socket to charge. Prince Albert—known as PA to locals—holds the inglorious title of Canada's third most dangerous city, and I fully expected Epona to be stolen if I turned my back for even a second. So, I remained outside, watching Saturday night revellers stream by the bright lights of the casino as I sipped my hot coffee. I stretched my legs out in front of me and assessed my knees—minimal swelling, thankfully. Once I drained the cup, I peeled myself from the pavement and hit the road for Saskatoon, ninety miles away.

Everything went dark once I left city limits. I turned up the brightness on my front bike light and hoped my eyes would adjust. I wore a reflective vest and had a spare set of lights on hand, and a backup headlamp just in case. After all those nights of barrelling into pitch-black obscurity during the

Trans Am, I was prepared for this. My tires hummed along the wide highway shoulder as I relished the sensation of being alone with the cool summer night.

. . .

I had departed the Husky gas station in Saskatoon alongside half a dozen randonneurs at 5:00 a.m. that morning, embarking on a 600-kilometre brevet that would take us in a gigantic rectangle: first east through rolling prairie to Humboldt and Tisdale, then north to Melfort, west to Prince Albert, and finally south to Saskatoon via Duck Lake. While the others aimed to overnight at the halfway point in Melfort and arrive at the Husky just under the forty-hour time limit, my goal was to finish as fast as I possibly could. No sleep, just efficient refueling and a steady pace. A month post-race, my body had recovered from the damage I'd inflicted on it during the Trans Am (except for the numbness and tingling in my fingertips, which continued to impede my ability to type for months). I was ready—no, desperate—for a fresh challenge. I missed the intense and deeply satisfying sense of purpose I felt during those long days in the saddle during the Trans Am, and wondered how close to the twenty-four-hour mark I could finish the 600-kilometre ride. I dropped everyone an hour in, apologizing profusely for my rude departure.

"Go get it, girl," Marj had said.

I waved farewell and I tucked into the aerobars, getting comfortable for the interminable day and night that lay ahead.

. . .

The Tim Hortons coffee didn't pack enough kick and by 2:00 a.m., I was flagging. Without warning, my front wheel plunged into a pothole. A jolt of adrenaline shot through me as I clenched the handlebars, trying to regain control.

Focus, Meaghan. Eyes on the pavement. Rubber side down.

I was on the home stretch, but with seventy miles separating me from the Husky gas station in Saskatoon where I had started that morning, it certainly didn't feel that way. Night's slippery tentacles were taking hold. I would have to fight tooth and nail to fend them off until sunrise bloomed on the prairie horizon.

My phone lit up with a message. Not Marj, but Matthias.

Hey, still riding?

Yup! But dude, I'm getting tired. And it's super dark. And I think I spotted a coyote.

Keep going. You've got this, Hackinen.

Thanks! Not sure if I do, but I appreciate your faith.

It would have been Sunday morning for him, and I wondered what he was up to. Matthias and I had stayed in touch since the Trans Am. We kept each other up-to-date on our summer rides and shared the daily minutiae that decorated the fabric of our lives; in our frequent back-and-forths, he had even taught me how to use emojis. Memories of our time together still threaded through my thoughts. I didn't say it out loud—not to Matthias or Tyler or anyone else—but I missed him. Did he miss me as well?

I toggled the cursor on my eTrex navigator and calculated that if I could maintain pace, I should be able to complete the 600-km brevet in twenty-seven hours. Nothing would be open when I passed through Duck Lake, but no matter. I had muffins.

My phone buzzed again. Another message from Matthias: *In case you need some motivation.* The accompanying image was of his clean-shaven thighs in Lycra, shorts hiked an inch above his razor-sharp tan lines.

I grinned, my insides warming. Then I put my head down and hammered all the way back to Saskatoon.

I zipped past strip malls in Wildwood, Lakeridge's luxury homes, then hooked a left on the Yellowhead Highway heading east toward Yorkton. As cars, trucks, and big rigs rumbled by, I felt myself swept up in the hustle, like a young child desperate to keep up with the quick-paced play of older cousins. I pedalled harder. My thoughts danced from carefree afternoons cannonballing into the backyard pool to road trips with my sister, the two of us blasting Radiohead's *In Rainbows* as we cruised through the sun-scorched Fraser Valley in our parents' red minivan toward a long weekend of rock climbing near Skaha Bluffs, Penticton.

Then, something—a pebble ricocheting from a car tire, a walloping gust from a passing semi-trailer—would fix me firmly in the present: the flex and release of hamstrings, quads, and glutes as air rushed in and out of my lungs. Next to the din of traffic on a highway with no end in sight, my life—and also my problems—appeared miniscule, and therefore manageable.

. . .

I detonated my relationship with Tyler on September 11th. I had been questioning our future since returning home from the Trans Am. Tyler wanted to get married and have kids, but I said I needed time to think about it. Over the summer, I came to realize the life I wanted was one of adventure and new experiences in faraway places—polar opposite to the happily-ever-after *Little House on the Prairie* existence Tyler imagined us settling into. Once I realized our futures were irreconcilable, the decision to end things arrived abruptly.

The unravelling, not so quick.

I would be the one to leave the Weird House. Fine. But have you ever looked for a cheap, centrally located space in a university town after the start of the semester? It's all but impossible. I made a mental note to time my breakups better in the future.

My professional life had simultaneously taken a nose-dive. The return of semester coincided with an increase in the hours of operation at the student-run health clinic where I coordinated volunteers, and an influx of newbie volunteers. During shift, I felt like a toy in the off-leash dog park I passed on my daily commutes: tugged from all sides, torn between trying to compose thoughtful reference letters for med school applicants, excavate the daily onslaught of emails from my inbox, and offer guidance to volunteers who were witnessing for the first time the realities of systemic racial inequality and fentanyl. A week into the semester, I became overwhelmed: I had never wanted a career in healthcare, and with my background in archaeology and creative writing, I was immensely underqualified to navigate the complicated real-world circumstances I had waded into, let alone provide leadership to others. I began taking timeouts in the bathroom to regain composure as a quivering lip escalated to frustrated tears.

Previously, I had relished September on the Prairies—the cooler evenings and the avenues coloured rusty orange with big-leaf maples. Now, I felt constrained, as though someone had lassoed my chest, the rope cinching tighter as each day went by.

I should have been hunting for a place, but after struggling through a shift at the clinic, I failed to complete any other task. My roommates would come home to find me comatose on the basement sofa next to the house's enormous white cat, my fears about work, finding a home, and surviving another two weeks of emotionally-charged encounters with my ex exploding in my head like firecrackers.

I needed to get out.

. . .

Bradwell became my destination, a familiar fifty-mile out-and-back route that took less than three hours, if the wind cooperated. The terrain was unexceptional, mimicking Kansas with its golden tongues of wheat and hay bale-dotted fields, but I didn't mind. The second I clipped in—that satisfying union of body and machine—the lasso around my chest eased. I craved freedom and release. Road cycling delivered. I took in a lungful of crisp air and smelled, for the first time, autumn's earthy musk. As I hurtled toward Bradwell, I relished complete engagement in the act of pedalling, kinetic energy surging from head to heel as I fought to hold onto the ludicrous pace I'd set. After ten minutes I backed off, squeegeeing sweat from my brow with a jersey sleeve before I transitioned into a more relaxed clip and set my imagination free again to wander.

Aside from immediate logistical concerns, I avoid dictating where my thoughts go when I'm cycling. The random, sporadic nature of the mind is both magnificent and puzzling. There is an underlying logic I neither understand nor question, but more often than not I find myself honing in on an issue that has troubled me for weeks. On the road, I experience a clarity of thought rarely obtained in everyday life. This proved especially true during my breakup with Tyler.

My mind skipped from one thing to the next as I cycled past the turnoff for Clavet—camping trips to newspaper headlines to Christmas mornings—until it travelled far enough to disassociate from my body. Free floating like a hot-air balloon over the sea of cut wheat. I could view myself exteriorly, and what had felt impossible—packing my scattered possessions into boxes and loading them into a moving van; saying goodbye to a houseful of friends and animals that had grown comfortingly familiar; surviving another shift at work—became tasks, and nothing more. All I had to do was map out the sequence in my head and skip merrily down the yellow brick road to contentment. I reached the turnaround in Bradwell feeling as though I'd discovered a way to clear the hurdles I had previously feared to face.

That evening, I returned home just as darkness set in. Tyler's Explorer was in the driveway. He'd picked up takeout vermicelli bowls from Thien Vietnam.

"Thought you'd be hungry," he said.

He was right.

I'd been avoiding him for days, but here we were. Seated at the table together—me in my sweat-soaked cycling kit, him in his pressed work shirt and tie—dousing noodles with Sambal Oelek and commiserating about the inconvenience posed by road closures downtown. For a moment, the clock had turned back, and I knew we could live out these final days in peace. I didn't have to creep around the house any longer. After dinner, I tidied up and sat down at the table with my laptop.

I recognized what I had to do next.

The house hunt wasn't easy. Most suites I looked at were ant-infested dives. Once, a landlord sent me away before I even stepped foot in the door, saying he only accepted male tenants.

"Then why did you bother to invite me to view the place?" I asked.

He shrugged. I kept searching.

. . .

Over the following weeks, I spent a few more coffee breaks hiccupping away tears in the bathroom at work. But speeding down Saskatchewan's highways on Epona—even for an hour—kept me sane. From the vantage point of the saddle, I could view my life with the same single-mindedness of purpose that propelled me across America. I didn't have to complicate matters or let my emotions rule over me: I just needed to set a goal and follow through. After I ticked an item off the list, I could advance to the next. Simple.

A few days shy of my move-out date, I found a shared basement suite with faux wood panelling, dusty shag carpets, and a broken stove the landlord promised to fix. I also decided to look for a different job—more in line with my background in writing—but that could wait until after I moved out.

Tiny avalanches of snow swept over the tops of my boots as I trudged toward the post office. It would have been a ten-minute ride, but I chose to walk, fearing that even the studded tires of my winter bike would fail to cut through the sudden dump of powder that Saskatoon had received. If anyone had bothered to actually shovel their sidewalks, I lamented, this would be much quicker. I consoled myself by thinking of the trek as an opportunity to tone my calves. Despite the tedious pace, my mood remained bright. I was on a mission.

My backpack carried precious cargo: six manila envelopes addressed to various Canadian publishing houses, each containing a query letter, annotated table of contents, and sample chapters of my manuscript. I had procrastinated too long. Rolf's words from that chilly Colorado night echoed in my head: "If you're a writer, why aren't you trying to get your work out there?"

That was months ago, but we had stayed in touch, our conversations peppered with reminders of his conviction in me. Every few weeks I'd receive a message, a ride recap followed by a gentle inquiry about what I was working on, and if I'd had any luck finding a publisher. Even from afar, he unflinchingly called attention to the discrepancies that existed between what I claimed as my passion—writing—and where I placed my time and energy daily.

I typed out explanations of how I was too busy breaking up with my long-term boyfriend, hating my work, and moving, but always deleted them. Rolf was right: enough with excuses. Besides, order had been re-established in my routine. I'd settled into the new place and found an exciting contract position in communications at a provincial sports organization where I hoped to put my writing skills to use.

I knew that stiff competition meant the likelihood of finding a publisher remained slim. On the other hand, I also realized that I was guaranteed to fail if I didn't try. I spent October revising my manuscript chapter by chapter, putting together a solid query letter, and researching publishing houses accepting creative non-fiction manuscripts. Then I purchased new ink cartridges, a brick of paper, and manila envelopes that I addressed in my neatest printing. Now, all I had to do was drop the submission packages off at the post office and wait.

. . .

Snow continued to tumble over the top of my boots, and by the time I reached the post office, my toes swam in water. Thankfully, the fleece lining kept my feet warm. The Shoppers Drug Mart which housed the post office also stocked an array of pre-packaged food items and kitchen appliances. I wandered the aisles after I dropped off the precious envelopes, wondering if there was anything I needed to buy. In a week, Matthias would be visiting. He had recently found himself single as well, and decided to use his upcoming vacation time to fly out and see me in the midst of a Prairie deep freeze. I was ecstatic.

Unfortunately, the dump I moved into after splitting with Tyler was an embarrassment: dark, cramped, and dingy. I didn't even know where Matthias would put his bags. Between the single bed and desk in my tiny, windowless basement bedroom, there remained just enough square footage to set up the indoor bike trainer I purchased—and no room for anything else. Then I remembered that I could fold up the trainer, tuck Epona into the garage for a week, and spend time getting to know Matthias without bicycles in the picture.

One thing at a time, I reminded myself, repeating the mantra that had seen me through the past months. One thing at a time. I grabbed a bag of coffee beans and a package of maple cookies and headed toward the check-out.

"What about this?" asked my father, pointing toward my wooden dresser. "Donation pile, or load it into the van?"

"Let's leave it on the curb," I said. "I'm sure someone will collect it."

We each took an end and hauled the dresser outside to join a bookshelf and miscellaneous chairs on the driveway. By sunset, only a solitary bar stool remained.

"I don't think we'll fit much more in the van once we pack your bikes," warned my father.

I looked around my bedroom: assorted work clothes, stacks of paper featuring short story drafts from my MFA in Writing Program. Tough decisions needed to be made regarding what to keep, and what to toss. I situated myself in the midst of the mess and began stuffing garments into a black garbage bag destined for the thrift store, and papers into a transparent recycling bag. Sorting and reshuffling my possessions without sentiment until the room was empty.

Finally, I was ready to say *hasta la vista* to Saskatoon.

. . .

Things had gone well with Matthias that winter. Our friendship had grown into romance, kindled after his return to Germany by bi-weekly video chats that left my heart singing. We talked about our favourite authors and books—it turned out we both harboured a penchant for stories featuring dysfunctional families and wayward protagonists. I traded an illustrated copy of Douglas Coupland's *Generation X* for Jonathan Franzen's *The Corrections*; he also introduced me to Haruki Murakami's meditative memoir, *What I Talk About When I Talk About Running*, a narrative that inspired my thinking about both endurance sports and the process of writing.

I even flew out to visit Freiburg in March, the two of us taking a road trip to Tuscany to enjoy some early season cycling in Italy before snow melted in the Prairies. By vacation's end, I had decided to quit my job and fly back to join him that summer. In the meantime, I obtained a year-long visa for Germany that would allow me to work and study, and booked a one-way flight to Frankfurt.

Matthias and I had signed up for an epic bicycle adventure from North Cape, Norway to Tarifa, Spain, and after that I would return to stay with him in Freiburg.

. . .

"So, you're in love," said my father, shouting over the van's clanking engine and fuzzy FM radio reception, as we drove 800 miles from Saskatoon to Kelowna.

I nibbled a string of red liquorice and fixed my eyes on the horizon. We were headed west onto the windy plains, daylight fading with every mile as we approached the Alberta border.

"I don't know," I replied, honestly. "Guess I'm going overseas to find out."

Over the past few months, I had considered my options, and it all boiled down to this: fly to Europe and get to know Matthias better, or stay in Saskatoon and spend the rest of my life wondering if I had passed up the romantic opportunity of a lifetime. The first option harboured risk and uncertainty, but I would gladly accept disappointments over the heartbreak of not knowing. Besides, that year's particularly severe winter had pushed me over the edge, and I decided that even if Matthias and I didn't amount to anything, I could no longer stay in Saskatoon. I wasn't meant to live in a snow globe six months out of the year: I longed for the mild winters of the West Coast where I'd grown up.

Far from being disappointed when I announced my departure, my work colleagues appeared thrilled.

"A transatlantic romance? That is so exciting," they gushed. "Send postcards!"

"I'll be back for my book launch," I promised.

After months of rejection letters, I had given up hope of finding a publisher. Then the day before I flew out to visit Matthias in March, I received a follow-up call from an independent literary publishing house in Edmonton, Alberta. I signed a contract before the week was over—complete with advance—still in shock.

Looking back, perhaps securing a book deal contributed to my decision to leave. I had taken a chance—dedicated months of my life to researching, writing, and editing a manuscript—and it had eventually paid off. Perhaps this gamble would be worth it as well.

"Coffee, love?"

Brian stood at the Nespresso machine in his compact kitchen. A massive picture window provided a glimpse of typical Swiss countryside: charming red farmhouses and evergreen pasture that was home to dairy cattle. Brian's face was gentle, relaxed. In contrast, my movements were tense, insides roiling like a pit of garden snakes.

"Yes, please."

"I'll make you a latte," he offered. "Then we'll go for a nice long ride."

I nodded, then slouched against a cupboard. The rhythmic chimes of cowbells echoed through the kitchen, signalling the cattle's swaying heads as they grazed. Brian offered me the drink with one hand, patting me on the shoulder with the other.

"There you go, love. Enjoy."

I wish I could tell you that things worked out between Matthias and me, but they didn't. During the two months of carving a north-to-south route through Europe, we shared experiences that I will treasure for a lifetime, from cycling into the midnight sun in frigid Nordic hinterlands, to romantic candle-lit dinners in French auberges.

But some things aren't meant to be. When September rolled around, it was time for me to go home.

"You were dumped," said Marj, never one to mince words. We remained in contact over Skype, but the clarity of her statement stung as smartly as if she were standing beside me.

Since this is the story of a long-distance bicycle race and not a critical examination of my own romantic shortcomings, I'll spare the details of our uncoupling and get to the point: Matthias dropped me off at Brian and Stacey's place in Fiaugères, Switzerland, a few days before my hastily booked return flight from nearby Geneva.

. . .

I spent four days with Brian and Stacey. It was a transitional time: a chill had stiffened the air, hinting toward coming autumn. Brian worked as an endurance cycling coach, and we trained every day, sometimes with his clients. I memorized the route to a nearby farm where we collected fresh eggs, and which backroads avoided the busy route up from Lake Geneva. Brian also agreed to coach me for the upcoming World 24 Hour Time Trial Championships, and we fleshed out a training plan. Dinners were accompanied by Pinot Noir and several types of cheese, conversations about my summer gallivanting from the birthplace of my ancestors in Scandinavia to the French Riviera, as well as Brian and Stacey's recent race around Denmark.

"Do you regret anything?" asked Stacey. She was in one of her sensitive moods, and I decided to open up. "No," I said. "Not in the slightest."

I wanted adventure, and I found it. Not all relationships have happily-ever-after endings. If my experience during the Trans Am taught me anything, it was that I wanted to live boldly. Take risks. Be the type of person who meets the moment to embrace life in all its bittersweet beauty, instead of someone who pines away at home. My romance with Matthias had been a journey—and a considerably more enjoyable one than the cross-country road race where our paths first crossed, if I'm being honest—but now it too had ended.

Brian, Stacey, and I raised our glasses over the kitchen table. The next day, I would board a plane bound for San Diego, where I would continue training for the late-October time trial alongside the palm-lined beaches of Southern California.

"To the Trans Am," I said. "Where we first met."

"To the Trans Am," repeated Brian and Stacey, our glasses tinkling in the pleasant notes of river pebbles.

Endings are never easy, but from my experience, they are never really endings, either.

The cascade of changes set in motion during the Trans Am Bike Race will continue for years to come. I look forward to exploring the road ahead, wherever it may lead.

Acknowledgements

Shifting Gears: Coast to Coast on the Trans Am Bike Race is based on my personal, subjective experience. I have aimed to present events as witnessed from my point of view, and weave together the threads of meaning that have surfaced in the aftermath. Some names have been changed to protect the privacy of individuals.

I am indebted to the contributions of early readers—Maureen Harris, Coleen Hackinen, Lynda Tammen, Russell Matthews, Marjory Oneschuk, and Carol Wray—who provided encouragement, insight, and thoughtful critiques. A massive thank you to the hardworking team at NeWest Press for their role in bringing this experience into print—and an extra special thanks to my editor, Anne Nothof, for her keen eye and enthusiasm for this project. I'd also like to acknowledge financial support from the BC Arts Council.

Shifting Gears is, in many ways, a love song to my experience as a competitor: stories born from a desire to express my enduring appreciation and gratitude for the individuals and geography I encountered during this coast-to-coast sojourn. To Matthias Rau, Rolf Moser, Brian Welsh, Nuno Lopez, and Mitchell Potter—a gushing, heartfelt thank you. I doubt any of you fully comprehend the extent to which you have impacted my life. I'd also like to thank the dotwatchers, competitors—Amy Lippe in particular, who always proved just out of reach—race organizers, and gas station attendants for making the Trans Am Bike Race the unforgettable event that it was.

Sadly, these pages also encompass tragedy. It is no small thing that a life was lost during the 2017 edition of the Trans Am Bike Race. Eric Fishbein was a father to three and a friend to many. He died on June 17, 2017, in Kansas. The following year, John Egbers—who ended his 2017 race attempt early after an injury—returned to the start line. On June 14, 2018, John stopped to pay tribute to Eric's roadside memorial in Kansas, writing the words "We are all diminished by one" on the wooden post. Twenty minutes down the road, John was hit from behind and sustained severe injuries that would lead to his death in hospital a few weeks later. During the writing process, I often found myself sidelined by re-imaginings of what could have been. Yet life is an uncertain thing. Though I mourn the loss of two vibrant men, I remain grateful to have met both Eric and John in passing.

Glossary of Terms

Adventure Cycling Association or ACA (noun): America's oldest non-profit member organization focused on travel by bicycle. Established in 1973, the Adventure Cycling Association advocates for safer cycling in the US, publishes cycling routes and maps, and provides guided trips. Headquartered near the TransAmerica Bicycle Route in Missoula, Montana.

Aerobars (noun): Also known as tribars; a type of handlebar extension with padded forearm rests that allow the rider to achieve a more aerodynamic position by drawing their body forward, with the added bonus of taking accumulative strain off of the wrists.

Ancien (noun): A veteran in the sport of randonneuring; a Paris-Brest-Paris finisher, or someone who has completed some other 1,200-kilometre brevet.

Asterisk (noun): A symbol (*) added to a racer's finishing time denoting an infringement of race rules.

Bivy bag or bivy sack (noun): A compact weather-proof covering that goes around your sleeping bag; a minimalist tent. Unsuitable for those harbouring a fear of confined spaces.

Brevet (noun): Also known as randonnée; within the sport of randonneuring, a ride that follows a predetermined route with designated control points, undertaken within a specified time limit. Riders must have their cards verified or stamped at the control points and complete the ride within the limit to be recognized as an official finisher. Common brevet distances are 200, 300, 400, and 600 kilometres; distances are typically totalled in kilometres, not miles. Other events include shorter populaire brevets, team fleche events, as well as 1,000- and 1,200-kilometres challenges.

Control (noun): A set location in an event where riders must stop to have their brevet card validated by receiving a stamp or signature. Controls are often located in establishments offering amenities such as food or shelter. Failure to stop at a control and receive verification, or arriving outside the controls time window, is grounds for disqualification.

DNF (abbreviation): Did not finish; to quit a race.

Dotwatcher (noun): A label derived from the popular pastime of following racers "dots"—representing racers' real time location on the course as broadcast from their GPS devices—from the comfort of your computer, tablet, or cellphone screen.

DQ (abbreviation): Disqualified; a racer director will assign a DQ for serious or repeated violation of race rules.

Epona (noun): Goddess protector of horses, donkeys, and mules in Gallo-Roman religion. Also, the name of the hero Link's horse in the video game *The Legend of Zelda: Ocarina of Time*.

Grand Brevet (noun): Also known as Grand Randonnée; a randonneuring event that is 1,200 kilometres or longer, such as Paris-Brest-Paris in France, Boston-Montreal-Boston in North America, or London-Edinburgh-London in the United Kingdom.

Hot foot (noun): Also known as Metatarsalgia; a burning pain in the ball of the foot that can radiate toward the toe caused by pedal pressure or foot swelling in cycling shoes. Hot foot can be extremely painful; severe cases can feel as though someone is holding a blowtorch to the foot.

Lanterne Rouge (noun): A distinction awarded to the last-place finisher in a cycling event. French for "red lantern," the term originated in reference to the red lantern hung on the caboose of a railway train. Signalmen and station masters were reassured to look back and see the "lanterne rouge", as it meant that none of the couplings had disconnected, and the train was still whole.

Paris-Brest-Paris or PBP (noun): An iconic out-and-back 1,200-kilometre grand brevet through the Brittany region in France, starting and finishing in Rambouillet on the outskirts of Paris, and travelling to Brest on the Atlantic Coast. Dating back to 1891, Paris-Brest-Paris, or PBP as it is affectionately known, holds the title of the world's oldest long-distance cycling event. Like the Olympics, PBP only takes place every four years; the route must be self-navigated and completed within a 90-hour window, with riders moving self-supported between control points.

Race clock (noun): The race clock begins with 00 hours. The first day of a multi-day race is therefore Day Zero, with Day One beginning once 24 hours has passed on the race clock.

Randonnée (noun): See brevet.

Randonneur (noun): Someone who has completed a 200-kilometre brevet; a lifelong title.

Randonneuring (noun): Also known as Audax in the UK, Brazil, and Australia; a non-competitive discipline in ultra-distance cycling where participants (or randonneurs) complete designated routes (known as brevets) within a predetermined time limit, stopping at specified controls to have their brevet cards verified. While self-sufficiency is prized, drafting or riding in pairs or groups is permitted, and camaraderie among riders is one of the hallmarks of the sport.

Race Across America or RAAM (noun): A long-running supported bicycle road race from Oceanside, California to Annapolis, Maryland. Racers are required to organize their own support crews and vehicles, and must cross 55 check points along a pre-determined route within strict time limits. The event spans 3,000 miles over twelve states; racers can compete solo, or as part of a two, four, or eight-person relay team. The cost and logistics associated with RAAM are considerably higher than for self-supported events like the Trans Am Bike Race.

Scratch (verb): To quit a race.

Shermer's Neck (noun): A condition unique to cyclists that occurs when the muscles around the neck give out with fatigue after prolonged use. Named after Michael Shermer, who experienced the ailment during his 1983 Race Across America attempt. The onset of Shermer's Neck is sudden and debilitating.

Spot Tracker or Spot (noun): A common GPS tracking device use by outdoor enthusiasts as well as participants in ultra-cycling races.

Tracker (noun): Another term for Trackleaders, the website where riders real-time GPS locations display the most up-to-minute race rankings. Also slang term for Spot Tracker.

Trail angel (noun): A term used to identify someone who provides unilateral support, typically in the form of nourishment, hydration, shelter, or encouragement, to long-haul travellers such as through hikers, bicycle tourists, or race competitors.

Transcontinental Race or TCR (noun): A self-supported ultra-distance bicycle race across Europe. Established in 2013 by ultra-cycling pioneer Mike Hall, the TCR is a forerunner in the now-eventful race calendar, and regarded as one of the world's toughest ultra-endurance races. The route varies from year to year; winners typically finish between 7-10 days. The TCR differs from the Trans Am in that competitors are not provided a race route to follow, but must self-navigate between mandatory checkpoints.

MEAGHAN MARIE HACKINEN is a writer and cyclist from Vancouver, BC. Her two-wheeled adventures have taken her from Haida Gwaii to Mexico's high plateaus, across Canada and the United States, and, most recently, from North Cape to Tarifa along some of Europe's highest paved roads. Her writing explores relationships, experiences on the road, and encounters with wild places. Her creative non-fiction, poetry, and prose can be found in literary journals and cycling magazines. She has an MFA in Writing from the University of Saskatchewan and currently resides in Kelowna, BC.